Trusting Records

THE ARCHIVIST'S LIBRARY

Volume 1

Editor-In-Chief

Terry Eastwood, *University of British Columbia, Canada*

Editorial Board

Luciana Duranti, *University of British Columbia, Canada*
Maria Guercio, *University of Urbino, Italy*
Michael Piggott, *The University of Melbourne, Australia*

Trusting Records

Legal, Historical and Diplomatic Perspectives

by

Heather MacNeil
University of British Columbia, Canada

KLUWER ACADEMIC PUBLISHERS
DORDRECHT / BOSTON / LONDON

A C.I.P. Catalogue record for this book is available from the Library of Congress.

ISBN 0-7923-6599-2

Published by Kluwer Academic Publishers,
P.O. Box 17, 3300 AA Dordrecht, The Netherlands.

Sold and distributed in North, Central and South America
by Kluwer Academic Publishers,
101 Philip Drive, Norwell, MA 02061, U.S.A.

In all other countries, sold and distributed
by Kluwer Academic Publishers,
P.O. Box 322, 3300 AH Dordrecht, The Netherlands.

Printed on acid-free paper

Printed in the Netherlands.

To my mother, Agnes MacNeil

Table of Contents

Acknowledgements

This book is a revised version of the doctoral dissertation which I completed for the Individual Interdisciplinary Studies Program at the University of British Columbia. I would like to thank the Social Sciences and Humanities Research Council of Canada for the doctoral fellowship that enabled me to carry out my original research.

For valuable inspiration and advice during the preparation of the dissertation I am indebted to my thesis supervisor Luciana Duranti and to the members of my supervisory committee – Terry Eastwood and Charles Dollar of the School of Library, Archival and Information Studies, Marilyn MacCrimmon and Anthony Sheppard of the Faculty of Law, and George Egerton of the Department of History – all of whom were unfailingly generous in sharing their knowledge and unswervingly supportive of my efforts.

Finally, I would like to thank Ronald Hagler for his meticulous and merciless editing of this book, and Ian McAndrew and Marta Maftei for their tireless efforts in formatting the text and preparing the index.

Introduction

Trust is "confidence in or reliance on some quality or attribute of a person or thing, or the truth of a statement."[1] When something is said to be trustworthy it means that it deserves, or is entitled to, trust or confidence. When a record is said to be trustworthy, it means that it is both an accurate statement of facts and a genuine manifestation of those facts. Record trustworthiness thus has two qualitative dimensions: *reliability* and *authenticity*. Reliability means that the record is capable of standing for the facts to which it attests, while authenticity means that the record is what it claims to be.

These two qualities – reliability and authenticity – are of particular interest to legal and historical practitioners. The complementary relationship between the disciplines of law and history is evident in their evolution. From antiquity until the fifteenth century, the rhetorical tradition linked the two. During the sixteenth and seventeenth centuries, as historical and legal scholarship gradually moved away "from the literary analysis of classical texts and toward an assessment of the accuracy of somewhat more recent historical data,"[2] the examination of records as evidence became a central concern of both disciplines. Historians and lawyers alike "sought to date documents and assess the good faith, knowledge, and credibility of those who initially had prepared them."[3] The need to authenticate medieval documents in particular led to the development of the science of diplomatics in the seventeenth century. By the eighteenth century, diplomatic science had been introduced into European faculties of law and by the nineteenth century, it had become one of the auxiliary disciplines of history. It formed, moreover, a part of the foundation for the discipline of archival science, which emerged in the same period.

Legal and historical practitioners both need to ensure that records are trustworthy so that justice may be realised or the past understood. For records created by bureaucracies, that trustworthiness has been ensured and protected through the mechanisms of authority and delegation and through procedural controls exercised over recordkeeping. As bureaucracies rely increasingly on electronic information and communication technologies to create and maintain their records, it is vital to explore whether traditional mechanisms and controls are adequate to the task of verifying the authenticity and degree of reliability of these new records, whose most salient feature is the ease with which they can be invisibly altered and manipulated. The technological complexity and dynamic nature of electronic recordkeeping systems require new legal interpretations of what constitutes "a circumstantial guarantee of trustworthiness" and "best evidence". Legal commentators note that, with the increasing use of computer-generated evidence in the courtroom, courts must determine "whether the legal system is in need of new rules of evidence or stricter foundation requirements to deal adequately with computer-generated evidence."[4] Recent historical literature addressing the implications of information technologies for historical methodology also reflects historians' concern that the complexity and volatility of electronic records may defeat their efforts to establish the authenticity of such records and to assess their likely degree of reliability.

During the spring of 1996, the trustworthiness of electronic records became a focal point of hearings held by the Canadian Commission of Inquiry into the Deployment of Canadian Forces to Somalia. The Commission was established in 1995 for the purpose of investigating "the chain of command system, leadership, discipline and actions and decisions of the Canadian Forces, as well as the actions and decisions of the Department of National Defence in respect of the Canadian Force's participation in the peace enforcement mission in Somalia during 1992-93."[5] As part of its investigation, the Commission requested access to National Defence Operations Centre (NDOC) logs, which were maintained in an automated database and which contained a record of all message traffic coming into National Defence headquarters from Canadian Forces' theatres of operation. During its review of the logs, the Commission discovered "a number of unexplained anomalies, including entries containing no information, entries missing serial numbers, and entries with duplicate serial numbers. The concern was that there may have been deliberate tampering with these logs."[6] Subsequent investigations "revealed no evidence to support the theory that tampering had occurred, but could not eliminate the possibility."[7] The investigations did reveal, however, a number of other serious problems with the NDOC logs, most of which appear to have resulted from a lack of standard operating procedures with regard to the log, a completely ineffective database security system, and a lack of system audits, among other things. The Commissioners determined that "NDOC logs are not a reliable record of transactions at the operations centre. Even apart from the question of deliberate tampering, the logs were compromised by problems with the data-base system and the absence of proper procedures for the operators."[8]

On the basis of its analysis, the Commission concluded that the Department of National Defence had failed to ensure the maintenance of a complete record of in-theatre message traffic to Headquarters. Specifically, it had failed to institute standard operating procedures to ensure that the logs were accurately recorded; to provide personnel with a clear understanding of the purpose of maintaining the logs; to provide adequate training to duty officers; and to use system audits to ensure that the record was being properly maintained.[9] Their findings led the Commission to recommend that the proper maintenance of NDOC logs be ensured by implementing the following:[10]

> (a) an audit procedure to ensure that standard operating procedures provide clear and sufficient guidelines on the type of information to be entered and how the information is to be entered;
>
> (b) an adequate data base system, which includes software controls to ensure accurate data entry in each field and appropriate training for operators and users of this system; and

(c) increased system security to an acceptable standard compatible with the objective of national security, including restricting access to authorized persons using only their own accounts and passwords, and extending the use of secure (hidden) fields to identify persons entering or deleting data.

The problems identified by the Commission have a bearing on both the reliability and the authenticity of the NDOC logs. The absence of standard operating procedures for recording entries in the log compromised their reliability while the lack of system audits and security procedures compromised their authenticity. The Commission's recommendations demonstrate the connection that continues to be drawn between the trustworthiness of records and the integrity of procedural controls over their creation and maintenance and underscore the role of changing technology in implementing and enforcing those controls.

The findings also imply that legal and historical practitioners will find it more and more difficult to reconstruct past events on the basis of surviving electronic records. Notwithstanding these concerns, many historians believe that the computer may actually enhance the authenticity and degree of reliability of records because electronic systems are capable of capturing more of the context in which electronic records are created and used within bureaucratic organisations than was possible with traditional recordkeeping systems. While neither the legal nor the historical discipline has identified a comprehensive set of methods for ensuring, or enhancing, the reliability and authenticity of electronic records, both agree that such methods need to be built into the design of electronic record systems.

Such need is also a recurring theme in the archival literature since, as preservers of records, archivists have a vested interest in ensuring the creation and maintenance of reliable and authentic records. In recent years, some archivists have undertaken to re-assess and adapt the concepts, principles, and methods of diplomatic science to meet the needs of contemporary recordkeeping. In so doing, they have succeeded in transforming it from a tool for retrospectively assessing the trustworthiness of medieval records into a standard for the creation and maintenance of reliable and authentic electronic records.

The purpose of this book is to explore the trustworthiness of records as evidence from the perspectives of law and history and to examine recent efforts to develop methods for ensuring the trustworthiness of electronic records based on diplomatic concepts and principles. It is organised into four chapters. The first traces the evolution of record trustworthiness from the compilation of the Justinian Code in the sixth century to the publication of Langlois and Seignobos' *Introduction to the Study of History* at the end of the nineteenth century, including the birth of diplomatic science in the seventeenth century. The second, third and fourth analyse the criteria and methods established by law, history, and contemporary archival diplomatics, respectively, for determining the trustworthiness of records in general, and electronic records specifically. Chapter 2, on legal methodology, focuses on the rules governing the admissibility of documentary evidence in common law jurisdictions generally and in Canada specifically. The rules relate to modes of authentication, the production of documentary originals (the best evidence rule), and the business records exception to the hearsay rule. To assess the extent to which new technologies for creating and storing records have affected these rules, the chapter also examines the revisions to the Canadian Evidence Act proposed by the Uniform Law Conference of Canada to address electronic record issues. While the interpretations and amendments to the legal rules described in this chapter are Canadian, they are consistent with and often draw upon interpretations and amendments to legal rules developed in other jurisdictions. Chapter 3, on historical methodology, focuses on the techniques of external and internal criticism that historians typically use to test the authenticity and degree of reliability of records in general and organisational records in particular. To assess the impact of new technologies on these techniques, two recent court cases that focused on electronic record issues and involved historians as plaintiffs are analysed as examples. The final chapter focuses on the application of the principles, concepts, and methods of diplomatics and archival science to records created in an electronic environment. It will examine specifically a research project entitled "The Protection of the Integrity of Electronic Records" whose goal was to identify and define the nature of an electronic record and the conditions necessary to ensure its reliability and authenticity on the basis of those principles, concepts and methods.

Each disciplinary chapter examines not only the methods and rules of that discipline for assessing record trustworthiness but also the assumptions and generalisations concerning observation, recording, and bureaucratic recordkeeping that underpin them in an effort to highlight common themes. Such examination will demonstrate how the criteria for record trustworthiness have changed over time and gauge the extent to which legal, historical, and diplomatic methods for evaluating it are adequate to the task of establishing warranted claims to knowledge about the past.

Chapter One

The Evolution of Legal and Historical Methods for Assessing the Trustworthiness of Records

Concern for the trustworthiness of records has been expressed since antiquity; many of the concepts and methods associated with this concern originated in Roman law. Over the centuries, from the compilation of the Justinian Code in the sixth century[1] to the publication of Langlois and Seignobos' *Introduction to the Study of History* at the end of the nineteenth century, procedures to ensure, and later verify, trustworthiness were gradually incorporated into European law and the emerging discipline of history.

1.1 The Roman Era

In the Roman law, as codified by Justinian, the trustworthiness of records as evidence was embodied in the concepts of perpetual memory and public faith. The former is explained by Luciana Duranti:

> The most ancient archival documents, either in the original or as transcriptions of lost originals, contain a formula, usually placed at the end of the salutation: *in perpetuum, ad perpetuum*, or *ad perpetuam rei memoriam*. This formula established the function of the document with respect to the fact it was about. Because only the present can be known, a device was necessary to freeze the fact occurring in the present before it slipped into the past, and the document, as embodiment of the fact, had the function of converting the present into the permanent.[2]

Perpetual memory was linked originally to records and subsequently to archival institutions. In both cases, the concept was not intended to communicate the idea of eternity or eternal preservation, but, rather, the idea of continuity, stability, endurance, and trustworthiness.[3] The preservation of evidence and memory were inextricably linked through the concept of perpetual memory.

If perpetual memory expressed the role of a record with respect to the fact it was about, the concept of public faith expressed the role of the archival institution in relation to the society it served.[4] A record endowed with public faith was capable of constituting proof of whatever it was about. Roman jurists such as Ulpianus asserted that such faith could only be conferred on a record that had been preserved in a public place, i.e., a temple, public office, treasury or archives. In the Justinian Code, an archives is defined as " *'locus publicus in quo instrumenta deponuntur'* (the public place where records are deposited) often with the addenda *'quatenus incorrupta maneant,' 'fidem faciant,'* and *'perpetua rei memoria sit'* (so that they remain uncorrupted and serve as authentic evidence, and so that a continuing memory of the acts to which they attest be preserved.)"[5] Public faith thus referred to the authenticating function of archives. As Duranti explains, depositing records in an archives

> was a procedural requirement for all completed acts meant to generate consequences. ... In other terms, the requirement existed only for documents of actions intended to create, maintain, modify or extinguish relationships among physical or juridical persons. Such a passage enabled the acts to have continuing effects by endowing them with authenticity. It did not change their nature, but made their reliability enduring by confirming it and guaranteeing its preservation.[6]

Because archives had the capacity to authenticate records, both public and private, only those "persons or corporations invested with sovereign power had the right to establish one in their own jurisdiction."[7]

The Roman law of evidence reinforced the privileged status accorded to documents invested with public faith. According to J.T. Abdy, among the means of proof accepted by the Justinian Code, "public documents [i.e., documents produced from the custody of, or created by, government officials and therefore invested with public faith] were considered of so high a nature, that not only did they prove themselves, but greater weight was attached to them than was given to any other species of evidence, whether oral or written. On the other hand, private instruments [e.g., letters, memoranda, and all sorts of informal writings] were never admissible, if they were not properly subscribed and witnessed, i.e., by three witnesses".[8] M. Carr Ferguson has identified a third category of document recognised by Roman law, i.e., quasi-public documents, consisting of documents that had been properly notarised. If sufficiently attested, they were ordinarily granted the weight of public documents.[9]

Practical rules to ensure the trustworthiness of records and recognise forgeries were also introduced in the Justinian Code. Among the titles in the Digest, Codex, and Novellae dealing with evidence are rules referring to the authentication of documents, attestation, signatures, seals, registration, comparison of handwriting, the requirement to produce documentary originals, the protocols necessary in notarial documents and the regulations affecting notaries, the faith reposing in public and quasi public documents, and forgery.[10]

The problem of forgery appears to have been widespread in Roman times. As Duranti observes:

> The problem of distinguishing genuine documents from forgeries was present in the earliest periods of documentation, but until the sixth century no attempt was made to devise criteria for the identification of forgeries. Even legislators did not demonstrate interest in the issue basically because of the legal principle

commonly accepted in the ancient world that authenticity is not an intrinsic character of documents but is accorded to them by the fact of their preservation in a public place, a temple, public office, treasury, or archives.[11]

However, when private persons began to deposit false records in public archives to lend them public faith, it became necessary to introduce a number of sanctions to ensure the authenticity of records. According to Ferguson, three different methods of preventing forgery are discernible. The first guard against forgery was the requirement that documents of a public or quasi-public nature be executed with great formality, sealed with wax in such a way that the document could not be altered, and witnessed by several responsible witnesses. The second guard applied primarily to private documents whose genuineness was disputed by one of the parties. In such cases, "the question was resolved by a comparison of handwriting with a genuine specimen. ... A required minimum of three handwriting experts gave their opinions after taking the oaths of impartiality."[12] A final deterrent "was the punishment of forgery or any concealing, destruction, or falsification of documents under the *lex Cornelia*. Punishment could range in various cases from corporal punishment to death, depending on the rank of the accused and the nature of the forgery."[13]

The concept of public faith thus was expanded to include the preparation of records in accordance with legally prescribed forms to permit public officials to determine their authenticity. The significance that now attached to documentary form had a number of consequences. First, it created a need for expertise in the compilation of certain legal documents, out of which grew the notarial profession. Secondly, only original documents or authenticated copies of those documents were granted any probative capacity. This adaptation reveals the roots of the Common law's "best evidence" rule as it still relates to the production of documents. Thirdly, creators of records began to separate documents prepared by notaries in accordance with prescribed forms from other documents. A split between the so-called "archives treasure," consisting of the documents embodying completed acts and endowed with public faith, and the "archives sediment," consisting of the documents generated in the routine conduct of affairs, became increasingly apparent. The former were consciously set aside and preserved as continuing proof of past events; the latter were allowed to accumulate and eventually disappear. As a consequence of this split, public faith gradually extended to documents kept in secure custody over a long period of time. According to the Roman jurist Tertullianus, antiquity provided records with the highest authority because the more removed the records were, in the past, from the facts to which they attested, the more impartial they could be considered. Their trustworthiness derived from the fact that they were not generated for a present purpose. This "antiquity" criterion of public faith survives today as the ancient document rule in evidence law.[14]

1.2 The Middle Ages

The Middle Ages inherited many of these legal concepts, though they necessarily underwent some adaptation. While public archives continued to perform an authenticating function, their number diminished between the fourth and the ninth centuries. During that period "only the papal archives survived as a major public repository."[15] Thomas Noble suggests that, "one of the characteristics of the transition from Roman to medieval times was a change in probative value from the public document in the archives to the private copy in the hands of the recipient."[16] As a consequence, the trustworthiness of a record came, increasingly, to depend on its method of compilation and the authority of its writer.

In Italy and the countries of written law bordering on the Mediterranean, the highest degree of trustworthiness was conferred on documents compiled by notaries. Since Roman times, it had been accepted that records created by and maintained in the custody of a person endowed with public faith by a sovereign authority were capable of making public faith. Notaries (*tabelliones* in Roman times) were endowed with such faith and invested with the competence for both compiling and preserving authentic documents. Despite the erosion of much of the apparatus of central government in the post-imperial period, a professional notariate seems to have continued to exist, or at least re-emerged, by the ninth century in Italy.[17] According to Peter Burke:

> From the eleventh century, if not before, Italy – or at least, the many towns of the north and centre – was becoming what might reasonably be called a 'notarial culture', with a high proportion of notaries in the population (eight per 1,000 in Florence in 1427), thanks to the high demand for the registration of wills, contracts of marriage, apprenticeship and partnership, and other legal 'acts' and 'instruments.' Italy was not alone in this respect. The notarial culture seems to have extended over much of the Mediterranean Christian world in the later Middle Ages.[18]

By the middle of the twelfth century, the growing demand for notaries who, in addition to running their own businesses, held positions in the papal and imperial chanceries and in the offices of city-states, resulted in the establishment of a course of study in notarial arts at the University of Bologna. The compilation of documents and, thus, methods of authentication, became standardised across much of Europe as a consequence. During the same century, Armando Petrucci observes, "the private document drafted by a notary underwent a profound transformation from the *charta*, whose credibility as legal proof rested on the subscriptions to the text, to the *instrumentum*, which had the force of legal proof because it was drafted by a professional invested with *public fides*."[19]

The validity of a notarial document derived not only from the authority of the notary who compiled it, but also from the technical form of its composition. The signing and dating of documents provided specific indicators of their authenticity. According to M.T. Clanchy, "a notary provided safeguards against forgery usually by writing the document in his own hand and by appending to it his name and an individual *signum* which he drew with a pen. If dispute arose, the notary could be cross-examined or, if he were dead, reference could be made to other documents signed by him or to a register in which an exemplar of his style and *signum* was recorded."[20] In addition, each document was precisely dated by the year, month, day, and, for some transactions, even the hour, at which it was issued or received, as well as the place at which it was issued or received, for the purpose of settling potential subsequent disputes about its authenticity. The fact that a notary signed a document did not mean that the statements in it were true in themselves, simply that they were considered to be true in the eyes of the law.[21]

By the end of the twelfth century, the notarial system had extended from Italy to southern France and become firmly established in those regions. It extended as well to some parts of northern France, notably Flanders and Normandy and somewhat later, notaries began to establish themselves in Germany. But their influence in these regions was restricted. The notarial system also began to appear in England in the thirteenth century, but here too, it remained a foreign custom and notaries were usually only employed in the drawing up of certain restricted types of diplomatic documents and certain types of private contracts of an international character.[22]

In those countries that did not adopt the notarial system, the affixing of a seal was the most generally used method of authenticating documents. The sealing or signing of a document by its sender or promulgator had been the two most important methods of documentary validation since Roman times. The practice of using seals for this purpose fell away in the period of the German conquests, and was limited for several centuries to the royal chancelleries. It was revived, however, during the eleventh century and flourished between the twelfth and fifteenth centuries.

The rise of the seal ushered in a new era for written documents. According to Arthur Giry:

> The seals of sovereigns, barons, prelates, churches, and municipalities were from the very beginning used to guarantee the authenticity, not only of those instruments in which the owner of the seal bound himself or was otherwise a party; but also of all documents to which it was desired to give (in legal phraseology) an "authentic" character – including contracts and deeds of private persons (other than the owner of the seal). It was natural, particularly in the regions where notaries public were unknown, for such private persons to have recourse, when executing documents that affected legal rights, to those superior authorities whose seals could give authenticity to the document.[23]

In law, a clear distinction was drawn between the seals of superior authorities and those of merely private persons. As Giry points out, although a private

person could use his own personal seal to indicate his personal sanction or
liability on private letters, receipts, and so on:

> deeds or like instruments, which bore no other mark of validation
> than the seal of a private individual were not deemed to be
> drawn in "public form" and were treated in law as merely
> "documents under private signet," as the modern expression has
> it. ... Ever since the beginning of the 1200s we find the laws and
> treatises using the expression "authentic seal" ("sigillum
> authenticum"); under this term the lawyers recognised only the
> seals of persons or groups having a legal jurisdictional authority,
> viz., sovereigns, feudal lords, bishops, churches, and
> municipalities.[24]

In the jurisdictions that employed seals, sovereigns provided special kinds of seals,
known as "contract-seals," and appointed an official keeper of this seal whose duty
it was to grant to the deeds of private persons the guarantee of the royal seal. In the
course of the thirteenth century, bishops, archdeacons, and abbots also came to
possess seals of jurisdiction in the exercise of their ecclesiastical powers. In
England in 1237 the Council of London passed an ordinance granting not only
bishops and their deputies, but, also, priors, deans, chapters, and others, the right to
validate contracts by their seals.[25]

The principle of conferring authenticity on the documents of private persons
by affixing the seal of a superior jurisdictional authority was also common during the
middle ages in the northern (or "customary") regions of France. To provide proof of
a contract the party would present himself before a judge and there formally
acknowledge the execution of the contract. This acknowledgement was recorded by
the judge in the form of a letter, validated by his seal.[26] The practice of attesting
private deeds by public or well-known seals gave to transactions a publicity
which was the most valuable sort of attestation.

The affixing of a seal did not simply furnish a record with a means of
authenticating its genuineness. It also rendered that record indisputable as to the
terms of the transaction it recorded, thus dispensing with the need to summon
witnesses to the transaction. As the use of the seal became more habitual, the old
regime of proof by transaction-witnesses gradually disappeared and by the
fourteenth century, such witnesses were almost superfluous. Instead, when a
transaction was made in writing, the parties relied for their future proof on the
opponent's seal found affixed to the document, which thereby made its terms
indisputable by him as representing the actual terms of the transaction between the
two parties. [27] This legal value of the seal stemmed originally from the Germanic
principle concerning the indisputability of the King's word according to which "Who
gives him the lie forfeits life." The King's seal to a document therefore rendered its
truth incontestable. As the use of the seal extended downward from the King to the
people at large it carried this valuable attribute along with it.[28]

The seal's dominance as a means of proving the authenticity of public and private documents eventually diminished after the fifteenth century with the rise of the written signature and the use of paper as a writing material. It remained in use, however, for formal documents of the royal chanceries and, in the form of a signet, for private individuals.

From the twelfth century onwards, written proof had become widespread even in agreements between ordinary people and methods for ensuring its legal trustworthiness were well established. Nevertheless, the evidential capacity of written proof, i.e., its ability to establish a fact in an actual legal dispute, remained a matter of some debate in both Roman-canonical law and customary law. Before proceeding to a discussion of that debate, however, a brief excursus on the transformation of evidence law in the medieval period is in order.

During the twelfth and thirteenth centuries, trial by ordeal and trial by battle, the standard methods of deciding litigation in early medieval Europe, were gradually replaced on the Continent by the Roman-canonical system of "learned" or "legal" proofs, and in England by the jury trial. Both these new systems of inquiry, however differently they went about it, attempted to supplant irrational means of proof with rational ones and to transform judicial proceedings into rational investigations of the truth of conflicting allegations. On the Continent, responsibility for fact-finding was given to professional judges. As Barbara Shapiro explains, the Roman-canonical inquisition process "was designed to obtain 'full proof,' defined by clearly established evidentiary standards which rigidly specified the quality and quantity of proof. A specified number of witnesses were required to prove facts, and once 'full proof' had been achieved, conviction was automatic. The judge ... was essentially an accountant who totalled the proof fractions." In England (with the exception of the ecclesiastical courts which adopted the Roman-canonical tradition), responsibility for fact-finding was given to a jury, and for a number of centuries the jury trial required little in the way of rules of evidence. The jurors were men of the neighbourhood and it was assumed that they would know the facts and incorporate their own knowledge in their verdict. Juries thus arrived at findings of fact "guided by common sense and common knowledge."[29]

In the system of legal proofs that emerged as part of the transformation of the law of evidence in Continental Europe, public documents were accorded full proof in a court of law; private documents were accorded half-proof. A public document was supposed to prove itself, i.e., provided that it gave no indication of falsification, its contents were accepted as valid in the absence of proof to the contrary. The proviso, however, was a significant one. As Levy explains it:

Two opposing tendencies emerge in the twelfth century; one of them favouring written proof and distrusting testimony because of the fallibility of human memory ... the other, to the opposite effect. The latter view prevailed. Between 1206 and 1209, a decretal of Innocent III gave the preference to depositions of four witnesses over the provisions of a notarised document confirmed by the declarations of a notary.[30]

The principle that oral testimony prevailed over written proof passed into the customary law and was expressed in sayings such as 'witnesses prevail over letters' or 'viva voce witnesses overcome letters.' Levy attributes the distrust of written proof to the fact that, in the Middle Ages, in the learned Roman-canon law, the written document was seen as a kind of testimony. According to Levy, "canonists of the twelfth and thirteenth centuries, post-glossators of the fourteenth, call 'attestationes,' or even 'testimonia' what are in reality only written documents."[31] As testimony, documents clearly constituted an inferior form of proof because they could not be interrogated in the way a witness could be:

> The truth is that for the men of the Middle Ages, written proof, as in the case of proof by testimony, is two different kinds of one and the same type of proof the nature of which is testimony. But while in the one case the witnesses are living and present, in the other case they are absent and as if dead. One speaks of the "vox mortua instrumentorum" which is opposed to the living voice of witnesses. A true witness can be examined face to face; one can question him, notice whether he hesitates or vacillates, if he flushes, if he grows pale: one can ask him the source of his knowledge of the facts. ... Furthermore, several witnesses, two at least, are necessary, and their statements must agree; while a written document remains impassive. The parchment on which it is inscribed is "only the skin of a dead beast" on which "the pen of the scrivener can note anything."[32]

The distrust of documentary modes of proof was understandable, given that many medieval charters were forged and the authenticity of genuine ones was often difficult to prove. Medieval forgeries are difficult to evaluate because although in many cases, both the document and the information in it were spurious, in other cases, while the document itself was spurious, its contents could well have been accurate in the essentials of the information recorded. Clanchy has described the forgery or "renewal" of documents during the medieval period as a product of the cultural transition from oral memory to written record. Monks were among the most prolific fabricators of charters, a fact Clanchy attributes partly to the monastic tradition and its preoccupation with posterity.[33] Forgeries represented an attempt by monastic charter makers to fill the gaps and correct

> the anomalies in written record which kings and other past benefactors appeared to have negligently left. It was the responsibility of the beneficiaries and not of the donor to see that adequate documents were supplied. In the non-literate past, people had been accustomed to the flexibility of speech and memory and they applied similar criteria at first to the written record. A charter was inaccurate and should be corrected if it failed to give the beneficiary a privilege which the donor had obviously

intended it to have, had he still been alive to express his wishes. Writing, or the lack of it, should not be allowed to annul or invalidate previous pious gifts. From this point of view 'forgery' is an inappropriate term to apply to renewals of evidence which were intended to ensure that a monastic house was adequately provided with charters to defend its patrons and saints against rivals. ... Where there was doubt they were determined to establish the truth for posterity. By truth about the past they meant what really should have happened. For a monastic house there was a providential truth, which was higher than the random facts.[34]

Viewed from this perspective, monastic forgery – the manufacture of evidence to serve the purposes of posterity – constitutes a creative adaptation of the Roman concept of perpetual memory.

Rules for the prevention and detection of forgery had been introduced by canon lawyers in Italy and were widely known throughout Europe. In a *summa* dating from the last quarter of the twelfth century, Huguccio, the best canonical authority on forgeries, recommended that, where there was doubt about the authenticity of a decretal, the papal registers should first be consulted.[35] The papal chancery had begun to keep registers containing the unabridged transcription of the most important records created in the chancery from around the fourth century. The registration of documents was modelled on Roman imperial practice and served the purposes of perpetual memory by preserving evidence of the positions the papacy had taken and to which it might need to refer in the future. If the document could not be found in the papal registers (a common occurrence since only the most important documents were registered), other tests with regard to "the style and substance of the text, the physical characteristics of the parchment, the *bulla* and its attaching thread" were recommended. These rules "were subsequently promulgated generally by Innocent III, who had been Huguccio's pupil at Bologna."[36]

These rules were difficult to enforce however, particularly in England, where there were no systematic registers of ecclesiastical documents. Instead, English canonist glossators "recommended testing forgeries by the customary oral method of swearing oaths and producing witnesses."[37] Moreover, even Innocent III is known to have been deceived at least on one occasion by forged papal bulls. In a case in the Roman *curia* in 1205, Thomas of Marlborough, abbot of Evesham, submitted, as evidence of a claim, two papal bulls in the name of Constantine I, who had been pope from 708 to 715. The bishop of Worcester challenged the bulls on the grounds that they were "'forgeries in parchment and script, thread and *bulla*.'"[38] The documents were then handed to Innocent III who felt the parchment, tugged on the *bulla* and thread and, on the basis of that physical examination, pronounced the bulls genuine. According to Clanchy, "the papal judgement in Evesham's favour encouraged Thomas to copy the bulls of Constantine I ... into his chronicle for future reference. The copies demonstrate that the bulls were undoubtedly forged and ... it is likely that [Thomas] had played a major part in deceiving the pope."[39] The case "suggests that, although by 1200 the papal *curia* had developed rules for detecting forgeries of recent decretals, it had no effective means of checking documents which claimed to be hundreds of years old." Clanchy observes:

> Neither the papal curia nor lesser courts had anything to gain by scrutinising forged charters with strict regularity. Decisions had to be reached in cases even when both parties produced forged documents. Conventions seem to have existed among the higher clergy within which forgery, while not being openly approved of or acknowledged, was at least tolerated. Every ruler in Europe, from the pope downwards, had suspect title-deeds if historically authentic writings were to become the yardstick of authority.[40]

As Clanchy makes clear, "it was not that literate standards of documentation were unknown, but rather that they could not be uniformly or readily applied to particular cases, because literate ways of doing business were still too novel."[41] In legal disputes, therefore, parties continued to rely heavily on the authority and the testimony of witnesses in order to establish the authenticity of documents making political or religious claims.

1.3 The Renaissance

The discovery of a coherent and internally consistent method for assessing the trustworthiness of documents created in a past for which there were no living witnesses depended upon a scholarly awareness of the difference between the past and the present and on the capacity of documents to reveal historical facts as well as legal facts. Movement in this direction is discernible from around the fifteenth century with the emergence of Renaissance humanism. As Donald Kelley explains:

> Renaissance humanism represented not merely new knowledge of and new appreciation for classical antiquity ... but a major reorientation in thought. What happened, in brief, was that the mere problem of gaining access to the past began to supersede the problem of how to make use of it. Increasingly, scholars were struck by the distance and the disparity between themselves and men of former ages. ... Even those humanists who ... tended to idealise antiquity could not avoid the fact of historical change, so conspicuously reflected in the vicissitudes of literary style, social customs, and religious practices. ... Wrestling with this anthropological dilemma ... led them toward what was, in effect, a principle of cultural relativity.[42]

Philology, a creature of Renaissance humanism, provided a specific impetus to the elaboration of a more sophisticated method for determining the trustworthiness of a document, based on an assessment of the plausibility of its content relative to the legal, historical, and social context in which it was generated. By focusing scholarly attention on the language, form and historical context of documents, philologists "established a new logos upon the assumption that language reproduced, if it did not actually create, the configurations of reality."[43] The establishment of the new logos was a result of a new respect for particular facts and for original sources. Though their understanding of them was limited, philologists introduced the concepts of cultural context and anachronism into scholarly discourse.

Lorenzo Valla's critique of canon law and, in particular, his exposure of the fraudulent Donation of Constantine, the cornerstone of papal supremacy in temporal matters, is one of the most famous examples of philological criticism in the fifteenth century.[44] The history of the donation is neatly summarised by Olga Zorzi Pugliese:

> It was an age-old belief that the Emperor Constantine the Great (d.337) had donated temporal power to Sylvester I, Bishop of Rome (314-55), after recovering from leprosy. This gift, supposedly granted back in the fourth century, was the justification many popes of the late Middle Ages had cited, either sincerely or through guile, for their intervention in political affairs and their claim to the right to investiture. However, the document reporting the alleged donation, that is the *Constitutum Constantini* charter, was actually drawn up in the eighth century, probably in Rome, and an abridged version of it was incorporated into Church law, through Palea's interpolations, four hundred years later in the mid-twelfth century. The document consisted of a series of declarations which Constantine supposedly made in the year 313; in them he stated the primacy of the Church of Rome and of its head, declared the power of the pope to be superior to that of the emperor, announced his decision to transfer the seat of the empire to Byzantium, and granted land and other privileges to Sylvester.[45]

Earlier scholars had questioned the legality of the donation but Valla's *The Falsely-Believed and Forged Donation of Constantine*, published in 1440, provided the most compelling proof that the document was fraudulent and that the donation had never been made.

According to Pugliese, what is striking about Valla's treatise, apart from his conclusion, is his painstaking analysis of the text of the donation document, in which he exposes a number of cultural anachronisms, linguistic discrepancies, and geographical oddities.

> Among the references made to the customs and attire of the protagonists involved in the alleged granting of power, the charter refers to the pope's bejewelled diadem when, in fact, silk caps were still worn by pontiffs at the time. The word *datum* (given or dated) appears in a closing phrase of the text, when such usage was reserved for the drafting of letters to be delivered to a specific addressee. The mention of Constantinople too is an obvious blunder, he finds, since the city had not yet been founded and at that time the site was known as Byzantium. Along with examples of grammatical barbarisms, Valla detects implausible linguistic

practice in words like *satraps*, alien to the vocabulary employed in the fourth century to describe the political organization of the Empire.[46]

Valla also finds reason for suspicion in the fact that the text itself is located in the interpolations rather than in the body of Gratian's *Decretum* (a synthesis of Church law compiled by Gratian, a twelfth century Italian professor of law and moral philosophy). The charter is nowhere to be found in the oldest compilations of Church law.[47]

Apart from the internal evidence provided by the prose and location of the charter text, Valla also discovers a dearth of external documentation that would support the view that the donation had taken place. Historical works written at the time made no mention of the event. As Valla declares, "Let all the Latin and Greek histories be consulted, let all the other authors who mention this period be cited: you will not find a single discrepancy regarding this matter ... [the] historian would not have kept silent about the donation of the Western Empire had it taken place."[48] Nor, argued Valla, had any commemorative coins come down: "If ever you had ruled over Rome, an infinite number of coins would be found commemorating the Supreme Pontiffs, whereas none are to be found either of gold or silver, and no one remembers having seen any."[49] The plausibility of Constantine willingly surrendering temporal power is also challenged on psychological grounds. Since rulers instinctively seek to enlarge their territory rather than diminish it, why, asks Valla, "do you declare as being credible that which is contrary to the opinion of men?"[50] In Valla's view, the textual, historical, and psychological inconsistencies that riddled the donation document testified against its verisimilitude and, hence, authenticity.

Donald Kelley summarises the key components of the philological paradigm that emerges through Valla's treatise as follows:

> First, ... Valla demanded a return to human "reality," for he was convinced that knowledge could be attained only through the examination of particular things. ... In the second place, Valla called for a return to original sources; for style was an organic part of doctrine, and antiquity had to be allowed to speak in its own inimitable accents. ... Lastly, and inevitably, Valla adopted an attitude that was both pluralistic and relativistic. Every age had literally to be understood in its own terms, and truth could no more be separated from its cultural environment, or from its cultural style, than form could be separated from matter. Thus Valla's method was fundamentally comparative as well as historical. Valla's historical thought was founded, in short, upon the recognition of a principle of individuality, of a determinable process of temporal change, and of a kind of cultural relativism.[51]

Valla's treatise proved that textual criticism could "erode or even destroy the claim to authority for a document which for centuries had been accepted despite some doubts. A single scholar could now cast doubt even on essential parts of tradition."[52]

From that point forward, philology, or source criticism, became an increasingly accepted means of determining the trustworthiness of historical documents and is intimately connected to the beginnings of a critical historical method.[53]

Some of the most significant developments in the evolution of the historical method occurred in the context of the flowering of historical legal studies. Academic jurists of the sixteenth century, especially those of France, were deeply influenced by humanism in general and philology in particular. Jean Bodin's writings on the principles of public law, for example, were based on a historical "comparison and synthesis of all the juridical experience of all the most famous states."[54] As Bodin and others turned to the sources of the past, questions about the trustworthiness of those sources, inevitably, were raised: questions concerning the types of sources and their relative authority, the tests of documentary authenticity, and the indications of an author's biases. Aspects of these questions had certainly been discussed earlier but it was only with the juristic revolution that these questions were systematically related and developed as a methodology of criticism.[55] As Barbara Shapiro notes, "[b]oth as historians and lawyers, French scholars searched for reliable witnesses and sought to date documents and assess the good faith, knowledge, and credibility of those who initially had prepared them."[56]

The trustworthiness of historical sources was challenged most strenuously by the Pyrrhonists, a group of radical sceptics who questioned the very grounds of historical belief.[57] The Pyrrhonists believed that historical knowledge was not possible because all such knowledge was filtered through unreliable sources. The sources of unreliability, they argued, were manifold: a witness to an event who is a participant in that event might be able to provide more accurate detail about it, its underlying motives, and so on, but he is likely to be partial since he is a participant in that event. On the other hand, a witness who is not a participant in the event has the advantage of disinterestedness but the disadvantage of not possessing any privileged access to the event.

The Pyrrhonist attacks on the grounds for historical belief were, fundamentally, attacks on the trustworthiness of historical sources as testimonies of past events. As Jacques Le Goff reminds us, the importance of testimony to historical methodology may be traced back to Greco-Roman antiquity and, more specifically, to Herodotus, for whom "testimony *par excellence* is personal testimony, the kind in which the historian can say: 'I saw, I heard'":

> The "great" historians of Greco-Roman antiquity dealt exclusively or preferentially with the recent past. After Herodotus, Thucydides wrote the history of the Peloponnesian War, a contemporary event, Xenophon dealt with the Spartan and Theban hegemonies, which he had witnessed firsthand (404-362 B.C.), Polybius devoted his *Histories* chiefly to the period from the Second Punic War (218 B.C.) to his own time (c. 145 B.C.), Sallust and Livy did the same, Tacitus went back to the century preceding his own and Ammianus Marcellinus was interested especially in the second half of the fourth century. Nevertheless,

from the fifth century B.C. onward, ancient historians were capable of collecting good documentation on the past, but that did not prevent them from being primarily interested in contemporary or recent events.[58]

It is not surprising then that in secular history the rules of historical method that began to emerge in the sixteenth century focused on the trustworthiness of earlier chroniclers of history both as witnesses and as recorders of events.

Jean Bodin and another academic jurist, François Baudouin, made perhaps the most significant contributions to historical method during this period. Bodin developed standards for assessing the reliability of historical sources while Baudouin articulated rudimentary rules for establishing their authenticity. Baudouin believed that "historical studies must be placed upon a solid foundation of law ... and jurisprudence must be joined to history."[59] Consequently, the rules he formulated were based on contemporary legal practice. As he explains:

In court ... *viva voce* evidence is normally demanded because it can be subjected to direct interrogation; in history, conversely, and "especially in one which is not of our age," the characteristic form of information is a "testimony" not a "testifier". But although written information is peculiarly historical, it is not necessarily ruled out of court. ... Indeed, in the special case of public records, it is not only admitted by the lawyer, but may even be preferred to oral testimony. The evidence of history, accordingly, may be justified by legal practice. But this is only on condition that it conform to the rules on written instruments.[60]

Baudouin further points out that in a court of law when a witness' statement is read rather than delivered orally it must be presented verbatim and intact since any alteration or suppression would amount to a dictation of his testimony. He referred to the fact that in the probate of contracts, wills, and other acts the original signed document is preferred to a copy and must be produced if it is extant (the best evidence rule). The inference Baudouin draws from these legal rules to history is that "derivative accounts" must be completely excluded in favour of the "source" or what he calls "archetype."

The juriconsults, certainly, when it is a matter of the faith and probity of instruments, do not stop at what are called *exemplars*, but require the *authentica* or 'archetypes.' And shall we, in the question of some ancient history, prefer more recent witnesses to those who were very ancient and classic, so to speak? And shall a secondary and interpolated narrative be of greater credit than the first and the intact?[61]

The general principle underlying the rule requiring the privileging of the account closest to the event, is, as Baudouin puts it, that:

> The newer and more recent a narration of the past, the more
> mendacious it normally becomes. For as wine grows weaker the
> more it is diluted, and at last becomes devoid of taste, as a rumour,
> the longer it progresses, recedes even further from the truth and
> constantly increases in its falsity, so a history, which has been
> tossed about in many repetitions, and besprinkled with the words of
> many versions, will often be at last contaminated, and thus
> degenerate to fable.[62]

In making such an assertion, Baudouin draws an historical analogy to the legal rule
excluding hearsay testimony although he accepts that in history, as in law, it may be
necessary to accept the testimony of secondary witnesses if no alternative exists or
if the author is considered judicious and not too distant from the event.[63]

In his assessment of Baudouin's contribution to critical historical method,
Julian Franklin suggests that Baudouin's criticism demonstrates "the beginnings of
an operationally significant distinction between original and secondary
documents."[64] His conception of what constitutes trustworthy historical evidence,
however, is still fairly crude, as Franklin makes clear:

> Baudouin, to begin with, does not distinguish, in the general class
> of original materials, between original narrative relations, in which
> events are consciously interpreted, and documentary records or
> "remains," in which transactions are more likely to be noted
> unreflectively, and hence often with more reliability. It is true, of
> course, that, like Bodin and other authors of the period, he is
> enormously impressed by "public monuments," by which are meant
> official records. ... The official monuments are generally regarded
> [however] ... as narrative in different form. And insofar as he
> accords them special status, the ground is not the distinction
> between documentary remains and narrative relation but between
> a publicly attested history and a version that is merely private. For
> the sixteenth century, therefore, the ideal type of source is still the
> literary narrative.[65]

Baudouin's privileging of public documents over private ones harkens back to
Roman and early Church law which also conferred a higher degree of
trustworthiness on public documents.[66]

Baudouin's work is also flawed by the fact that he treats the distinction
between an early and late narrative and the identification of a prime observer as
self-evident when, in fact, these can often only be established by a systematic
comparison of versions since many sources were undated and the relationship
among various testimonies complex. Moreover, as Franklin points out, Baudouin
assumes:

> that the distinction between prime and derivative accounts is an
> aspect of entire works, as though the whole of any secondary

history were directly borrowed from a single older version and so
on back to the "first and the intact." But a derivative account may
sometimes be composed from several sources, and even in
contemporary narratives the individual assertions may often be
derivative, so that, strictly speaking, the distinction between original
and secondary should be applied to statements, not to entire
works.[67]

Notwithstanding its limitations and lack of refinement, Baudouin's approach to
source criticism signals the beginnings of "an impressive system of external or
preliminary criticism."[68]

Baudouin's contribution lay primarily in his elaboration of methods for
evaluating the *authenticity* of an historical source. Bodin's contribution, on the other
hand, lay in his elaboration of methods for evaluating the *reliability* of the authors of
historical sources. In *Methodus ad facilem historiarum cognitionem*, Bodin identifies
a number of rules and standards for identifying a good historian and for determining
the circumstances under which he may be trusted. Though they underwent some
considerable re-statement, Bodin's rules were based on ones originally laid down
by Polybius who maintained that "the good historian ... must be reliably informed
as to the facts, which means ... that he must have either witnessed them himself
or directly questioned persons who were present."[69] However, unlike Polybius, or
Baudouin for that matter, Bodin gives tacit authority to a secondary author on the
grounds that he is more detached from the event and, therefore, a more trustworthy
source. As Bodin states it, "[a] historian of somewhat later date is in a better position
to speak frankly and is somewhat less susceptible to bias than one who was too
close to the event."[70] From Bodin's perspective, an author's reliability derives more
from his research habits, i.e., his willingness to go to the sources and his sense of
obligation in reporting them correctly, than it does from his proximity to the event.

Bodin recognised that all historians, even good ones, are susceptible to
bias. Among the potential sources of bias he identifies are patriotism, religious faith,
attachment to a cause, self-interest, self-aggrandisement, and fear, any of which
may compromise the trustworthiness of the author's account of events. The biases
Bodin cites are analogous to those cited by the Pyrrhonists in their sceptical attacks
on history. But whereas the Pyrrhonists found in such biases "indications of
complete depravity and ... the sole motivations from which history is written," Bodin
treated them as psychologically normal.[71] Moreover, unlike the Pyrrhonists, he
balanced his account of the various circumstances in which bias may be expected
with an enumeration of circumstances in which bias is unlikely to occur. Accounts
which do not implicate the author's interests one way or another or which contain
admissions in conflict with his interests, for example, are presumed to be less
biased.[72]

In Franklin's estimation, Bodin's critique represents a clear theoretical
advance beyond the generalities of Baudouin:

For [Baudouin], as for the skeptics, an historian is either "good" or "bad" as such, and his willingness to tell the truth is either to be accepted or rejected as a whole. It is correctly recognised, of course, that a good historian is only a "probable" authority, and that his particular assertions are not to be followed if implausible. But his authority as such, being a judgement of his total personality, creates the same presumption for everything he says. With Bodin, however, the standpoint is more clearly psychological, and there is a corresponding shift in emphasis from the judgement of an author as a whole to an estimation, from the bearing of his interests, of his attitude towards different topics. In other words, the idea of a "choice among historians," of their discrimination into lists of "good" and "bad," is partially transformed into the judgement of specific statements.[73]

Bodin's elaboration of potential sources of bias suggests that the concept of internal criticism as a means of establishing the reliability of a document was understood in the sixteenth century, even if that understanding was somewhat crude. More than anything, the works of Bodin and Baudouin demonstrate the beginnings of a doctrine of historical method, i.e., a distinction between original and secondary sources, a means of establishing the authenticity of documents, and a set of psychological criteria for determining the bias of a source.[74] The contributions of these two jurists became sources for the subsequent tradition and continued to be cited in works of historical criticism throughout the seventeenth and eighteenth centuries.

1.4 The Seventeenth Century

The seventeenth century witnessed a number of refinements in historical methodology. By its end, the distinction between original and derivative authorities had become, in Arnaldo Momigliano's words, "the common patrimony of historical research." The work of antiquarians played a conspicuous role in the refinement of that distinction which Momigliano explains in the following way:

By original authorities we mean either statements by eye-witnesses, or, documents, and other material remains, that are contemporary with the events which they attest. By derivative authorities we mean historians or chroniclers who relate and discuss events which they have not witnessed but which they have heard of or inferred directly or indirectly from original authorities. We praise original authorities – or sources – for being reliable, but we praise non-contemporary historians – or derivative authorities – for displaying sound judgement in the interpretation and evaluation of the original sources.[75]

R.G. Collingwood has further observed that the systematic examination of authorities for the purpose of determining their relative credibility also resulted, by the end of the seventeenth century, in the transformation of "authorities" into "sources."

> As soon as it became understood that a given statement, made by a given author, must never be accepted for historical truth until the credibility of the author in general and of this statement in particular had been systematically inquired into, the word 'authority' disappeared from the vocabulary of historical method, except as an archaistic survival; for the man who makes the statement came henceforth to be regarded not as someone whose word must be taken for the truth of what he says, which is what was meant by calling him an authority, but as someone who has voluntarily placed himself in the witness-box for cross-examination. The document hitherto called an authority now acquired a new status, properly described by calling it a 'source', a word indicating simply that it contains the statement, without any implications as to its value.[76]

The credibility of historical testimony (*De fide historica*) was a recurring theme in historical writing of the seventeenth and eighteenth centuries.[77] According to Anthony Grafton:

> Writers ... like the German F.W. Bierling ... addressed the wider problem of establishing rules for the criticism of sources. Long before Ranke had made archive-diving fashionable, Bierling had pointed out ... that archives can mislead. He admitted that many of his contemporaries thought this impossible, but a careful analysis of their content proved his point. Archives consisted, he argued, chiefly of documents created by ambassadors and other public officials. But such men normally had to report on deliberations to which they did not have direct access and the intentions of monarchs who did not speak frankly. Their reports, in short, contained "what the ambassador guesses to be true or considers to be memorable, not always what is true."[78]

It was also during the seventeenth century that historical scholarly procedure began to take into serious account the need for the historian to demonstrate his own trustworthiness in his use of the sources. Anthony Grafton has described the emergence of the footnote in its modern form "as part of an effort to counter scepticism about the possibility of attaining knowledge about the past."[79] Grafton credits Pierre Bayle, the compiler of the *Dictionnaire historique et critique* (begun in 1690 and published in 1696), with primary responsibility for establishing the footnote as a standard part of scholarly procedure. Given that his contemporaries considered Bayle a Pyrrhonist, the attribution is somewhat ironic. The *Dictionnaire* was a historical dictionary of ancient, medieval, and modern persons and places, supported by a vast apparatus of references and citations. In it, Bayle exposed numerous errors and contradictions between different historians and chroniclers, between different texts, and within the texts themselves, and maintained that the historical record of all periods and places had been corrupted by massive falsification. Not surprisingly, many readers viewed the Dictionnaire as an act of subversion, designed to undermine religious orthodoxy and, more generally, any notion that it was possible to achieve precise knowledge about the past. Nevertheless, Grafton points out, "Bayle emphasized the rules of good scholarship as well as the defects of bad. And in doing so he stated, formally, rules of scholarly procedure."[80] In defending his dictionary, Bayle asserted that "it is necessary to bring to bear proofs, to examine them, confirm them, and clarify them. In a word, this is a work of compilation." Grafton credits Bayle with making compilation "a term of pride":

> More elegant writers, who refused to provide the evidence in full, had brought scholarship into discredit. Bayle's vast accumulation of passages from other texts, of exegesis, summary, and rebuttal, was a profound exercise in truth-seeking – the only one indeed, that could allay the fears of readers rightly discouraged by the normal methods of uncritical scholarship: "And because many frauds are committed in the citations of authors, and those who honestly abridge a passage, do not always express the full force of it, it is incredible how much judicious persons are grown distrustful."[81]

By the end of the eighteenth century it had become an unquestioned assumption on the part of historians "that a serious work of history must have notes; that these must lead the reader to the original sources and represent them accurately; that notes in fact provided the diagnostic test of a historian's critical expertise."[82]

Jurists and other secular historians of the sixteenth and seventeenth centuries laid part of the foundation on which systematic methods for determining the trustworthiness of documentary sources could be built. Ecclesiastical historians during that same time period laid another part of that foundation. As Grafton explains, source criticism had long been a concern of ecclesiastical history.

> [Ecclesiastical] historians … wrote as controversialists and believers: as Jews seeking to prove the Torah older than Homer or as Christians determined to prove the priority of a doctrine or an institution. The genre's ends determined its form: not the neat, classical prose of the political historians, but a mixture of technical arguments and supporting documents, the latter quoted verbatim in the text proper. Documents performed two functions, each vital: they supported the theses put forward by the author and they gave the reader a distinct, vivid sense of what it had meant to be a faithful Jew or a Christian in a distant and more difficult world.[83]

Much of the impetus for the flourishing of ecclesiastical history in the early modern period was provided by doctrinal conflicts of the Reformation and Counter-Reformation. George Huppert writes: "Among intellectuals the Reformation was at bottom an historical question, as they kept battling each other with documents to support their notion of what the primitive church had been like and measuring the historical variations of their opponents from this standard."[84] Intellectuals and theologians alike adopted for their own purposes the antiquity criterion of trustworthiness that had existed in law since the time of Tertullian. The words of the Protestant theologian, Nicolas Vignier, in 1599, are indicative:

> Therefore one has to go back to the sources and say with our Lord Jesus Christ: it was not always thus since the beginning. ... Jesus Christ is my antiquity, said St. Ignatius, and not to obey him is manifest perdition. My authentic archives are his cross, his death, his resurrection ... . That which comes first is the most true, said Tertullian. That which is at the beginning is first: that which is of the Apostles is at the beginning. It is therefore a very necessary thing to know what doctrines were held from the very beginning in the Church and to see graphically represented the various mutations experienced by the Church.[85]

1.4.1 THE BIRTH OF DIPLOMATICS

In the seventeenth century, the diplomatic wars (*bella diplomatica*) waged within the Catholic Church by Bollandists and Dominicans gave birth to a whole range of modern technical disciplines aimed at determining the trustworthiness of historical documents, among them, paleography, sigillography, and diplomatics. In 1675, the Bollandists published the second volume of the *Acta Sanctorum*, "in which the testimonies related to the lives of single saints were evaluated for the purpose of separating the facts from the legend."[86] The second volume included an introductory essay by Daniel Van Papenbroeck, who outlined general criteria for establishing the authenticity of diplomas (e.g., donations, privileges) of Merovingian and other rulers of France before the year 1000. In applying these criteria, Papenbroeck brought into disrepute all the Merovingian diplomas, most of which were preserved in the Benedictine Monastery of Saint-Denis.

Six years later, Jean Mabillon, a monk of Saint-Denis who was compiling the lives of Benedictine saints, responded by publishing a six-part treatise *De re diplomatica libri VI*. Mabillon defined the new science of *diplomatic* as "the establishment of 'certain and accurate terms and rules by which authentic instruments can be distinguished from spurious, and certain and genuine ones from uncertain and suspect ones.'"[87] In the first two parts of the treatise Mabillon stated the principles of diplomatic criticism, i.e., the tests by which charters can be identified as true or false. In Part I, he defined the different kinds of charters and examined the main materials generally used for documents as well as the ink and kinds of writing. In Part II, he examined the language of the documents, the characteristic parts of medieval charters, the seals, and the systems of chronology used in dating them. On the basis of this examination, "Mabillon stated what, for a particular time and place, was the correct form for a genuine document, and presented ... the general principles of diplomatics."[88] The remaining four parts of his treatise were devoted to proofs and illustrations of these principles and the manner in which they were to be applied. The sixth part consisted of more than two hundred documents copied from the originals, with notes and arguments demonstrating why they should be considered authentic.

The fundamental assumptions of Mabillon's treatise were that the context of a document's creation is made manifest in its physical and intellectual form and that this form can be separated from the document's content and examined independently of it. By comparing documents created in different periods and issued by different chanceries, and discovering the attributes they shared, as well as those they did not share, Mabillon was able to articulate the necessary and sufficient elements of documents and identify the purpose each fulfilled in the document as a whole.

Apart from identifying the visible manifestations of documentary elements, Mabillon looked at the document conceptually as embodying a system of both external and internal elements consisting of *acts*, which are the determinant cause of documentary creation, *persons* who concur in its formation, *procedures*, which are the means by which acts are carried out and the *documentary form* itself which binds all the elements together. By decontextualising and universalising all the elements of documentary creation, Mabillon established a methodology for determining the authenticity of documents across juridical systems and over centuries. By focusing attention on the importance of chancery procedures in the establishment of norms for documentary creation, he provided future diplomatists with the tools for assessing the conformity of the document's formal elements with those established by chancery procedures. The uncharacteristic absence (or presence) of certain elements provided grounds for doubting the document's authenticity.

Mabillon's achievement is summarised by Leonard Boyle in the following way:

> Above all else, Mabillon formulated a ... comprehensive and compelling statement of documentary criticism ... when he argued that any proper evaluation of the character, content and authenticity of a given document must take account of internal as well as external criteria; of the changing fashions of composition, handwriting, and style from area to area and from age to age; and of the history, personnel, and usages of chanceries, notarial offices, and scriptoria from place to place and from period to period.[89]

Marc Bloch declared the year 1681, the year of the publication of *De re diplomatica*, to be "truly a great one in the history of the human mind, for the criticism of the documents of archives was definitely established." In Bloch's view, the publication of Mabillon's treatise marked "the decisive moment in the history of the critical method" because from that day forward, methodological doubt became the starting point of historical inquiry.[90] For Jacques Le Goff, Mabillon's contribution to historical method resides in the fact that his work "teaches that the agreement of two independent sources establishes the truth and, taking his inspiration from Descartes, [Mabillon] applies the principle of 'everywhere making enumerations so complete and so general' that one can be 'sure of not having omitted anything.'"[91]

The purpose of diplomatics was to establish the authenticity of medieval records across legal systems and over time. The meaning diplomatics ascribed to authenticity, however, differed somewhat from its original legal meaning. Since antiquity, authenticity had been associated with the concept of public faith. To declare a document authentic was equivalent to saying that the document was recognised as true by the juridical system in which it was created. The legal trustworthiness of a record and methods to guarantee public faith focused on external means of ensuring the recognition of the record by the legal system in which it was created (e.g., preservation in a public place, compilation by a notary). A record's legal truth was considered a sufficient guarantee of its historical truth. Diplomatics, on the other hand, sought to establish a record's historical truth as well as its legal truth on the basis of its documentary truth. Moving from the observation of perceptible matters of fact (the elements of the document itself) to assertions about imperceptible matters of fact (the past in which the document was created), diplomatic methodology transformed written facts into historical sources and nurtured the belief that knowledge about a past to which there was no direct access could, nevertheless, be attained by examining its documentary traces.

The diplomatic method for assessing the trustworthiness of a record represented a significant departure from earlier methods in its approach to adducing evidence. Earlier methods had relied on external evidence, i.e., evidence derived from circumstances or considerations outside of the document (e.g., the evidence of witnesses, the evidence of authority); diplomatics relied instead on internal evidence (the evidence embedded within the document's physical and intellectual form). Ian Hacking maintains that the concept of internal evidence was unknown before the late seventeenth century. In making this claim, he distinguishes between verisimilitude, which "is a matter of one thing being or not being what it seems or pretends to be" and internal evidence, which "is a matter of inferring one thing from another thing."[92] According to Hacking, the arguments Lorenzo Valla makes in his exposure of the fraudulent donation of Constantine are based on verisimilitude rather than on inference. Valla looked at the document's contents, the claims it made, and the prose style in which it was couched, and concluded that the Donation did not resemble a true document of the fourth century: it lacked verisimilitude.[93]

The rules of textual criticism enunciated in Mabillon's treatise, on the other hand, reflect the new conception of evidence as inference (or inductive evidence). Mabillon treated stylistic aberrations and historical anachronisms found within a document's formal elements as evidence that a document was faulty or fraudulent. In this case, one thing (a particular abbreviation or script) served as evidence against the claim that the whole document was sound. Diplomatic analysis translated a document into a system of internal signs or traces that pointed to a reality beyond them. Each trace was a small window into the past in which the document was created.

1.4.2 THE EMERGENCE OF RATIONALIST EMPIRICISM

The introduction of the concept of evidence as inference provided a necessary precondition for the emergence of a new philosophy of rational belief based on probability rather than certainty.[94] That philosophy, in turn, radically altered the epistemological framework in which assessments of record trustworthiness would be subsequently carried out. Many of its tenets were laid out in 1689 in John Locke's *Essay Concerning Human Understanding*[95] which, according to Barbara Shapiro, "represented a culmination of earlier efforts to redefine and clarify the varieties of knowledge and certainty."[96] For Locke, knowledge manifested itself in three forms: intuition, demonstration, and sensation. Knowledge by demonstration was "the showing the agreement or disagreement of two ideas, by the intervention of one or more proofs, which have a constant, immutable, and visible connexion one with another."[97] Since such knowledge was necessarily "short and scanty," determinations of the truth or falsity of propositions concerning most matters of interest or consequence in life must be based on judgements of probability. Locke defined probability as "the appearance of such an agreement or disagreement, by the intervention of proofs, whose connexion is not constant and immutable, or at least is not perceived to be so, but is, or appears for the most part to be so, and is enough to induce the mind to judge the proposition to be true or false, rather than the contrary."[98] Conformity with one's own experience or the testimony of others' experience provided the grounds for such judgements; in judging the testimony of others, the number, integrity and skill of the witnesses, the consistency of the testimony's parts and contrary testimonies were all to be taken into consideration.[99] Assent to any proposition was to be based on the strength of the evidence. "One places a level of confidence in the proposition that is proportioned to its probability on that satisfactory evidence. If the proposition is highly probable on the evidence, one believes it very firmly; if it only is quite probable, one believes it rather weakly; etc."[100]

The ideas of Locke and others concerning the relationship between probability and evidence exercised a significant influence on the emerging disciplines of law and history.[101] As Barbara Shapiro points out, Locke and other philosophers, such as Robert Boyle, assumed that documentary evidence fell under their general theory of evidence and knowledge:

> For example, both [Locke] and Boyle noted that an attested copy of a record is good evidence that an event occurred, but that an unattested copy is not as good. The testimony of a witness is good evidence that an event has occurred, but "a report of his report is not and will not be admitted in a court of law. The further from the source, the weaker the evidence becomes."[102]

Legal and historical scholars came to agree that in investigating issues of fact, demonstrable or infallible proof should not be insisted upon and that determinations of fact in history and adjudication were no different from those in other investigations. From that time on, the truth of any proposition would be established by reasoning from the relevant evidence and it would be measured, not in terms of absolute certainty but rather in terms of probability, which would always be a matter of degree.

1.5 Eighteenth and Nineteenth Century Developments in Evidence Law

These ideas concerning the relationship between knowledge, belief, and evidence, which culminated in a new theory of epistemology, known as rationalist empiricism, exercised a formative influence on the Anglo-American tradition of evidence scholarship that was beginning to take shape in the eighteenth century. The first specialised study of legal evidence in that tradition, Sir Geoffrey Gilbert's *The Law of Evidence*, was based explicitly on Lockean theories of knowledge. In the opening paragraphs of his treatise, Gilbert asserted that

> It has been observed by a very learned man [identified at the bottom of the page as "Mr. Locke"] that there are several degrees from perfect certainty and demonstration, quite down to unprobability and unlikeness, even to the confines of impossibility; and there are several acts of the mind proportioned to these degrees of assent, from full assurance and confidence, quite down to conjecture, doubt, distrust, and disbelief.
>
> Now what is to be done, in all trials of right, is to range all matters on the scale of probability, so as to lay most weight where the cause ought to preponderate, and thereby to make the most exact discernment that can be, in relation to right.[103]

Gilbert accorded to written evidence "the first place in the discourses of probability" on the grounds that, unlike human memory, which was fallible, "contracts reduced to writing are the most sedate and deliberate acts of the mind and are more advantageously secured from all corruption, by the forms and solemnities of the law".[104] The greater part of his treatise was occupied with establishing a hierarchy of written evidence, with the memorials of the legislature and the King's courts of justice at the top of that hierarchy and private documents at the bottom.

The Law of Evidence was considered the leading work of its kind for at least a half century (first published in 1754, it was last re-issued in 1801).[105] In the early part of the nineteenth century, however, it was subjected to a scathing critical analysis by another legal theorist in the Rationalist tradition, Jeremy Bentham, who found Gilbert's entire work pervaded by a strain of "anility, garrulity, narrow-mindedness, absurdity, perpetual misrepresentation, and indefatigable self-contradiction".[106] Bentham's attack on Gilbert's theory of evidence in *An Introductory View of the Rationale of Judicial Evidence* drew needed attention to the two separate aspects of record trustworthiness and sharpened the contours of its legal scope and meaning. What raised Bentham's ire was Gilbert's assertion that written evidence, as a matter of general principle, was more trustworthy than oral testimony.[107] In making such an assertion,

Bentham argued, Gilbert failed to distinguish between what Bentham termed "makeshift evidence" (i.e., unoriginal evidence such as hearsay and casually written evidence) and "preappointed evidence" (i.e., evidence specifically created with a view to being used as evidence and thereby invested with securities to ensure its trustworthiness).[108] He maintained that Gilbert's apparent inability to distinguish among different kinds of records possessing different degrees of trustworthiness betrayed a more fundamental inability to distinguish between the trustworthiness of a record as a record and its trustworthiness as a statement of facts. "Two questions which [Gilbert] confounds at the very outset, and is never tired of confounding, are the question of authenticity and the question of verity – the question concerning the authenticity of a script, and the question concerning the verity of the assertion contained in it."[109] Gilbert had placed first in the hierarchy of written evidence the legal memorials of the legislature and of the king's courts of justice which were deposited at the Treasury of Westminster. According to Bentham, such records were notoriously lacking in both authenticity and verity, being: "Compounds or reservoirs of truths and lies undistinguishably shaken together, penned by nobody knows who, and kept under the orders, how seldom soever, if ever, actually subjected to the eyes of the judges of Westminster Hall."[110] In Bentham's view, the authenticity and reliability of records were matters to be proven, not presumed.

Bentham returned to the conceptual distinction between authenticity and verity in his monumental work, *The Rationale of Judicial Evidence*. In the *Rationale*, he substituted the word, "fairness" for "verity," but the distinction he had earlier established remained the same:

> A distinction must here be observed, between evidence of authenticity, and evidence of fairness. Authenticity may be proved by similitude of hands: it may be proved, provisionally at least, *ex tenore*, with or without the other presumption *ex custodia*. To the question of fairness, none of these media of proof, it is evident, can apply. A bond is produced in evidence: the obligor may have been in a state of insanity or intoxication when he executed it: he may have executed it with the fear of a pistol or a dagger before his eyes, or in a state of illegal imprisonment, to which he had been subjected for that purpose. Of none of these modifications will the signature, or the custody of the instrument, or the tenor of it, afford any sort of warning.[111]

Bentham's acerbic critique of Gilbert's rules of evidence effectively invalidated the notion that written evidence should be treated as inherently more trustworthy than oral evidence It did not, however, invalidate the rationalist assumptions on which Gilbert based his theory of the law of evidence. During the nineteenth century, several treatises on the law of evidence were written.[112] According to Twining, all of these share a number of common assumptions, among them: (1) knowledge about particular past events is possible; (2) the establishment of the truth of alleged facts in adjudication is typically a matter of probabilities, falling short of absolute certainty; (3) judgements about the probabilities of allegations about particular past events can be reached by reasoning from relevant evidence presented to the decision-maker; (4) the characteristic mode of reasoning about probabilities is induction; and (5) judgements about probabilities have, generally speaking, to be based on common sense logic and experience, which may be supplemented, in appropriate circumstances, by specialised scientific or expert knowledge.[113] These assumptions constitute the core of the rationalist tradition of evidence scholarship, a tradition that has continued into the twentieth century, primarily through John Henry Wigmore's *A Treatise on the Anglo-American System of Evidence in Trials at Common Law*, which provides the theoretical foundation for the Common law rules of evidence.[114]

By the end of the nineteenth century, rules for assessing the authenticity and reliability of records as evidence were firmly embedded in Anglo-American Common law. The rules governing the authentication of records, e.g., authentication by age (the ancient documents rule), by official custody, by official seal, and by comparison of handwriting could be traced back to Roman law and had been standard features of medieval legal procedure. The rule requiring the production of documentary originals (the best evidence rule) can also be traced back to Roman law; it did not, however, enter the Common law until the eighteenth century. There had been a rule of pleading in profert since at least the fifteenth century which required that documents on which a claim was based must be presented to the court but the rule only applied to sealed writings and to civil cases. Other documents might be placed before the tribunal or witnesses might simply make reference to documents without producing them. This practice was increasingly seen as irregular and by the eighteenth century it was a rule that an original document must be produced, unless unfeasible, to prove its terms.[115]

At Common law, the reliability of business records as testimonial assertions was dealt with under the regular entries exception to the hearsay rule. The roots of that exception extended back to a seventeenth century doctrine that permitted the shop-books of parties to be entered into evidence since, as parties to an action, they were prohibited from testifying. The rule disappeared by the end of the seventeenth century as the self-serving nature of its usage became apparent. Subsequently, the courts began to allow the admission of books of regular entries prepared by third parties, including clerks of a party, if the entrant was deceased at the time of trial. The regular entries exception was firmly established by 1832.[116] Although one of its underpinnings was necessity (the death of the entrant), the exception was also justified on the grounds of a circumstantial probability of trustworthiness.

1.6 Nineteenth-Century Developments in Historical Method

The nineteenth century was also an important period for the codification of historical methods for determining the trustworthiness of records as historical sources. In 1898, Charles Victor Langlois and Charles Seignobos published *Introduction aux études historiques*. It was immediately translated into English and published later the same year as *Introduction to the Study of History*.[117] The *Introduction* represented the culmination of efforts to identify the scope of historical criticism, define the various categories of historical evidence, and establish procedures for determining their authenticity and reliability.[118] The principles of historical evidence that were codified in the nineteenth century were built on a tradition of philological or source criticism dating back at least to the fifteenth century. During the eighteenth century, philological studies blossomed, particularly in the philosophical faculties of German universities, and provided the intellectual formation of the most influential nineteenth century historians. Leopold von Ranke studied classical philology under Barthold Georg Niebuhr and considered Niebuhr's work "a model of the method of historical research."[119]

The methods practised by Ranke and codified by Langlois and Seignobos reflect an aspiration to achieve a "scientific history." The trustworthiness of documents was assessed, accordingly, by means comparable to that employed by the "objective" sciences, and involved the decomposition of a document into a series of statements that were subsequently refined until they resembled a scientific observation. "Scientific history" was based on the claim that:

> history ... is primarily concerned with facts and their causal
> connection – how they acted upon each other. The historian
> works with materials contemporary with the time on which he
> focuses, or at least with early reports about the past, preferably
> documents, whose exactitude and reliability have to be subjected
> to critical examination. Like any other science, therefore, history
> has its own method, the critical method, and Ranke is
> understood to have extended the critical method of philology to
> the entire study of the past. Research in the sources of the past,
> using the critical method, became the precondition and the
> centre of historical scholarship. ... By making the establishment
> of the facts of the past the main aim of historical criticism, Ranke
> set up a clear priority among the sources of history. The first
> place belonged to archival research.[120]

Ranke's clear preference for primary sources had the effect of diminishing the value that previously had been granted to derivative sources, including histories written before 1800.

In previous centuries, Leonard Krieger observes, historians had "looked for a literal truth in the report conveyed by the documents and methodically vetted for error, fraud, interpolation, or other extraneous matter that might distort the faithful translation of past reality in the reports. The scientific historians ... saw in those same reports mere indications, or symbols, of a past reality which had to be reconstructed from the traces left in the documents."[121] This shift in perspective is evident in Langlois' and Seignobos' manual, in which they assert that "the facts of the past are only known to us by the traces of them which have been preserved. These traces, it is true, are directly observed by the historian, but, after that, he has nothing more to observe; what remains is the work of reasoning, in which he endeavours to infer, with the greatest possible exactness, the facts from the traces. The document is his starting-point, the fact his goal."[122]

As historians began to distinguish between the past and its traces, and between documents and historical facts, they also began to draw a clearer distinction between authenticity and reliability. When Mabillon first formulated the principles and methods of diplomatic criticism, authenticity, in the diplomatic sense, referred to the presence in a record of all the elements of form required to enable it to be its own competent witness. Because of the tight controls exercised over the procedures of documentary creation and the limited number of documentary forms produced during the medieval period, early diplomatists did not distinguish between a record's authenticity and its reliability; it was assumed that if a document could be proved trustworthy in form, its contents could be considered trustworthy in fact. With the rise of the state from the sixteenth century onwards, and the consequent increase in the number and variety of documents being produced, such an assumption could no longer be sustained. By the end of the nineteenth century, Langlois and Seignobos were echoing Bentham in their warning to historians not to equate authenticity with historical truth:

> To say that a document is authentic is merely to say that its origin is certain, not that its contents are free from error. But authenticity inspires a degree of respect which disposes us to accept the contents without discussion. To doubt the statements of an authentic document would seem presumptuous, or at least we think ourselves bound to wait for overwhelming proof before we impeach the testimony of the author. ... These natural instincts must be methodically resisted. A document ... is not all of a piece; it is composed of a great number of independent statements, any one of which may be intentionally or unintentionally false, while the others are *bona fide* and accurate. ... It is not, therefore, enough to examine a document as a whole; each of the statements in it must be examined separately; *criticism* is impossible without *analysis*.[123]

The distinction between reliability and authenticity was reinforced in the separate procedures governing the external and internal criticism of documents identified by Langlois and Seignobos.

Authenticity was dealt with under the procedures for external criticism which sought to establish whether the document was an original or a copy; and, if it was a copy, identifying its source, and comparing different versions of the same text in order to ascertain the most authoritative copy. It also attempted to identify the origin of the writing, its author, place, and date, to determine whether there had been any interpolations or continuations made to the text by other authors. In carrying out these procedures, the historian was expected to investigate the document's handwriting and language, the events mentioned in the text, as well as looking at external evidence for clues to confirm or refute its purported authorship.

For medieval documents, external criticism included the application of concepts and principles of diplomatics. The original purpose of diplomatics had been to determine a record's authenticity for legal purposes and that purpose continued into the eighteenth century when its concepts and principles were incorporated into the curriculum of many European faculties of law. By the end of the nineteenth century, however, under the influence of classical philology and the scientific school of historiography, diplomatics had emerged as an auxiliary science of history and a discipline in its own right. The emergence of diplomatics as an academic discipline was helped along by the founding of the École des chartes in France in 1821 and the Austrian Institute of Historical Research in Vienna in 1854. Both institutions aimed to promote the study of the auxiliary sciences of history and, particularly, paleography and diplomatics.

The diplomatist's task was to prepare the ground for the historian by:

[Constructing] a building site for historical material that had been rigorously edited, dated, and critiqued. [The diplomatist] implemented a negative type of critique, if one can call it that, revealing falsifications, separating the wheat from the chaff, and also the straw (the formulary) from the grain (indisputable facts); or to take another metaphor which has had its moment of glory, to destroy the outer crust of the formula, within which the mineral of the data remains captive if it is not reached by the expert intervention of the diplomatist.[124]

In the two centuries that had elapsed since the publication of *De re diplomatica*, diplomatic methodology had undergone some refinement but Mabillon's work remained the standard book on methodology. By the end of the nineteenth century, it had been replaced by manuals such as Harry Bresslau's *Handbuch der Urkundenlehre für Deutschland und Italien*,[125] Arthur Giry's *Manuel de diplomatique*,[126] and Cesare Paoli's *Programma scolastico di paleografia latina e di diplomatica*.[127] The nineteenth century also witnessed significant advances in diplomatic doctrine, due largely to the efforts of Austrian diplomatists such as Théodor von Sickel[128] and Julius Ficker.[129]

As state archives and private collections were opened, and more and more documents became available for publication and study, published editions of medieval charters and other diplomatic texts began to appear with increasing frequency. As the corpus of documentation became increasingly varied, so too did diplomatic analysis. Various branches of diplomatics began to take shape, focusing on chronology (i.e., systems of dating documents), sigillography (i.e., bulls and seals), documentary forms, the status of transmission of documents, various types of copies, the procedures governing documentary creation, the procedures governing specific chanceries, and, of course, the criticism of forgeries, which had given diplomatics its original purpose.[130]

According to Langlois and Seignobos, if a record was found to be a forgery, it was immediately eliminated from any further consideration. If it was found to be authentic, it was then subjected to internal criticism, the purpose of which was to assess the credibility of a record as testimony of the facts contained within it.[131] Specifically, it attempted

> ... by the help of analogies mostly borrowed from general psychology, to reproduce the mental states through which the author of the document passed. Knowing what the author of the document has said, we ask (1) What did he mean? (2) Did he believe what he said? (3) Was he justified in believing whatever he did believe? This last step brings the document to a point where it resembles the data of the objective sciences: it becomes an observation.[132]

Nineteenth century historians emphasised the close connection between the personality of an author and the account he presented on the grounds that such account inevitably reflected the intellectual formation and interests of its author as well as the ideas and preoccupations of the world in which he lived. In Ranke's words: "every writing, not only its value and importance, but in a certain sense its life, depends on the relationship between subject and object, between author and his topic. The first task of every critical examination is to make this relation visible."[133] Internal criticism accomplished this task in three stages. The first stage, *interpretive criticism*, was directed toward establishing the literal and actual meaning of the words used by the author in his account. The second stage involved *the negative criticism of the good faith and accuracy of the author*. It assessed the extent to which the author could be trusted as an observer and/or recorder of events. The third stage consisted of *the determination of particular facts*, in which the author's account of an event was compared to other accounts to see where they coincided and where they diverged.

In their manual, Langlois and Seignobos stressed that internal criticism, "can *prove* no fact; it only yields probabilities. Its end and result is to decompose documents into statements, each labelled with an estimate of its value – worthless statement, statement open to suspicion (strong or weak), statement probably (or, very probably) true, statement of unknown value."[134] On the other hand, two statements, insufficient in themselves, "may confirm each other in such a manner as to produce a collective certainty."[135]

1.7 Conclusion

In the period of time bracketed by the compilation of the Justinian Code and the publication of *An Introduction to the Study of History*, the concepts and methods for ensuring record trustworthiness underwent considerable refinement. Originally associated exclusively with the truth of a record as a record, i.e., its authenticity, trustworthiness gradually came to embrace, as well, the truth of a record as testimony of the facts contained within it. The concepts and methods associated with trustworthiness were also affected by changes in the conception of records as evidence. In antiquity and through much of the middle ages, records were seen primarily as manifestations of legal facts. Renaissance humanism and the emergence of philology encouraged scholars and jurists to consider them also as manifestations of historical facts, i.e., as facts specific to a particular time and place. By the late seventeenth century, with the emergence of a new concept of evidence as inference, records began to be seen in yet a new light: as sources from which historical or legal facts might be inferred. The new concept of evidence as inference was intimately connected to the emergence of a new philosophy of rationalist belief which asserted that the truth of most propositions cannot be established with any certainty; it could only be measured in degrees of probability, based on reasoning from the relevant evidence. As Carl Joynt and Nicholas Rescher observe, in their discussion of evidence in history and the law:

> Facts are not evidence for one another *per se*, for the very idea of evidence rests upon the mediation of our *knowledge* regarding the relationships between facts. ... Evidence, as a probabilistic concept, is based upon reference to our information about things: it concerns itself with our *knowledge* about states of affairs, and not with states of affairs *per se*.[136]

By the end of the nineteenth century, a recognisable set of legal and historical methods for assessing the trustworthiness of records as evidence, operating within a framework of probabilities, was well established. As the next two chapters demonstrate, that tradition continues to provide the foundation of modern legal and historical methods for determining record trustworthiness.

Chapter Two

Trusting Records as Legal Evidence: Common Law Rules of Evidence

The Anglo-American and Canadian rules of evidence which constitute the subject of this chapter belong to the legal tradition known as Common law.[1] As a tradition, it is distinct from the Romano-Germanic law of evidence, which forms part of the Civil law tradition.[2] Since a legal tradition constitutes the cultural framework in which evidence law operates, it is appropriate to begin this chapter with a brief look at the historical background and salient characteristics of Common law and Civil law systems of adjudication.[3] The specific purpose of this preliminary exploration is to provide a broader socio-historical perspective on the Anglo-American and Canadian rules governing assessments of record trustworthiness before proceeding to a more detailed examination of the rules themselves.

2.1 Common law vs. Civil law Procedure

In England, the increasing regulation of documentary evidence in the eighteenth and nineteenth centuries was at least partly attributable to the disappearance of the self-informing jury. For a number of centuries after its inception in the twelfth century, the jury trial had required little in the way of rules of evidence. It was assumed that the jurors, who were men of the neighbourhood, knew the facts in the dispute and thus could incorporate their own knowledge in their verdict. By the eighteenth century, however, jurors were no longer the main witnesses to the facts in dispute and so courts could no longer rely on the authority of their personal knowledge of the facts of the case as a basis on which to render a verdict. Increasingly jurors had to render a verdict on the basis of the witnesses and documents placed before them.[4] Given that the jury was empowered to render a verdict that was virtually impervious to challenge on the grounds of faulty analysis of evidence, the development of rules governing the admissibility of evidence was seen as a necessary protection against the danger that a lay jury might overestimate the probative value of certain kinds of evidence, underestimate their inherent weaknesses, or reason from them inappropriately.[5] By the end of the nineteenth century, this development had resulted in a split in the trial court between judicial regulation of the means of proof and lay adjudication of the facts at issue. The trial judge would screen evidence outside of the presence of the jury to determine whether it would be admitted in the proceeding and the jury subsequently would determine how much weight would be given to the evidence admitted. This rigorous separation of questions of law (concerning the admissibility of evidence) and questions of fact (concerning the weight of evidence), and between the trier of law and the trier of fact remain today salient traits of the Anglo-American fact-finding process.

Transformations in the law of evidence on the Continent, where the jury had never been a significant factor, offer a striking contrast to these Common law developments. Since the twelfth century, Continental fact-finding procedures had been regulated by the Roman-canonical system of legal proofs, which accorded a precise numerical value to each item of evidence. During the eighteenth and nineteenth centuries the system came under increasing attack by Enlightenment philosophers and revolutionary politicians for the secretive, undemocratic, and authoritarian ways in which it was applied. By the early nineteenth century, the legal control of proof had become intellectually discredited and politically suspect.[6] The Roman-canonical system was, consequently, rejected and a new evidentiary regime based on the principle of free evaluation of evidence, or free proof, took its place.[7] The system of free proof did not give the fact-finder (who continued to be a professional judge) licence to ignore logical or common sense canons of valid inference. It did, however, liberate him from binding legal rules concerning the analysis of evidence.[8]

The rebellion against the Roman-canonical regulation of proof was inspired, in large part, by a conviction that "the probative weight of evidence [was] a matter ... too contextual to be captured in a web of categorical legal norms."[9] As Damaška explains, the revolutionary condemnation of the system of legal proofs brought with it not only an antipathy to rules of weight.

> It also gave rise to a climate of opinion hostile to the adoption of rules excluding evidence on the ground that it is of dubious probative value. For if one takes the view that the probative effect of evidence depends on the infinite particularity of experience, then rules resting on an ex ante judgement of probative value easily appear as potentially dangerous overgeneralizations. To legislate on a subject so deeply contextual is like legislating against a chameleon by reference to its color ... this "antinomian" attitude was thus responsible for the fact that on the Continent, the adoption of Anglo-American intrinsic admissibility rules was never seriously contemplated, despite the widespread postrevolutionary attraction of Continental lawyers to Common law forms of justice.[10]

These historical developments partly explain why today in Civil law jurisdictions there are virtually no rules rejecting probative evidence on the ground that it may be misused or misconstrued. The dearth of rules may also be explained by the fact that in Civil law countries, the trial court is unitary rather than split as is the case in Common law jurisdictions. In Civilian legal proceedings, professional judges or, in some cases, a mixed tribunal composed of professional judges and lay assessors function both as triers of law and triers of fact, rendering the separation of admissibility and weight artificial and irrelevant. Moreover, Continental trial judges, unlike Common law juries, are obliged to justify their factual findings in a written opinion and so the need to compensate for the inscrutability of jury verdicts or the self-interest of litigating parties, which is a principal rationale for Common law admissibility rules, is not a compelling one.

The assessment of evidence in Common law and Civil law jurisdictions is also influenced by the divergent sources of law on which each depends. In Anglo-American (or Common law) jurisdictions, the two main sources of law are statutory law and the Common law. Statutory law is the body of law created by statute, a statute being a formal written enactment of a legislative body, whether federal, provincial, or municipal. Common law refers to the "body of law that develops and derives through judicial decisions as distinguished from legislative enactments."[11] The Common law thus refers to "judge-made" or "case" law, the contours of which are shaped by the accretion of judicial precedents. Its authority is reinforced through the doctrine of *stare decisis*. According to that doctrine, the decision of a higher court within the same jurisdiction acts as binding authority on a lower court within the same jurisdiction.

In Civil law jurisdictions, the main source of law is the Civil Code, which lays out the guiding principles of the legal system in a single authoritative text. Whereas the Common law and statutory law of Anglo-American jurisdictions embody the rule of experience and inductive thinking, the codification of law in Civilian jurisdictions embodies the rule of reason and deductive thinking.[12] The differences between statutory law and codification specifically are described by Brierley and MacDonald in the following way:

> The legislative style of a Code differs from that of a statute both in the degree of abstraction at which it is cast and in its normative referent. A statute or regulation is usually directed to a particular problem, defined not in terms of a legal category, but in terms of the application of a legal category to an identifiable set of facts. The form of a statute therefore tends to be casuistic and remedial. In contrast, an artfully drawn Civil Code will contain ... expressions of legal norms articulated at a level of abstraction that allow them to serve over a wide variety of particular instances ... a Code aspires to promise meaningful generalities that can accommodate a range of future facts in all their diversity.[13]

Civilian judges, unlike Common law judges, are not permitted to make law: only Civil legislators have that power. Judges are only empowered to apply and, to a limited extent, interpret the law.[14] For that reason, the doctrine of *stare decisis* does not exist as such in Civil jurisdictions.[15]

Thus, in Common law jurisdictions, the regulated evaluation of evidence takes place within a legal framework that is more changeable and less predictable. In Civil law jurisdictions, on the other hand, the free evaluation of evidence takes place within a legal framework that is less changeable and more predictable.

In his comparison of evidence and fact-finding precision in Common law and Civil law jurisdictions, Damaška observes that Common law adjudicators "are traditionally strongly attached to individualised justice and strive to arrive at the just result in the light of concrete circumstances of the case."[16] Precedents, rather than detailed and precise rules, constitute the decisional standard in the Common law system, resulting in a greater degree of uncertainty and fluidity in that standard.[17]

Formal standards and precise rules are, on the other hand, a characteristic feature of the continental system of Civil law. In a Civil law context, "decisionmakers are relatively more concerned about uniformity and predictability: they are much more ready than the Common law adjudicator to neglect the details of the case in order to organise the world of fluid social reality into a system."[18] Precise rules contained in authoritative texts constitute the decisional standard, resulting in a greater degree of certainty and stability.[19]

All of these differences between the Common law and Civil law traditions are a reminder that legal assessments of record trustworthiness are context-dependent and will be interpreted in different ways depending on the perspective and values of the social system in which it is being assessed. Bearing that in mind, we can now proceed to a more detailed examination of the Common law rules of admissibility relating to documentary evidence.

2.2 Rules Governing the Admissibility of Documentary Evidence

The Anglo-American and Canadian legal rules governing the use of documentary evidence demonstrate a substantial degree of continuity with those established at the end of the nineteenth century. The authoritative compilation of the law of evidence in trials at Common law continues to be *Wigmore on Evidence*,[20] which has been revised and expanded a number of times since it first appeared in 1904. In the last twenty-five years, the Common law rules have been refined and extended, and supplemented by statutory law, in order to accommodate the modern reality of modern recordkeeping. What follows is an examination of the Anglo-American rules governing the reliability and authenticity of documentary evidence in general and business records in particular, the specific expression of these rules in Canadian Common law and statutory law, and recent amendments to the Canada Evidence Act that address the specific trustworthiness of electronic records.[21]

In Common law countries the specific purpose of evidence law is to ensure the integrity of decisions reached in adjudication. The legal rules governing the admissibility of documentary evidence further that end by requiring that records meet a certain standard of trustworthiness before they are admitted as evidence in court. Admissibility means that a particular fact is relevant, and that it has also met the requirements of specific auxiliary tests and extrinsic policies. As Wigmore makes clear, it does not mean "that the particular fact has demonstrated or proved the proposition to be proved, but merely that it is received by the tribunal for the purpose of being weighed with other evidence."[22] The admissibility of evidence is determined by the judge, the weight of evidence is determined by the trier of fact, usually the jury.

At Common law, the rules of admissibility are grouped into three categories. The first deals with the probative value of specific facts (rules of relevancy), the second includes rules that attempt to increase or safeguard probative value (rules of auxiliary probative policy), and the third consists of rules based on extrinsic policies (e.g., rules excluding privileged communications) rather than on probative value.[23] For the purpose of the present discussion, only the first two categories are pertinent.

Relevancy means "applicability to the issue joined. ... Two facts are said to be relevant to each other when so related that according to the common course of events, one either taken by itself or in connection with other facts, proves or renders probable the ... existence or non-existence of the other."[24] As the definition shows, the rules of relevancy governing evidence are rooted in the Lockean tradition of rationalist empiricism and, more specifically, in the theory of logical relevancy. The first principle of that theory is expressed in terms of the relationship between evidence and probability. Peter Tillers explains the principle in the following way: "Knowledge of facts is always a matter of probabilities. We may acquire knowledge of matters of fact by drawing inferences from evidence, but these inferences can only alter the probability that some fact does or does not exist and can never establish with certainty that some fact does or does not exist."[25] Inferences, in turn, rest on generalisations based on common sense experience and logic:

> We draw an inference when the existence of one fact, the factum probans, alters our estimate of the existence of another fact, the factum probandum, but we do not draw that inference because of any intrinsic relationship between the factum probans [the existent fact, i.e., the evidence] and the factum probandum [the hypothetical fact, i.e., the proposition]; we draw that inference because we hold some principle that leads us to believe that the existence of the factum probans makes the existence of the factum probandum more or less probable. These connective principles are called "generalizations" or "evidential hypotheses," and they are furnished by experience or logic. They take the form of relative frequency statements that assert that when events of type A occur, events of type B occur with a certain frequency (e.g., "very often," or "almost always").[26]

Finally, inferences from evidence usually involve a series or chain of inferences and a chain of inferences is only as strong as its weakest link. "The greater the number of links in the chain -- the greater the number of intermediate inferences -- the weaker the final inference produced by the chain of inferences."[27] These principles of logical relevancy provide the overarching framework in which assessments of the trustworthiness of evidence in general and documentary evidence in particular are made.

The rules dealing with documents in general and business records in particular are rules of auxiliary probative policy and are "designed to strengthen here and there the evidential fabric and *to secure it against dangers and weaknesses pointed out by experience.*"[28] Within that broad category are rules governing the authentication of documents, the rule requiring the production of an original document (the best evidence rule), and the rule governing the admissibility of business records as an exception to the hearsay rule. The legal rules relating to authentication and best evidence address the authenticity of a record; the rule relating to business records address its reliability.

2.2.1 COMMON LAW AND STATUTORY PROVISIONS GOVERNING THE RELIABILITY OF RECORDS

The Hearsay Rule
At Common law, the hearsay rule is an analytic rule, the purpose of which "is to subject a certain kind of evidence to *tests calculated to exhibit and expose its possible weaknesses* and thus to make clear to the tribunal the precise value it has."[29] The rule requires the application of two interconnected tests for trustworthiness: cross-examination and confrontation. The theory underlying the rule is that witnesses' assertions must be tested by cross-examination and confrontation in order to expose any deficiencies, distortions, or suppressions.[30] According to Wigmore, "the chief questions that arise in connection to this rule are whether the rule has in a given case been satisfied by adequate opportunity for cross-examination, whether certain classes of testimonial assertions are to be received exceptionally without undergoing these tests, and where the line is to be drawn between utterances to which the rule does and does not apply."[31]

Hearsay evidence, as defined by McCormick, is "testimony in court, or written evidence, of a statement made out of court, the statement being offered as an assertion to show the truth of matters asserted therein, and thus resting for its value upon the credibility of the out of court asserter."[32] Under normal circumstances, such statements are excluded on the grounds that they cannot be tested by cross-examination. Ewart explains the inherent unreliability of statements made in documents in the following way:

> All documents, if offered in evidence as proof of the truth of their contents, are hearsay. Since documents can only "tell" a trier of fact that which their makers have "told" them, they inevitably make in-court assertions about statements made by someone else outside of the courtroom. ... The view that all documents are hearsay if offered as evidence of the truth of their contents is reinforced when consideration is given to the usual reasons proffered in support of a rule against hearsay evidence. These include the inability to observe the demeanour, credibility, and personality of the declarant whose statement is in issue, the

inability to qualify, clarify or cast doubt upon the statement by cross-examination, and the fact that ordinarily the declaration, unlike the rest of the evidence before the court, will not have been given under oath.[33]

Nevertheless, as Wigmore points out in his introduction to the exceptions to the hearsay rule, in certain cases, the circumstances in which the statement was made make its probable trustworthiness practically comparable to that of statements tested by cross-examination. Moreover, it may not be possible to test a witness' assertion. The witness may be dead, out of the jurisdiction, insane, or otherwise unavailable at the time of trial. If the testimony is to be taken at all, therefore, it must be taken in its untested shape. These two conditions – a circumstantial probability of trustworthiness and necessity – create the overarching principles of all the exceptions to the hearsay rule.

The Business Records Exception to the Hearsay Rule
In his discussion of these two principles in the specific context of the business records exception to the hearsay rule, Ewart argues that the principle of trustworthiness

> is by far the more compelling: a court can feel relatively comfortable in breaking new ground if it has been satisfied that the circumstances of the document's creation provide an adequate substitute for the traditional safeguard of cross-examination. The proponent of a document should seek to persuade the court that the document, *because of the circumstances of its creation*, is inherently reliable. If this is done, then the necessity doctrine can likely be satisfied simply by demonstrating that there is no other equally convenient way to put before the court the information in question.[34]

No uniform standard has been developed for measuring acceptable degrees of trustworthiness or necessity in particular cases. Instead, the principles tend to be applied on a case by case basis and different cases dictate different applications of the principles.

In Wigmore, three distinct but related reasons are given why entries that are recorded systematically and habitually in the ordinary course of business are likely to possess a degree of trustworthiness sufficient to justify their admissibility:

(1) The habit and system of making such a record with regularity calls for accuracy through the interest and purpose of the entrant; and the influence of habit may be relied on, by very inertia, to prevent casual inaccuracies and to counteract the possible temptation to misstatements ...

(1) Since the entries record a regular course of business transactions, an error or misstatement is almost certain to be

detected and the result disputed by those dealing with the entrant; misstatements cannot safely be made, if at all, except by a systematic and comprehensive plan of falsification. As a rule, this fact (if no motive of honesty obtained) would deter all but the most daring and unscrupulous from attempting the task; the ordinary man may be assumed to decline to undertake it. In the long run this operates with fair effect to secure accuracy.

(1) If, in addition to this, the entrant makes the record under a duty to an employer or other superior, there is the additional risk of censure and disgrace from the superior, in case of inaccuracies – a motive on the whole the most powerful and most palpable of the three.[35]

The traditional requirements for admitting declarations made under a business duty were that: the declarant had to be deceased; the declarant must have been under a duty to act and to record the thing done; the declarant must have observed the act; the act must have been completed; the declarant must have made the statement contemporaneously with the act; the declarant must not have had any motive to misrepresent; and collateral matters in the statement were inadmissible.[36] As Sopinka observes, strict adherence to these requirements often led to anachronistic results.[37]

In 1970, the Supreme Court of Canada restated and expanded the Common law exception in order to adapt it to the modern reality of recordkeeping. The case in question, *Ares v. Venner*,[38] involved a malpractice suit against a physician in which nurses' notes were sought to be admitted. The Court's decision reflected a more flexible approach to the exception, one that placed less emphasis on technical rules of exclusion and more emphasis on the principles of necessity and trustworthiness underlying the rules. The Supreme Court determined that the records were admissible on grounds of both necessity[39] and trustworthiness.[40] The trustworthiness of the notes was based on the fact that in a hospital where a patient's health is at stake, every effort would be made to keep accurate notes; secondly, since the nurses had no interest, apart from their duty, in keeping such notes, they had no motive to misrepresent the information in them; thirdly, the nurses were unlikely to have any independent memory apart from the notes they made; therefore, the notes would be superior to any oral testimony the nurses might give. The Court determined that all of these factors created a circumstantial probability of trustworthiness, which justified admitting the nurses' notes without requiring the declarants to be called as witnesses.[41]

Ares v. Venner resulted in at least two changes to the Common law exception. First, it eliminated the traditional requirement that a declarant be deceased. Secondly, it opened the door to courts admitting recorded opinions, so long as those opinions "fall within the declarant's normal scope of duty."[42] Certain of the traditional common-law requirements, however, remain unaffected by the *Ares* decision. At Common law, the general principle of testimonial evidence, i.e., that the person whose oral or written statement is received as testimony should speak from personal observation or knowledge, applies to declarations made in the course of a business duty. A testimonial assertion requires the presence of three elements: observation, recollection, and communication.[43] *Ares* and subsequent court decisions have confirmed the traditional requirement that the declarant have personal knowledge of the information recorded.[44] Subsequent court decisions have also maintained that the *Ares* doctrine only applies to records kept pursuant to a business duty on the grounds that only those records possess a circumstantial guarantee of trustworthiness.[45]

The modern common-law exception to the hearsay rule, in the wake of *Ares v. Venner,* thus appears to make admissible a record containing an original entry, made contemporaneously, in the routine of business, by a recorder with personal knowledge of the thing recorded, as a result of having done or observed or formulated it, who had a duty to make the record, and who had no motive to misrepresent the information in it.[46] Ewart suggests that the most significant consequence of *Ares v. Venner* is not so much "the specific relaxations of the Common law rule enunciated therein, but rather the inculcation of an attitudinal shift from exclusion towards expanded admissibility of hearsay."[47] The principled approach adopted in *Ares* also has been applied to situations outside the hospital setting.[48]

Although it has been adapted to meet the reality of modern recordkeeping, the Common law rule is still fairly restrictive and prohibits the admissibility of a large variety of business records. To allow for greater admissibility of modern business records, new exceptions have been developed by legislation, specifically through the addition of business record provisions to the federal, provincial and territorial Evidence Acts.[49] The provisions are modelled on comparable American statutes.

Under the Canada Evidence Act, records "created in the usual and ordinary course of business"[50] are admissible. The provincial Evidence Acts of British Columbia, Manitoba, Nova Scotia, Ontario and Saskatchewan have the additional requirement that "it must have been in the usual and ordinary course of business to create such records." The additional criterion has been defended on the grounds that it reinforces the record's circumstantial probability of trustworthiness by prohibiting the introduction of potentially self-serving evidence. The case cited in support of the additional criterion is *Palmer v. Hoffman,* an American case involving an action arising out of a railroad crossing accident.[51] In that case, the defendant attempted to admit into evidence a report of the accident made by the deceased train engineer to officials at the freight office. Although the engineer's report was made in relation to his employment, the Supreme Court of the United States held that it was inadmissible on the grounds that such reports have nothing to do with the day to day operation and management of the railroad business. While the Court acknowledged that most businesses are concerned with litigation and therefore are in the practice of taking statements from employees when an accident occurs, the primary purpose of such reports is to assist in the lawsuit rather than in the running of the railway business. The Court was concerned that admitting such reports could invite abuse since businesses might be motivated to introduce self-serving evidence, i.e., statements which reflect their own version of such events. The Court determined, therefore, that in order to come within the business records statute:

> it must be shown to be a record which is necessary for the systematic and mechanical conduct of the business as a commercial enterprise. ... The trustworthiness of business documents is based on the reliability placed on such records by the commercial world. In the absence of routineness, there exists the danger that the maker of the record may not be motivated to be accurate. It is the mercantile nature of the record which attracts trustworthiness, not just the fact that the document was prepared in the regular course of business.[52]

Sopinka observes that "the implied introduction into business record legislation that there be no motive to misrepresent is consistent with the requirements of the traditional common-law exception."[53] Although the Canada Evidence Act does not include the second criterion, there must be some demonstration that the document was made in the usual and ordinary course of business. The fact that a document was prepared by a business organisation may not be, in itself, sufficient to qualify it for admissibility.[54]

The provincial business record provisions require that the record be made at or near the time of the act, transaction, occurrence or event recorded. Although the Canada Evidence Act does not specifically require contemporaneous recording, it does allow the court to investigate the total "circumstances in which the information contained in the record was written, recorded, stored or reproduced, and draw any reasonable inference from the form or content of the record."[55] The Court in Setak v. Burroughs emphasised the significance of contemporaneous recording when it stated that:

> A substantial factor in the reliability of any system of records is the promptness with which transactions are recorded. Unless it appears from the context of the record, or the testimony of the witness introducing the writings or records into evidence that the act, transaction, occurrence or event described therein occurred within a reasonable time before the making of the writing or record, then such writing or record should not be admitted for the purpose of proving those matters. Where there is some delay in transcribing, then in each case, it would seem to me, the Court must decide, as a matter of fact, whether the time span between the transaction and the recording was so great as to suggest the danger of inaccuracy by lapse of memory.[56]

The connection statutory law draws between contemporaneous recording and trustworthiness is consistent with the Common law.[57] It is also consistent with the "ground-zero" theory of evidence that pervades Anglo American evidence law in general. As Kim Scheppele characterises it:

> This theory implicitly adopts a conception of truth that takes for granted a strong relationship between informational accuracy and relevance on the one hand, and the distribution of knowledge over time and space on the other. In other words, the ... law of evidence deems a piece of information to be true if it was produced close to the events that are in question in the lawsuit, the "ground-zero" of the metaphor. ... The reliability and relevance of knowledge, like the extent and scope of damage, are thought to lessen with distance in time and space from the original event.[58]

The most significant difference between the Common law exception and legislative business record provisions is the latter's acceptance of hearsay and even second-hand or double hearsay. The Evidence Acts of British Columbia, Manitoba, Saskatchewan and Ontario explicitly state that the lack of personal knowledge by the maker of the record does not affect its admissibility, though it may affect its weight.[59] However, courts have been consistent in asserting that second-hand hearsay is only admissible under these provisions if the maker of the record and the supplier of the information recorded were both acting in the usual and ordinary course of business.[60] In confirming this requirement, Canadian courts have cited the decision of the New York Court of Appeals in *Johnson v. Lutz*,[61] an action arising out of a motorcycle accident. The Court in that case ruled that statements contained in a police officer's report were inadmissible because they were based on information provided voluntarily to the officer by a bystander, rather than on the officer's personal knowledge. Since the bystander was not under any duty to make a statement to the police officer, the trustworthiness of his statement was compromised. The Court held that "to come within the statutory provision ... it had to be shown not only that the maker of the record was acting pursuant to a business duty, but that the person from whom he received the information was acting under a business duty as well. It is the business element of the record which gives it credence and efficacy."[62] Ontario Courts have confirmed that

> the mere fact that recording of a third party statement is routine imports no guarantee of the truth of the statement. ... [the business record provision] of the [Ontario] Evidence Act should be interpreted as making hearsay statements admissible when both the maker of the writing or the entrant of the record, and the information or informants, if more than one, are each acting in the usual and ordinary course of business in entering and communicating an account of an act, transaction, occurrence or event.[63]

The same rationale is evident in *Adderly v. Bremner*[64] in which parts of a hospital record which related to occurrences taking place prior to admission and recorded as part of the patient's case history were held to be inadmissible because the statements made by the patient to his doctor and recorded in a hospital note were considered self-serving. Speaking for the court, Brooke, J. observed that he did not believe the Ontario Legislature intended "to open to a plaintiff a means of escaping the test of truth through cross-examination by resort to the hospital history record."[65]

The business record provision of the Canada Evidence Act lacks a subsection stating that a lack of personal knowledge will not affect the admissibility of the business record; the admissibility of hearsay under the federal Act, therefore, is not as straightforward as it is in provincial enactments.[66] Nevertheless, Courts have tended to interpret the provision as permitting the admissibility of hearsay and double hearsay. The issue was considered by the Court in *R. v. Grimba*, a case in which the Crown sought to introduce a fingerprint identification record obtained from the U.S. Federal Bureau of Investigation. The record was admitted on the grounds of its inherent trustworthiness:

> Section 30 was placed into the Act in 1968. ... It would appear that the rationale behind that section for admitting a form of hearsay evidence is the inherent circumstantial guarantee of accuracy which one would find in a business context from records which are relied upon in the day to day affairs of individual businesses, and which are subsequent [sic] to frequent testing and cross-checking. Records thus systematically stored, produced and regularly relied upon should, it would appear under s. 30, not be barred from the Court's consideration simply because they contained hearsay or double hearsay.[67]

In other court decisions, the weight of authority has favoured the admissibility of double hearsay under section 30.[68] The acceptance of hearsay under these conditions moves the criteria for the circumstantial guarantee of trustworthiness further from the traditional Common law criteria for testimonial assertion, i.e., observation, recollection, communication.

The modern Common law, in the aftermath of *Ares v. Venner*, allows the introduction of statements of opinion so long as they were given in the course of a business duty. Court interpretations of provincial business record provisions, however, have ruled such statements inadmissible.[69] The Ontario Court in *Adderly v. Bremner*, for example, excluded "hospital records, which contain subjective data such as a doctor or nurse's diagnosis, opinion or impression, on the ground that these do not constitute 'an act, transaction, occurrence, or event', within the meaning of the words in the provincial provision.[70] The wording of the Canada Evidence Act is less restrictive since it refers to "evidence in respect of a matter" rather than to "an act, transaction, occurrence or event". Sopinka suggests that "it could be argued that the use of the general word 'matter' contemplates records containing opinions and other subjective data."[71] Sopinka also finds support for a broader interpretation of the provincial provisions in McCormick who maintains that, "the opinion rule should be restricted to governing the manner of presenting courtroom testimony and should have little application to the admissibility of out-of-court statements."[72]

The Public Documents Exception to the Hearsay Rule
The hearsay exception granted to statements in public documents at Common law, also known as official statements, emphasises the circumstantial probability of trustworthiness that derives from the fact that the statement is recorded by a public officer in pursuance of an official duty.[73] The exception is supported by a presumption of due performance of duty.[74] As Wigmore explains:

> The fundamental circumstance is that an official duty exists to make an accurate statement, and that this special and weighty duty will usually suffice as a motive to incite the officer to its fulfilment. The duty may or may not be one for whose violation a penalty is expressly prescribed. The officer may or may not be one from whom in advance an express oath of office is required. ... It is the influence of the official duty, broadly considered, which is taken as the sufficient element of trustworthiness, justifying the acceptance of the hearsay statement.[75]

Although, in some cases, the presumption of official duty is, in Wigmore's words, "more a fiction than a fact," it is, nevertheless, "a fiction which we can hardly afford in our law openly to repudiate."[76] The circumstantial probability of trustworthiness is bolstered by the requirement that the subject matter of the statement be of a public nature, prepared for a public purpose, and with a view to being retained and kept as a public record.[77] English courts require, in addition, that the documents be made available to the public at all times on the grounds that, "where an official record is one necessarily subject to public inspection, the facility and certainty with which errors would be exposed and corrected furnishes a special and additional guarantee of accuracy."[78] While English courts require publicity as an incentive to accuracy, some Canadian courts have rejected it as a requirement.[79] Courts have also determined that the public official need not have personal knowledge of the facts recorded and the information may be supplied by private citizens.[80]

Many statutes contain provisions governing the admissibility of specific types of public or government records, which avoid the Common law restrictions. In addition, the various Evidence Acts contain broad provisions to simplify the admissibility of public records. For example, section 26 of the Canada Evidence Act[81] allows for the introduction of certified copies of government records, as satisfying the requirements of the hearsay rule, the best evidence rule, and authentication.

Assumptions Underpinning the Rules Governing Reliability
As the exceptions to the hearsay rule demonstrate, the legal rules governing reliability are grounded in a number of generalisations about the relationship between records and the reality they purport to represent. A specific assumption underpinning the business records exception to the hearsay rule concerns the

relationship between the observer/recorder and the event observed/recorded. Business records are assumed to reflect events in the real world. Their reliability depends therefore on the claim of the observer to have been present at those events. Accordingly, the exception to the hearsay rule aims to ensure that the record is an accurate reflection of those events, one that is uncontaminated by the distorting influence of time, space, bias, interpretation, or unwarranted opinion on the part of the observer/recorder. In other words, the observer/recorder must be present to witness and transcribe what Stanley Raffel calls "the world's speech," but he or she must not contaminate that speech.

> To be an observer is to be present, to 'be there'. ... However, although the observer must be concretely present, he is not supposed to make a difference. The contact of observation must be direct and unidirectional in that the contact flows from event to observer, so that the record can be direct and unencumbered by the observer's opinion. ... The achievement of the observer is the achievement of absence through presence. The responsible observer is one who can make what he observes responsible for what he observes. ... record users can know the event through the record because, since the record has not been affected by the observer, it becomes unnecessary to understand the observer in order to understand the record. The record speaks for itself.[82]

As Marilyn MacCrimmon points out, the belief that it is possible to separate the observer from the event he or she is observing:

> reflects the Cartesian model of the mind which assumed that "the natural operations of the mind do not err unless they are disturbed by incidental and extraneous factors such as prejudice, passion, or impatience." Descartes drew a sharp distinction between the mind and the body, assuming that each could be studied in isolation from the other. Under this model the mind is kept reliable by preventing the intrusion of distorting influences.[83]

This view of reality, however, shows little affinity with the one that has emerged from research in several disciplines, among them, philosophy of science, psychology, artificial intelligence, and literary theory. That research, according to MacCrimmon, suggests that, in fact, "it is impossible to see the world except through a lens shaped by our world experiences, culture and internal knowledge structures ... the observer is not separate from the system being studied and ... the act of the observation or measurement alters the thing observed.[84]

The limits of the Cartesian model are also implicit in the ground-zero theory of evidence, as Scheppele makes clear.

> The idea about truth embedded in the [ground-zero] theory is precisely that description without reflection is possible, and that

one can find somehow untainted or "raw" description that then
gets tainted or "cooked" in subsequent retellings. The theory
holds out the possibility that there is a version of events that has
no "spin" – an account of "what happened" that is the simple and
unvarnished truth. ... [However], as Ludwig Wittgenstein
reiterated perhaps most powerfully, seeing is never pure in the
first place, but is always "seeing as." In other words, the *first*
version of events *also* has a perspective embedded in it, like with
any other version of events.[85]

All of these observations concerning the problematic nature of facts in
adjudication point to some of the inherent limits of the legal rules governing the
reliability of business records.

2.2.2 COMMON LAW AND STATUTORY PROVISIONS GOVERNING THE AUTHENTICITY OF RECORDS

Authentication
Whereas the documentary exceptions to the hearsay rule are concerned with the
reliability of a record's contents, the authentication and best evidence rules are
concerned with its identity and integrity. The Common law rule requiring the
authentication of documents as a pre-condition to their admissibility is a
"quantitative" rule stating that, in given cases, "certain *kinds of evidence* [are] *to
be associated with other evidence* before the case will go to the jury."[86] The rule
is met by evidence sufficient to satisfy the court that the document is what it
purports to be. The need to establish the authenticity of a record is based on the
common sense assumption that whenever a claim involves any element of
personal connection with a physical object, that connection must not be
presumed, but shown. Records present a particular danger because, unlike other
physical objects, e.g., a piece of clothing or furniture, a record purports to declare
its ownership on its face, either by a signature or some other means, and fact-
finders might be inclined, on sight of a record, to accept that it is all that it
purports to be. Therefore, "the general principle has been enforced that a writing
purporting to be of a certain authorship cannot go to the jury as possibly genuine,
merely on the strength of this purport; *there must be some evidence of the
genuineness* (or execution) of it."[87] As Benning, J., explains, "no writing can be
received in evidence as a genuine writing until it has been proved to be a
genuine one, and none as a forgery until it has been proved to be a forgery. A
writing, of itself, is not evidence of the one thing, or of the other. A writing, of
itself, is evidence of nothing, and therefore is not, unless accompanied by proof
of some sort, admissible as evidence."[88] Of course, authentication is not required
if due execution is admitted.[89]

Evidence of execution or authorship may be direct or circumstantial.
Anthony Sheppard summarises the various forms such evidence can take:

Direct evidence of authentication may consist of the identification
of the document by the writer, a signatory, or an eye-witness to its

writing or signing. Circumstantial evidence of authentication may involve handwriting or typewriting identification by a witness who did not see the making or signing of the actual document but who can identify the writing. ... Comparison of hands is another form of circumstantial authentication. ... Finally, the reply letter doctrine is another method of authentication whereby a witness testifies that he received the disputed letter through the mail and it was in response to an earlier letter which he had mailed to the alleged author.[90]

At Common law, the authenticity of declarations made pursuant to a business duty is proved by the testimony of a witness who can testify about the record and the circumstances in which it was created. According to Ewart, "the authenticating witness will usually be someone who is familiar with, or who has supervisory responsibilities over the recordkeeping system, where such exists."[91]

Statutory provisions "have eased the requirement of proof of execution ... provided it can be shown that the document fits into the category envisioned by the statute."[92] In the federal and provincial Evidence Acts, for example, the authenticity of business records may be proved by foundation evidence that the records were made in the usual and ordinary course of business. Such evidence may be given orally or by affidavit.[93]

It has long been established under the statutory business record provisions that "the witness offering the required foundation evidence need not have any personal knowledge of the matters described or even of the general subject matter. Instead, it was sufficient if the witness could testify to the recordkeeping system in effect when the record was made."[94] As Ewart points out, "this is a logical requirement, since the Common law has always looked to the trustworthiness of the duty or system as a guarantee of the accuracy of the material recorded in the record."[95] Under section 26(1) of the Canada Evidence Act, government records are admitted under analogous conditions.

Under specified conditions, certain documents are presumed to be authentic. For public documents, the fact that the records have been found in official custody has long been accepted as sufficient external evidence of their authenticity.[96] Wigmore explains the grounds for such acceptance in the following way:

When in a government office permanent records are kept under the custody of an officer appointed to that duty, there is commonly little danger in inferring that records found there are genuine. It would be difficult as well as criminal to substitute or to insert false records. Moreover, the usual mode of authenticating such documents (as by proving the clerk's or officer's handwriting) would be both highly inconvenient, on account of its repeated necessity, and also often impossible on account of the change of officials as well as the antiquity of many portions of the records.

It seems, therefore, never to have been doubted that the *existence of an official document in the appropriate official custody* is sufficient evidence of its genuineness to go to the jury.[97]

Ancient documents are also presumed to be authentic.[98] An ancient document is any written document that is not less than thirty years old.[99] Such a document is presumed, under certain conditions, "to have been duly signed, sealed, attested, delivered, or published according to its purport."[100] The conditions supporting a presumption of trustworthiness are the long existence of the document,[101] together with its being found in a natural or proper place of custody and having an unsuspicious appearance.[102] Such conditions suffice, in combination, as evidence that the document was "fairly and honestly obtained and reserved for use, and ... free from suspicion of dishonesty."[103] The presumption is not based entirely on considerations of trustworthiness. Necessity is also a factor since, after a long lapse of time, it is difficult, if not impossible, to obtain testimonial evidence from anyone with personal knowledge either of the document's execution or the author's style of handwriting.

In interpreting the requirement that the document be found in a proper place of custody, courts have been consistent in asserting that "it is not necessary to show that it has come from the *most* proper custody; it is sufficient if it come from a place where it might reasonably be expected to be found."[104] The question of what constitutes proper custody is therefore left to the determination of the trial court on the circumstances of the particular case. Once the fact of proper custody is established, "there is no need to inquire what happened to the document between the date of execution and the date of production."[105] Sopinka points out, however, that, "in the case of documents of which the custody is imposed by statute on a particular person, the rule must perhaps be more strict, and any unusual custody must be properly accounted for."[106]

Authentication by official custody and by age date back to Roman times and are founded upon the principle of circumstantial evidence and, specifically, upon the application of the principle of current possession or existence of a record to prove its past execution. Authentication by official seal or signature also dates back to Roman times. It survives today in the form of a Common law rule that the genuineness of documents bearing the official seal or signature of a public official (including a notary) "*need not be evidenced otherwise than by the production for inspection of the document* bearing them."[107] The purporting seal or signature is sufficient proof that the document has been genuinely executed by the purporting official, whose official character is assumed without evidence.[108]

The Best Evidence Rule
If the purpose of authentication is to establish the identity of the record, the purpose of the best evidence rule is to establish its integrity. This rule, which requires the production of an original record, is "a rule of preference for the

inspection of the thing itself, in place of any evidence, either circumstantial or testimonial, about the things."[109] As stated by Wigmore, the rule stipulates that "in proving a writing, production must be made, unless it is not feasible, of the writing itself, whenever the purpose is to establish its terms."[110] That purpose is key to the legal understanding of what constitutes an "original." According to Wigmore, the original document whose production is required is:

> The document whose contents are to be proved in the state of the issues. Whether or not that document was written before or after another, was copied from another, or was itself used to copy from, is immaterial. The question becomes: is this the very document whose contents are desired to be, and in the now state of the issues by the substantive law may be, proved?[111]

The requirement to produce an original record when it exists is dictated by common sense and long experience which suggest that (1) a copy is always liable to errors; (2) an original may contain subtle details that may be missing from the copy and that may be significant in terms of the record's meaning; and (3) it is very difficult for oral testimony to reproduce the terms of a document accurately. The "best evidence" rule is intended to increase the probability of the record's trustworthiness by decreasing opportunities for deliberate or inadvertent falsification.[112]

The best evidence rule is sometimes referred to as a rule of primariness because its application requires that a distinction be drawn between primary (or best) evidence and secondary evidence. As elucidated by Henry, J., in *Gumm v. Cox* "evidence that carries on its face no indication that better remains behind is not secondary but primary."[113] Generally speaking, if a document is executed in duplicate or in counterparts, each duplicate or counterpart is treated as an original because it is created simultaneously with and by the same act of writing as the original.[114] A machine copy or photocopy of an original document, on the other hand, is secondary evidence because the reproduction follows the creation of the original.[115]

The essential principle of preferred evidence is that it is to be produced if it exists and is available. If it does not exist, or is unavailable, secondary evidence is admissible.[116] At Common law, secondary evidence is admissible if the original has been lost or destroyed, if production is inconvenient or impossible (e.g., an engraving on a tombstone), if the original is in the possession of another party and the party refuses or neglects to produce it, or if the original is in the possession of a third party and beyond the power of the party seeking to compel production.[117] For public and official documents, secondary evidence is admissible at Common law on the grounds that the removal of the original documents would create considerable inconvenience and risk. The secondary evidence may be an exemplification (verified under seal), or examined (verified under oath) or certified copies.[118] The Evidence Acts and other statutes also contain provisions "allowing sealed or certified copies to prove the contents of judicial or public books and documents and dispensing with proof of the genuineness of the seal or certification."[119] The business records provision of the Canada Evidence Act also allows a copy of a record to be admitted, if it is not "possible or reasonably practical" to produce the original. Two affidavits must accompany the copy of the record, the first giving reasons why it is not possible or reasonably practicable to produce the record, the second, sworn by the person who made the copy, identifying the source from which the copy was made and attesting to the copy's authenticity.[120]

A number of courts and legal commentators suggest that, while the best evidence rule continues to be valid in cases "where the terms of a contract, the authenticity of an affidavit or the validity of a will are disputed, or there is an issue whether a document has been altered, the modern Common law, statutory provisions, rules of practice and modern technology have rendered the rule obsolete in most cases and the question is one of weight and not admissibility."[121] McCormick, on the other hand, cautions against a total disregard for

> all other justifications for the rule. It has long been observed that the opportunity to inspect original writings may be of substantial importance in the detection of fraud. At least a few modern courts and commentators appear to regard the prevention of fraud as an ancillary justification of the rule. Unless this view is accepted, it is difficult to explain the rule's frequent application to copies produced by modern techniques, which virtually eliminate the possibility of unintentional mistransmission.
>
> Finally one leading U.S. opinion intimates that the rule should be viewed to protect not only against mistaken or fraudulent mistransmissions, but also against intentional or unintentional misleading through introduction of selected portions of a comprehensive set of writings to which the opponent has no access. This seems to engraft upon the best evidence rule an aspect of completeness not hitherto observed.[122]

The leading opinion to which McCormick refers is *Toho Bussan Kaisha, Limited v. American President Lines, Limited*[123] in which photostats of portions of records held in Japan that were prepared for litigation were excluded on the grounds that the duplicates did not constitute a full rendition of the original material.[124]

2.3 Admissibility of Electronic Records

Electronic records are a form of documentary evidence and so the traditional rules of evidence have been applied to them, either explicitly or by analogy. Computer records and other data derived from mechanical systems are admissible under the Common law exception to the hearsay rule[125] and computer records and output are included within the definition of "record" under the business records provision of the Canada Evidence Act.[126] Computer printouts have been admitted under the best evidence rule. As Sheppard observes, "the courts seem ready to admit [a computer printout] as the end product of a reliable system which summarises and replaces many records and papers."[127]

However, while most electronic records are being admitted in litigation, there remains some confusion on a number of fundamental issues. Observers point out that "courts have struggled with the traditional rules of evidence, with inconsistent results."[128] For example, a computer printout has been held to be both primary evidence[129] and secondary evidence.[130] Some Courts have allowed "the introduction of computer bank records under s. 29 of the Canada Evidence Act but have required as a condition of admissibility that a foundation be established to demonstrate the reliability generally of the input of entries, storage of information and its retrieval and presentation."[131] Other courts "have accepted the reliability of computers without stipulating any preconditions to the admissibility of their printouts under s. 30 of the Act."[132] The dominant test for the admissibility of computer printouts appears to be the rule enunciated in *R. v. McMullen* that, "the nature and quality of the evidence put before the Court has to reflect the facts of the complete recordkeeping process." The rule does not establish, however, which "facts" and how "complete" the foundation evidence for admissibility ought to be.[133]

2.3.1 THE CANADIAN UNIFORM ELECTRONIC EVIDENCE ACT

In 1998, in an effort to reduce the uncertainty and create consistency in the application of the rules of evidence governing electronic records, the Uniform Law Conference of Canada (hereafter ULCC) developed a model statute that establishes foundation requirements for admitting electronic records as evidence. The requirements are intended to ensure that electronic records meet a standard of trustworthiness equivalent to the one traditional paper records are required to meet.[134] Under the "Uniform Electronic Evidence Act," an electronic record is defined as "data that is recorded or stored on any medium in or by a computer system or other similar device, that can be read or perceived by a person or a computer system or other similar device. It includes a display, printout or other output of that data, other than a printout referred to in Sub-section 4(2)."[135]

Because "electronic records may be more vulnerable than paper records to undetectable modification, intended or unintended,"[136] the ULCC decided it was necessary to test their trustworthiness at the admissibility stage rather than leaving it until the weight of the records comes to be appraised. It offered four arguments in favour of a specific integrity test for admissibility. First, electronic records may be inherently so untrustworthy that it would be unfair either to apply less stringent rules of admissibility to electronic records than those applied to non-electronic records or to eliminate altogether any rules regarding record integrity at the admissibility stage. Secondly, information relevant to determining the trustworthiness of an electronic record is within the knowledge of the proponent of evidence; therefore, it is not unduly difficult to support its admission. Thirdly, if the proponent is not required to adduce foundation evidence to support the admission of an electronic record, the opponent will be forced to call her own witnesses to challenge the record's trustworthiness. Under these circumstances it will be difficult for the opponent to mount a successful challenge given that the best and, likely, only witness would be an employee of the proponent and, if such a witness is called, the opponent will not be able to cross-examine him. A fairer test of the record's integrity can be made, therefore, if the proponent is required to give foundation evidence at the admissibility stage. Finally, the requirement to adduce foundation evidence is bound to encourage responsible recordkeeping since anyone who wishes to introduce electronic records will have to withstand cross-examination on the records' trustworthiness.[137]

From the ULCC's perspective, the justification for a special rule for electronic records is the need to expose their special vulnerability to undetectable change. For that reason, the Uniform Electronic Evidence Act focuses on adjusting the best evidence rule since its traditional purpose is to establish the integrity of a record.[138] The application of that rule in a traditional recordkeeping environment requires that the proponent of evidence produce, whenever possible, the original document since alterations are more likely to be detected on the original. Its application in an electronic environment has proven difficult as court decisions have shown. Rather than search for what might constitute an "original" electronic record, the ULCC has chosen to direct its attention to the principle underlying the best evidence rule:

> The "function" of the best evidence rule is to ensure ... the integrity of the record to be produced in evidence. It is presumably easier to tell that an original paper record has been altered than to determine any alteration by viewing a copy. In the electronic world, there may or may not be an original paper version of the electronic record. Therefore, the search for integrity of an electronic record has to proceed in another way.
> As Ken Chasse said "the law should move from 'original' to 'system', that is, from dependence upon proof of the integrity of the original business document to a dependence on proof of the integrity of the recordkeeping system." Stated another way, the integrity of the recordkeeping system is the key to proving the integrity of the record, including any manifestation of the record created, maintained, displayed, reproduced or printed out by a computer system.[139]

Accordingly, in the Uniform Electronic Evidence Act, record integrity is replaced by system integrity.[140] The shift away from the record itself to the recordkeeping system that produced it is reflected in Section 4(1), which stipulates that, "where the best evidence rule is applicable in respect of an electronic record, it is satisfied on proof of the integrity of the electronic records system in or by which the data was recorded or stored."[141] This stipulation does not apply to a record that is produced using a computer but that lives its life on paper, for example, a letter generated using word-processing software which is then printed. In such cases, the ULCC argues, the reliability of the computer system is not at issue and the paper printout is considered the original. Therefore, Section 4 contains the proviso: "An electronic record in the form of a print-out that has been manifestly or consistently acted on, relied upon, or used as the record of the information recorded or stored on the printout, is the record for the purposes of the best evidence rule."[142]

In the Uniform Act, an electronic records system "includes the computer system or other similar device by or in which data is recorded or stored, and any procedures related to the recording and storage of electronic records."[143] Such procedures include "physical and electronic access controls, security features, verification rules, and retention or destruction schedules", which may or may not be embedded in the computer system itself.[144] Under Section 5, the integrity of the electronic records system is presumed

> (a) by evidence that supports a finding that at all material times the computer system or other similar device was operating properly or, if it was not, the fact of its not operating properly did not affect the integrity of the electronic record, and there are no other reasonable grounds to doubt the integrity of the electronic records system[145]

The section thus creates a presumption of integrity of the system based on evidence that includes the computer system that produced the record and the recordkeeping system in which it operated. Both are required to demonstrate integrity.[146] The test of integrity is a fairly simple one. According to the drafters of the Act, the decision to adopt a simple test at the admissibility stage was based on the fact that the integrity of most electronic records is not disputed. The intention of the Act is to point out the basic criteria on which the integrity of a record may be judged, not to render the process more difficult or to provide grounds for frivolous and expensive attacks on otherwise acceptable records.[147] Evidence of the integrity of the electronic records system "may be established by an affidavit given to the best of the deponent's knowledge or belief,"[148] and the parties to the proceedings have the right to cross-examine the deponent on the affidavit.[149]

The drafters considered but ultimately declined to endorse any particular industry standard as a minimum standard for electronic record trustworthiness. The Canadian Information and Image Management Society had requested that the Uniform Electronic Evidence Act provide legislative support for the National Standard on Microfilm and Electronic Images as Documentary Evidence by providing that records created and maintained in compliance with the National Standard would be admissible and presumed reliable. Moreover, a 1994 consultation paper prepared for the ULCC by Ken Chasse had recommended that an integrity test listing the factors to be considered in determining the admissibility and weight of electronic records be adapted from the National Standard.[150] In the end, however, the drafters of the Act decided against creating a statutory presumption of reliability based on the standard on the grounds that it constituted too high a standard for admissibility[151] and might encourage a tendency to not properly scrutinise the records further as to weight.[152]

Although the Uniform Electronic Evidence Act does not make compliance with recognised standards obligatory to the admission of electronic records, it does make compliance with them a relevant consideration. The Act states that:

> for the purpose of determining under any rule of law whether an electronic record is admissible, evidence may be presented [in any legal proceeding] in respect of any standard, procedure, usage or practice on how electronic records are to be recorded or stored, having regard to the type of business or endeavour that used, recorded or stored the electronic record and the nature and purpose of the electronic record.[153]

Record creators still face the responsibility to design systems that will provide a rebuttable presumption of integrity. Moreover, once an electronic record is admitted the opponent can challenge it on a number of grounds, including its lack of integrity. The rule thus provides an incentive to businesses to adopt standards that will facilitate the admissibility of electronic records and strengthen their weight once they have been admitted into evidence.

2.4 The Role of the Adversarial Process in the Legal Assessment of Record Trustworthiness

The ULCC's reluctance to impose precise and detailed standards for electronic records at the admissibility stage may be attributed to its steadfast belief that any weaknesses and deficiencies in the records that may have been overlooked at that stage will be exposed upon cross-examination. This belief, in turn, is rooted in the Common law's faith in the adversarial process in general and cross-examination in particular as the most effective means of establishing the trustworthiness of records. In an adversarial process, the facts of the case are provided to the fact finder in the form of two alternating one-sided accounts.[154] According to Dale Nance, "a principal justification for the adversary process is that the self-interest of the parties will bring about a thorough investigation and vigorous clash of evidence from which the relatively detached trier of fact will best be able to discern the truth."[155] There are, however, a number of epistemological frailties endemic in the practice of allowing two adversaries to control the development of evidence at trial. Damaška identifies three of the most salient pitfalls:

> [First,] it may be in the narrow interest of only one party, or in the common interest of both, that some items of information, which the witness possesses, do not reach the adjudicator – even though their relevancy in the quest for truth is beyond dispute …. [Secondly,] because the witness is limited to answering relatively narrow and precise questions, much information may effectively be kept away from the decisionmaker. … Accordingly, the factual basis for the decision may be incomplete. … [Thirdly,] the cross-examination technique, … with its challenge to the credibility of

witnesses, is a two-edged sword. ... Even with the best of intentions on the cross-examiner's part, reliable testimony may easily be made to look debatable, and clear information may become obfuscated.[156]

Electronic records, with their technological complexity, provide particularly fertile ground for inadvertent or deliberate misrepresentation, incomplete presentation, obfuscation and confusion.

To counteract some of the weaknesses of the adversarial process, Nance urges the courts to renew the Common law's original commitment to a best evidence principle. The argument for the continuing validity of a best evidence principle draws on its eighteenth century roots as a unifying principle of the Anglo-American law of evidence. It was asserted by Lord Gilbert in the first treatise on evidence at Common law in the following terms, "The first ... and most signal rule, in relation to evidence, is this; that a man must have the utmost evidence the nature of the fact is capable of."[157] In its original terms, the best evidence represented an epistemic ideal, embodying the obligation of the litigating parties to present the logically most probative evidence. By the end of the nineteenth century, the overarching principle of the law of evidence had shrunk to the context of the original document rule. Responsibility for diminishing its status is usually attributed to Thayer and Wigmore, both of whom argue that the adversarial process guarantees the production of the best evidence through the motivated self-interest of the litigating parties.

However, Nance points out, the argument is based on a number of faulty assumptions: first, it assumes that "strategically best" evidence (meaning "evidence which is strategically optimal from the point of view of the litigant unswervingly committed to victory at trial") will always coincide with "epistemically best" (meaning "the set of information, reasonably available to the litigant, that a rational trier of fact, expert or nonexpert, would find most helpful in the resolution of the factual issue"), when this clearly will not always be the case.[158] Secondly, it assumes that, even if one party presents "epistemically inferior" evidence, the opponent will be sufficiently motivated to present the better evidence, an assumption that ignores certain realities: opponents will not always have access to the better evidence; they may be prevented by legal or tactical obstacles from presenting the evidence; or they may be insufficiently diligent in obtaining the better evidence, or insufficiently effective in presenting it.[159]

Given the weaknesses and biases of the parties, Nance believes that judges ought to take a more active role in protecting the jury from them by placing reasonable limits on the range of choices given to litigants in proving a proposition, and by encouraging parties to produce more reliable evidence. Nance argues that, in performing this role, judges should intercede "only when there is a strong likelihood that the litigant has attempted to press a tactical advantage unreasonably inimical to the presentation of the epistemically best evidence, or that the litigant has unreasonably evaluated an otherwise legitimate consideration, as when the litigant's cost evaluation is palpably improper."[160]

Nance's equation of "best evidence" with "epistemically best evidence" complements the connection McCormick draws between "best evidence" and "completeness of evidence" in his argument for the continuing relevance of the rule pertaining to documentary originals. Taken together, their comments imply that, in relation to documentary evidence, the epistemically best evidence is, among other things, that which is most complete. The dimension of completeness is particularly pertinent to electronic records since structural and contextual elements of an electronic record may be stored separately from its content. In an electronic recordkeeping environment, adherence to a best evidence principle would entail an obligation on the part of the litigating parties to produce the record that contains all the relevant structural, contextual, and discursive elements that were present in the original. The foundation evidence supporting a presumption of integrity should be capable of demonstrating not only the reliability of data input and verification procedures, but also the completeness of the procedures for reproducing original presentation features and annotations, to the extent that these are relevant to an understanding of the record's content (or "terms"). This would entail, in turn, an obligation on the part of courts to come to grips with the question of what precisely constitutes a complete record and to assess the significance of missing elements.

2.5 Conclusion

Although the criteria for assessing the trustworthiness of records as legal evidence have changed over time, reliability continues to be associated with the observer/recorder's proximity to the event being recorded and to the closeness in time between observation and recording. In statutory law, the requirement that the observer and recorder be the same person has been relaxed, however, and the fact that both observer and recorder were acting under a business duty is sufficient evidence of a record's reliability to admit it. The observational principles on which the exception was originally based have not been abandoned. It is simply that the authority of bureaucratic controls, which constitute a somewhat different kind of observation, is now emphasized over the authority of personal observation. A similar shift in focus is apparent in the adaptations to the best evidence rule that have been proposed by the ULCC. There, the emphasis on the authority of the original record has been replaced by an emphasis on the authority of the system in which records are generated and maintained. The integrity of the electronic records system is ensured by verification controls and security procedures, which, like bureaucratic controls, constitute a kind of surveillance over the system and the individuals using it. The significance of observation, whether personal or bureaucratic, is also a prominent feature of historical methods for assessing the trustworthiness of records as historical evidence. Those methods will be examined in the next chapter.

Chapter Three

Trusting Records as Historical Evidence: Modern Historical Methods

In the nineteenth century, scientific historians like Ranke believed that the critical examination of documents would reveal the past "as it actually happened." Twentieth century historians are more constrained in the claims they make concerning the historian's capacity to know the past based on the evidence that has survived into the present. That notwithstanding, the techniques of modern historical criticism, like modern rules of legal evidence, reflect a substantial degree of continuity with those established at the end of the nineteenth century. Over the last fifty years, they have been refined, extended, and qualified in response to changes in recordkeeping practices and to shifting perspectives concerning the nature and limits of historical inquiry. This chapter explores the salient characteristics of modernist historical methods, some contemporary critiques of those methods, and the response of the historical community to the methodological challenges posed by electronic records.

3.1 Framework of Modernist Historical Methods

In *An Introduction to the Study of History*, Langlois and Seignobos used metaphors drawn from natural science to describe the historian's methods of revealing the past. In *The Historian's Craft*, Marc Bloch invokes metaphors drawn from police work and jurisprudence to describe those methods. James Wilkinson detects in Bloch's metaphors, and his work in general "a note of caution that is absent from the counsels of Langlois and Seignobos," and a greater awareness "that historians deal with human fallibility. ... [Bloch's] approach to evidence is cautious not simply because of the possibility of fraud but also because no single source can yield the whole truth."[1] Although modernist history no longer aspires to any single or fixed truth about the past, it has not abandoned the belief in the capacity of historical criticism to reveal what Gertrude Himmelfarb calls "partial, contingent, incremental truths."[2] For that reason, historical method continues to place "a premium on archival research and primary sources, the authenticity of documents and reliability of witnesses, [and] the need to obtain substantiating and countervailing evidence."[3]

David Hackett Fischer maintains that, within the historical discipline, "specific canons of historical proof are neither widely observed nor generally agreed upon. There is no historiographical Wigmore, Stephen, or Thayer and no body of precedents which is recognised as a reliable guide."[4] Nevertheless, there are certain generally accepted procedural checks and controls that guide historians' assessment of the trustworthiness of their sources and that constitute the core of modern manuals of historical methodology.[5] These are, for the most part, the same checks and controls that were codified at the end of the nineteenth century. The distinction between primary and secondary sources and between the trustworthiness of a record as a record (i.e., its authenticity) and its trustworthiness as a statement (i.e., its reliability or credibility),[6] are still considered valid, as are the analytic techniques of external and internal criticism.[7] Moreover, as Geoffrey Elton makes clear, in their search for answers to questions about the past, historians continue to operate within a framework of probabilities rather than certainties:

> History ... aims at explanations, which approximate to an unverifiable truth and are themselves subject to the continuous change, which is the one indisputable fact about history. Historical explanations themselves form part of the history told. The standards of acceptable proof in history thus are standards of acceptable probability controlled by expert knowledge of the evidence, and the historical account is in itself the nearest thing to a proof that the historian can obtain or proffer. He convinces insofar as he persuades others capable of judging that he has worked honestly and that the story he tells makes sense in light of the sources available illumined by a cautious understanding of people and their probabilities.[8]

Although the range of sources available to historians is considerably wider than it was in previous centuries, modern historical method still expresses a preference for primary sources, i.e., records created closest in time to the event they purport to record. According to Fischer, "the best relevant evidence, all things being equal, is evidence which is most nearly immediate to the event itself. The very best evidence, of course, is the event itself, and then the authentic remains of the event, and then direct observations, etc. We shall call this the rule of immediacy."[9] In the late twentieth century, records generated by bureaucracies in the course of administrative activity, as means to an end rather than as ends in themselves, dominate the category of primary sources.

The preference accorded to such records is, of course, a qualified one. As Marc Bloch explains, "It is not that this sort of document is any less subject to errors or falsehoods than the others. ... neither all ambassadorial accounts nor all business letters tell the truth. But this kind of distortion, if it exists, at least, has not been especially designed to deceive posterity."[10] Bloch's comments underline the fact that, although administrative records are frequently characterised as "unintentional" or "unpremeditated" evidence, the real distinction is between different kinds of intentionality. Michael Stanford, for example, categorises administrative records as "communicative evidence," i.e., "evidence [which] reveals the intention to communicate." Within the category of communicative evidence, he follows Bloch's distinction between evidence intended for the eyes of contemporaries only and evidence intended for posterity.[11] The qualified preference given to bureaucratic records provides the framework within which more detailed assessments of the authenticity and reliability of records are conducted.

3.2 The External and Internal Criticism of a Record

Establishing a record's authenticity continues to fall within the purview of external criticism, the purpose of which has always been to verify or establish the authorship of a record, its place and date of origin, its status as an original or copy, and the history of its transmission and custody over time.[12] Although the analytical techniques of external criticism are considered fundamental procedures, their application to records generated by twentieth century bureaucracies occupies very little space in modern manuals of historical methodology. Many historians view external criticism as a necessary task but one whose relevance for modern and contemporary records is limited. Leon Goldstein, for example, suggests that, "it is clear enough, that for periods prior to the emergence of modern conditions of publishing, these analytical techniques of external criticism may be very important, indeed indispensable to the practice of history, though for more recent periods they have, as Mandelbaum puts it, become 'superfluous in the majority of cases.'"[13]

Similarly, the purpose of internal criticism continues to be to establish the credibility of statements made in the record.[14] To do so the historian assesses the credibility of its author, both as a witness and as a reporter. As Shafer observes, "much of historical research is concerned with determination of the accuracy and value of observations of details made by witnesses of events. ... The ability of the witness to observe thus becomes a matter of prime importance."[15] The credibility of a witness is initially assessed in relation to her proximity in time and space to the objects or events on which she is reporting and her familiarity with or understanding of those objects or events. The credibility of the witness as a reporter is assessed in relation to the lapse of time between observation and reporting. According to Louis Gottschalk, "because reliability is, in general, inversely proportional to the *time-lapse* between event and recollection, the closer a document is to the event it narrates the better it is likely to be for historical purposes."[16] The historian is also expected to take into account the reporter's frame of mind and intent in composing the record. In assessing the reporter's frame of mind, the historian attempts to identify possible biases (both personal and cultural), or other legal, social, or cultural constraints that may affect his ability to report accurately.[17] In assessing the reporter's intent, the historian looks at the purpose for which the record was created and its intended audience to determine the likelihood of distortion, editing, or falsification in reporting the events. Finally, the historian attempts to find corroboration (or refutation) of the statements made in the record by comparing them with independent sources.

In contemporary manuals of historical methodology, it is not only the reporter's frame of mind that is considered in assessing the credibility of the record as a statement. The mind of the historian is also a factor since the many sources of both deliberate and inadvertent error that affect reporters, e.g., ignorance, bias, inadequate or selective perception, cultural difference, self-delusion will inevitably affect the historian's perspective on the evidence. As Shafer points out, "the historian must remember that he is looking at the evidence through the prism of his own culture and time."[18] Jacques Le Goff underlines this point when he asserts (echoing Croce) that

> All history is contemporary insofar as the past is grasped in the present, and thus responds to the latter's interests. This is not only inevitable but legitimate. Since history is lived time (*durée*), the past is both past and present. It is the historian's task to make an "objective" study of the past in its double form. To be sure, since he is himself implicated within history, he cannot attain a true "objectivity," but no other history is possible. The historian will make further progress in understanding history by putting himself in question in the course of his analysis, just as a scientific observer takes into account the modifications he may make in the object he is observing.[19]

Historians cannot transcend the perspective of their own time but they can at least be aware of the fact that they inevitably bring a set of assumptions about the world in their assessment of the evidence and, to the extent possible, expose those assumptions in their account.[20]

Many of the conditions identified in manuals of historical methodology as either inhibiting or promoting credible statements are analogous to legal rules of evidence governing testimonial assertions. In fact, the "three steps of historical testimony," identified by Gottschalk, i.e., "observation, recollection, and recording"[21] are practically identical to the elements of testimonial assertion identified by Wigmore in *Rules of Evidence at Common Law*. An account of events that serves the interests of the reporter (i.e., self-serving evidence) is considered inherently unreliable. On the other hand, an account that is detrimental to the interests of the reporter (i.e., statements against self-interest) or an account created under circumstances in which there is a strong motive for accuracy and little or no motive for distortion or falsification (i.e., statements made under a business duty), are considered inherently more reliable. Finally, a statement corroborated by one or more independent witnesses is considered more reliable than a statement that has not been so corroborated.

Moreover, historians writing on historical method often describe the process of internal criticism as a kind of interrogation, or cross-examination, in which records are forced to surrender information they had never intended to provide. Marc Bloch describes cross-examination as "the prime necessity of well-conducted historical research."[22] Michael Stanford draws on the same legal analogy when he suggests: "Historical evidence is our only witness to the past. Therefore the historian must interrogate it ruthlessly like a prosecuting lawyer."[23] And, according to Le Goff, "documents become historical sources only after having undergone a treatment whose purpose is to transform their mendacious function into a confession of the truth."[24] In all these statements, the record is seen as a recalcitrant witness that, nevertheless, can be made to render a more or less reliable account of past events, once the motives and biases of its author are identified and taken into account.

In Geoffrey Elton's view, the legal model is somewhat misleading as a metaphor for the historian's approach to documentary evidence. As he explains:

> I will admit that the legal model might be said to have a metaphorical or analogical validity – that the analysis of documents can be made to appear similar to the cross-examination of a witness. But the metaphor misleads. The cross-examined witness is asked about his claims to have seen or heard that to which he testifies; the analysed document is asked questions about its origin, its place in a series, its contents of common form, even perhaps its authenticity (did it exist when it says it did?) With a witness we endeavour to ascertain the reliability of a statement, with a document the meaning of its existence and of its relation to a complex of events, not observations.[25]

Although Elton's comments focus on the importance of context to an understanding of the *meaning* of records, it is clear that such context is equally important to an assessment of their *reliability*. Vernon Dibble underlines the specific significance of administrative-procedural context in assessing the reliability of records generated by organisations. He observes that the historical rules for evaluating testimony derive from inferences based on generalisations concerning the psychology of cognition (e.g., "testimony about specific details is likely to be more accurate than testimony about general conditions"), the psychology of memory (e.g., "testimony recorded shortly after an event took place is likely to be more accurate than testimony recorded long afterwards"), and the nature of communication (e.g., "testimony about ideologically relevant events addressed to people who share the witness's beliefs and values is likely to be more accurate than testimony addressed to audiences which do not share the witness's ideology").[26]

Such generalisations, however valid they may be for assessing the reliability of records generated by individuals, are an inadequate means of testing the reliability of records produced by organisations which have institutionalised procedures for recording facts and events. Such records are more accurately characterised, Dibble maintains, as a form of "social bookkeeping" rather than as a form of "testimony." With the various forms of social bookkeeping, it is not so much the intentionality of individual authors of records as it is the nature and extent of the bureaucratic controls exercised over those authors that determine the records' degree of reliability with respect to the events they purport to record. Dibble identifies a number of factors likely to influence the reliability of organisational records, among them: the extent to which interested parties have a hand in producing the record; the extent to which those parties are likely to check the record after it is first created; the extent to which they are free to alter the record; the extent to which such alteration, if allowed, makes for greater accuracy or for less,[27] the extent to which the creation of the record has built-in checks, apart from interested parties; the extent to which the events recorded are visible to the record-keeper; the extent to which communication between observers and record-keepers is assured and; the number of steps between observer and record-keeper.[28]

The connection Dibble draws between the administrative-procedural context of a record's creation and its likely degree of reliability is based on the same kinds of generalisations about the nature of bureaucracy that are operative in the business records exception to the hearsay rule discussed in the previous chapter. Reliability is measured in relation to the observer's and recorder's proximity to the event and the nature and degree of the procedural checks on record accuracy.

The administrative-procedural context enlarges the traditional conception of the observer's/recorder's presence in time and place. The bureaucratic controls exercised over observation and recording constitute, in effect, an additional level of observation in which the bureaucracy itself watches over observers and recorders. Reliability is ensured not only because the observer/recorder is close to the event recorded but also because the recording itself takes place within a framework of bureaucratic observation and surveillance. The degree of reliability then is the degree to which the bureaucracy shapes and constrains the speech of observers and recorders. The greater the constraints and controls imposed on recordkeeping by the bureaucracy, so the generalisation goes, the greater the degree of the record's reliability. In "Causation in Historical Study," Robert Sharman suggests that the author of a bureaucratic record

> has so little discretion as to what is recorded as to render the element of personal choice almost irrelevant. Now I admit that with certain types of records ... there is a larger area of discretion. A Colonial-Governor, for instance, writing despatches to London, may have a large amount of freedom as to what he records. Even this freedom, however, is exercised within certain limits. If he fails to answer specific enquiries from London, or if he forgets to report regularly on matters which the Secretary of State expects a Governor to report upon, Downing Street will soon call upon him for an explanation. And if a Viceroy has to render a true account of his stewardship, how much more diligent must a lowly official be in recording the transactions of his office.[29]

Sharman's comments underline the fact that in a bureaucratic environment recordkeeping represents a kind of controlled speech.

Sharman's discussion of the comparative authority of *attested* and *expository* statements also suggests other analogies between law and history in the inference of reliability each draws from the administrative context of a record's creation.[30] An attested statement, according to Sharman, is one whose reliability is guaranteed by the office responsible for registering it. An official convict transportation record, such as an indent list or assignment list, which states the fact that a convicted felon was transported to one of the Australian colonies may be relied upon by historians because such fact was attested by the authorities whose job it was to register such transactions. An expository statement, on the other hand, does not possess the high degree of reliability conferred on attested statements. As Sharman points out, it was the custom for the transporting authorities to take confessions from transported felons. The fact that the confession was made is itself an attested statement, but the official recording the confession cannot attest to the truth of the assertions contained within it. The distinction between attested and expository statements is consistent with legal assumptions about the reliability of events that occur outside the presence of the recorder. The portion of a hospital record that records the patient's case history prior to admission, for example, is not admissible under the business records exception to the hearsay rule because a patient's assertions about his or her prior condition cannot be substantiated by the doctor taking the case history.[31]

The fact that an expository statement does not possess the inherent guarantee of reliability that an attested statement possesses does not render it completely unreliable. As Sharman explains, an ambassador's reply to a despatch containing instructions as to how he should represent his country's interests at the court to which he is accredited will contain both attested and expository statements:

> That he received the instructions is an attested statement, and it can also be attested that he was given an audience by the Secretary of State for Foreign Affairs. But the ambassador will then enlarge on the sort of reception his representations met with, and possibly the promises made by the Foreign Secretary. It is more than likely that we can look upon these as only expository statements.[32]

While an expository statement contained in such a document lacks the kind of reliability granted an attested statement, its degree of reliability can nevertheless be measured on the basis of

> the extent to which it was accepted and acted upon in the office to which it was sent. The ambassador may have exaggerated the effectiveness of his interview with the Foreign Secretary, but if his report is received in good faith, and if subsequent policy is based upon the outcome of representations supposedly made, we come a long way nearer to accepting expository statements as of evidential value to enable us to determine both what actually happened and why it happened.[33]

In other words, a record that the bureaucracy treats as reliable may be taken as reliable for most intents and purposes.

3.3 Postmodernist Critiques of Historical Method

In recent years, modernist historical methods for assessing the reliability of a record have been challenged by new ways of looking at documentary sources. The reliability of any record depends on the question being asked of it and records considered unreliable as an answer to one question may be reliable as an answer to another question. Drawing on the legal model of evidence, David Hackett Fischer explains:

> ... sound evidence consists in the establishment of a satisfactory relationship between the *factum probandum*, or the proposition to be proved, and the *factum probans*, or the material which is offered as proof ... [It follows] that the criteria for a satisfactory *factum probans* depend in large degree upon the nature of the *factum probandum*. This is a pedantical way of saying that every fact in history is an answer to a question, and that evidence which is useful and true and sufficient in answer to question B may be false and useless in answer to question A.[34]

However, modernist historical methods for assessing record reliability tend to privilege a particular way of looking at records. The reliability of a record is measured specifically in relation to its fidelity to the event it purports to record. Speculating on the reasons underlying that standard of measurement, Mark Cousins comments:

> A primary source is preferred over a secondary source because – why? Because it is close to – what? A complex of relations is opened up by this question. A primary source is closer to what it refers to than a secondary source. The word 'closer' has itself two connotations. It is closer to the truth and it is closer to the event. Truth is the adequate representation of the event. The event is the object which may be referred to in truth. A primary source is then the more reliable witness to the event. The event is most reliably represented by a witness, by testimony which can best be trusted. Secondary sources are tainted, less reliable; they cannot be treated as convincing testimony; they lack reliability.[35]

The preference for primary sources over secondary sources, for unintentional evidence over intentional evidence, and for evidence given by a more or less neutral observer over that provided by an interested observer, are all based on an assumption that such evidence is the most credible testimony concerning the event to which a record refers.

Letters of remission from the fourteenth to sixteenth centuries are a good example of a source traditionally considered to be unreliable, "a tissue of counter-truths,"[36] whose fidelity to the event it purports to record is hopelessly compromised by the self-interest of the person recounting the event. Letters of remission were pardons, granted by the king upon a request for grace by a supplicant, and ratified by a court of law. They were normally reserved for crimes such as homicide where the offender had been or could be sentenced to death. Incorporated into the letter of remission was the supplicant's story of unpremeditated, unintentional, or otherwise justified murder, as told to a royal notary, either by the supplicant or by relatives.

By modernist criteria, a letter of remission is unreliable as evidence of the actual event the letter purports to record because it typically is recounted as a highly charged "pardon tale" of passion and contrition. The narrative is clearly crafted to elicit the sympathy and grace of the king. Nevertheless, it is reliable as evidence of the storytelling event itself. According to Natalie Zemon Davis, letters of remission provide valuable "evidence of how sixteenth-century people told stories (albeit in the special case of the pardon tale), what they thought a good story was, how they accounted for motive, and how through narrative they made sense of the unexpected and built coherence into immediate experience."[37] What makes them unreliable as factual accounts – their fictive (in the sense of shaping) elements – is precisely what makes them reliable as narratives of those accounts. Moreover, they are, Davis maintains, "one of the best sources of relatively uninterrupted narrative from the lips of the lower orders ... in sixteenth-century France."[38]

The understanding that records may be used to answer questions about events other than those they purport to record is not ignored altogether by more traditional historians. As Dibble makes clear, historians analyse social bookkeeping for the same reasons they analyse testimony: "in order to make decisions about the probable accuracy or completeness of the record." But, he continues, "historians are not interested only in accurate social bookkeeping. Inaccurate social bookkeeping can be just as valuable as testimony known to consist of lies and distortions."[39] Collingwood has pointed out that "anyone who has read Vico ... [knows] that the important question about any statement contained in a source is not whether it is true or false, but what it means."[40] The assertion, though overstated, is an important one because it emphasises that, for the historian, unlike the lawyer, the fact that a record is found to be unreliable with respect to the events it purports to record does not diminish its value as historical evidence.

The same observation holds true for inauthentic records. In law, a record that is found to be inauthentic is inadmissible as evidence.[41] Langlois' and Seignobos' manual, similarly, excluded inauthentic records from the historian's further consideration. Twentieth century historians are not so dismissive, recognising that a record's authenticity is only one dimension of its value as historical evidence. As R.C. Cheney explains: "Even the 'authentic' character of a record, which appeals to the lawyer and which an archivist is sometimes at pains to preserve, is not the criterion of its value as historical evidence. The tendentious official account or the forgery, once recognised as such, will be valuable to the historian precisely because it is not objective or not authentic."[42] The fact of forgery simply changes the kinds of inferences that may be drawn from the record. A 'false' document, according to Jacques Le Goff, "is also a historical document that can provide valuable testimony regarding the period in which it was forged and concerning the period during which it was considered to be authentic and used."[43]

Recognising the value of an unreliable or inauthentic record as historical evidence does not, however, absolve the historian of responsibility for establishing whether the record is, or is not, trustworthy. As Shafer makes clear, "the historian is interested in lies as well as truth, but he must be able to distinguish between them."[44] The fact of a record's authenticity and its likely degree of reliability are an essential first link in the chain of inferences from the *factum probans* to the *factum probandum*. Even in Davis' study of sixteenth century letters of remission, which emphasises the status of records as a form of persuasion rather than as a form of proof, the fidelity of the stories told in the letters to "real events" is taken into account (by comparing them with other contemporary accounts of the same events) in order to determine "what relation truth-telling had to the outcome of the stories and what truth status they enjoyed in society at large."[45]

The emergence of postmodernist history has resulted in a more general problematising of the presumed correspondence between evidence and reality underlying modernist historical methods for assessing record reliability. Carlo Ginzburg describes this presumption as a legacy of the scientific or positivist history of the nineteenth century, which tended to simplify the relationship between evidence and reality: As he explains:

> In a positivist perspective, the evidence is analysed only in order to ascertain if, and when, it implies a distortion, either intentional or unintentional. The historian is thus confronted with various possibilities: a document can be a fake; a document can be authentic, but unreliable, insofar as the information it provides can be either lies or mistakes; or a document can be authentic and reliable. In the first two cases the evidence is dismissed; in the latter, it is accepted, but only as evidence of something *else*. In other words, the evidence is not regarded as a historical document in itself, but as a transparent medium -- as an open window that gives us direct access to reality.[46]

Modernist historical methods are thus underpinned by the assumption that a necessary and meaningful relationship exists between the referent (a determinant reality – the past) and its expression (the record).

This assumption has been challenged specifically by structuralist and post-structuralist theorists who emphasise instead the arbitrary relationship between word and world, between the language that names reality and the reality that is being named. Roland Barthes, for example, maintains that the assertion of a direct relationship between referent and expression is nothing more than an illusion, a "sleight of hand":

The only feature which distinguishes historical discourse from other kinds is a paradox: the 'fact' can only exist linguistically, as a term in a discourse, yet we behave as if it were a simple reproduction of something on another plane of existence altogether, some extra-structural 'reality'. Historical discourse is presumably the only kind which aims at a referent 'outside' itself that can in fact never be reached.[47]

The problematising of the relationship between the past and its mode of expression is rooted in ideas developed early in the twentieth century by the structural linguist Ferdinand Saussure. Language, Saussure believed, is a system of signs. A sign is constituted by the union between a signifier, i.e., the physical form of the sign as we perceive it through our senses – the sound of a word for instance – and a signified, i.e., the user's mental concept of what the sign refers to. Between the signifier (or expression) and the signified (or referent) there is no necessary relationship; the form of the signifier is based purely on convention or agreement among its users.[48]

The radicalism inherent in the structuralist view of language (a radicalism unrecognised by the structuralists themselves) has been taken to its logical conclusion by the post-structuralists, a constituency of postmodern theorists, who stress the fragility of the link between the signifier and the signified and the consequently slippery nature of "meaning". Postmodern writing on history, specifically, stresses the contingent and indeterminate nature of historical knowledge in general, and the documentary conception of such knowledge in particular. As Linda Hutcheon explains:

All documents ... used by historians are not neutral evidence for reconstructing phenomena, which are assumed to have some independent existence outside them. All documents process information and the very way they do so is itself a historical fact that limits the documentary conception of historical knowledge. ... the lesson here is that the past once existed, but that our historical knowledge of it is semiotically transmitted.[49]

From this perspective, the past is not a foreign country waiting to be discovered, but, rather, "an empty space waiting to be filled by the historian."[50] A record is not a reflection of a determinant reality, but, rather, "a constituent agent in the reconstruction of a conception of the real."[51]

The shift in the status of the record as representation has been characterised by Michel Foucault as a transformation from *document* to *monument*. *Document* derives from *docere*, meaning 'to teach'. During the seventeenth century, French jurists associated *document* with *legal proof*. During the nineteenth century, under the influence of the positivist historical school, it acquired the meaning of *historical proof*, and was considered the foundation of the historical fact. The Latin term *monumentum*, on the other hand, is linked etymologically to the Indo-European root *men*, which is linked, in turn, to *mens* (the mind) and *memimi* (memory). The philological origins of the word *monument* suggest anything that recalls and perpetuates the past.[52] Foucault's description of the transition of the status of the record from document to monument plays on these conceptual associations and distinctions.

> History, in its traditional form, undertook to 'memorize' the *monuments* of the past, transform them into *documents*, and lend speech to those traces which, in themselves, are often not verbal, or which say in silence something other than what they actually say; in our time, history is that which transforms *documents* into *monuments*. In that area where, in the past history deciphered the traces left by men, it now deploys a mass of elements that have to be grouped, made relevant, placed in relation to one another to form totalities.[53]

What transforms a document into monument is the fact of its creation and use by a ruling authority. A *document* enjoys the status of a (more or less) unselfconscious remnant of the past, which the modernist historian translates into a statement of historical fact. A *monument* is understood to be a deliberate and self-conscious product of a society bent on shoring up and perpetuating its knowledge and power. The aim of postmodern historians, such as Foucault, is to penetrate beneath the documentary surface of a record to its monumental structure, which is its ideological meaning, decipher its conscious and unconscious intentionality, and expose the network of knowledge and power relationships operating in and embedded within it.

The three traditional aims of internal criticism, i.e., to assess the competence and sincerity of the record's author, determine the credibility of its content, and test it against other evidence, are insufficient because, as Le Goff explains:

> Whether we are concerned with documents that are conscious or unconscious ... the conditions under which the document was *produced* must be carefully studied. In fact, the structures of power in a society include the power of certain social categories and dominant groups to voluntarily or involuntarily leave behind them testimony that can orient historiography in one direction or another. Power over future memory, the power to perpetuate, must be recognised and defused by the historian. No document is innocent. It must be judged. Every document is testimony or evidence (*monument*) which we have to know how to destructure, to take apart. The historian must be able, not simply to discern a fake, to judge the credibility of a document, but also to demystify it.[54]

Armando Petrucci, an historian and paleographer, interprets Le Goff's comments as an assault, not only on the practice of internal criticism, but also on the foundations of traditional diplomatic theory and practice. Early in the twentieth century, the classical paleographer and diplomatist Cesare Paoli defined the document as "written evidence of a deed of a juridical nature, compiled observing certain specific forms which were intended to establish its trustworthiness and status as legal proof."[55] While he does not dispute the validity of this definition, Petrucci believes that it "makes the mistake of reducing the always projecting and variegated density of documentary sources to the pure and simple connection with the juridical event."[56] He finds in the remarks of the historian Mario Liverani a more profound characterisation of what the discipline of diplomatics should be, one that builds explicitly on the theme of document as monument:

> The 'true thing,' for now, is undoubtedly the text (or the refiguration, or in any case the documentary datum); next comes the ideological system of which this text is an expression; and finally, across these filters, one can get to the factual support that in itself one must realistically consider to be lost forever. We do not study physical acts ... but documents that are *word* acts of an ideological *language* whose reconstruction should be our preliminary and pre-eminent task, if not perhaps our only one.[57]

Variations on Liverani's theme have been explored in the context of "social" or "qualitative" diplomatics, a relatively new disciplinary stream that concerns itself more with exposing the discursive strategies employed in the production of documents than with determining their authenticity.[58] Petrucci's own diplomatic examination of the language used in the preambles of Italian documents written between the tenth and thirteenth centuries constitutes an exercise in demystifying and exposing "the linguistic masquerade, the semantic shell, appearance, sign, and interpretive voice that is the natural attribute of any text."[59] Petrucci finds in the formulas used by notaries in preparing preambles an increasing "preoccupation with affirming the validity of written evidence in comparison with the transience of oral evidence."[60] Preambles from the eleventh century contrast the permanence of documentary *memoria* with the *oblivio* of human memory. The concept of documentary memory is gradually accompanied, in the twelfth century, by that of *veritas* which, in turn, is linked, in the thirteenth century, to *publicitas* and *instrumentum publicum*. These shifts in the wording of the formulas used in preambles reflect the growing status of the document as an instrument of juridical power, as well as the growing status of Italy's professional notariate as an exclusive wielder of such power.[61]

Postmodernism stresses not only the power structure immanent in language (and, therefore, records), but also the indeterminate, sometimes duplicitous, nature of language and its dissociation from any presumed reality.[62] Linguistic communication is used for a variety of purposes and rarely with the sole intention to inform. According to J.L. Austin's theory of speech acts, when we make a statement, we perform at least three different acts. A *locutionary act* "is roughly equivalent to uttering a certain sentence with a certain sense and reference, which again is roughly equivalent to 'meaning' in the traditional sense." An *illocutionary act* is roughly equivalent to informing, warning, or ordering, i.e., "utterances which have a certain (conventional) force." A *perlocutionary act* is "what we bring about or achieve *by* saying something, such as convincing, persuading, deterring, and, even, say, surprising or misleading."[63] Austin's theory of speech acts demonstrates the different senses or dimensions of the use of language in speech acts, which apply to written as well as to oral communication.

In demonstrating those different dimensions, the theory also illustrates the limits of the historian's capacity to enter into the minds of those who lived in the past by analysing the documentary remains of that past. Every act of communication involves an act of translation and every speech act requires what Keith Jenkins describes as an "interpretation between privacies."[64] As Jenkins elaborates, "the philosophical problem of other minds" has been discussed by Wittgenstein, who

> considers whether it is possible to enter into the mind of another person we know well and who is beside one, and concludes that it is not. Historians, however, have disregarded this conclusion and have continued to raise questions that are based on the assumption that it actually is possible to enter lots and lots of minds, even minds we cannot possibly know well, and which are far away from us in space and time.[65]

In Jenkins view historians, such as Collingwood,[66] who believe that it is possible to enter into the minds and experiences of people in the past, simply ignore the fundamental limits and, ultimately, impossibility, of achieving such empathy.

Postmodern historical discourse usefully points out some of the limits of internal criticism, the concept of reliability, and the rationalist assumptions on which they are built. At the same time, the discourse betrays its own limits by the unremittingly sceptical stance some of its advocates adopt toward the possibility of knowing the past at all through its documentary traces. According to Gertrude Himmelfarb, postmodernist history "denies not only suprahistorical truths but historical truths, truths relative to particular times and places." In so doing, it denies "the reality of the past apart from what the historian chooses to make of it, and thus of any objective truth about the past."[67] The postmodernist views records and reality alike "as a 'text' that exists only in the present – a text to be parsed, glossed, construed, and interpreted by the historian, much as a poem or novel is by the critic. And, like any literary text, the historical text is indeterminate and contradictory, paradoxical and ironic, rhetorical and metaphoric."[68] An interpretation of an historical text, however, necessarily entails an interpretation about the past, and that interpretation must be supported by evidence. In a forum dedicated to a discussion of truth and objectivity in history in the wake of postmodernism, Raymond Martin observes that, while

> [h]istorians' feelings about [truth and objectivity] may affect profoundly how they *view* historical studies ... they seem unlikely to have much effect on how they actually *do* history. Historians

who want to be taken seriously have to support their interpretations by evidence, and by the same sorts of evidence, and in the same ways, whether they are objectivists, relativists, or skeptics.[69]

An historical investigation, if it is to have any validity, must strike a balance between textual representation and extra-textual reality. As Carlo Ginzburg points out, modernist historians have privileged the latter at the expense of the former; postmodernist historians, for their part, have privileged the former at the expense of the latter. Whereas traditional history has tended to treat documentary evidence as an open window, postmodern sceptics regard it "as a wall, which by definition precludes any access to reality."[70] In this respect, both the "theoretical naiveté" of modernist historians and the "theoretical sophistication" of the postmodernists find common ground in a rather simplistic assumption that the relationship between evidence and reality is a straightforward one when, in fact, it is more accurately characterised as a complex and mutually dependent one:

> Without a thorough analysis of [a record's] inherent distortions (the codes according to which it has been constructed and/or must be perceived), a sound historical construction [of the past] is impossible. But this statement should also be read the other way around: a purely internal reading of the evidence, without any reference to its referential dimension, is impossible as well. ... The fashionable injunction to study reality as a text should be supplemented by the awareness that no text can be understood without a reference to extratextual realities.[71]

Ginzburg's observations underline the point that modernist and postmodernist perspectives on historical methods should be seen, not as irreconcilable but mutually dependent: each perspective qualifies and corrects the excesses of the other.

3.4 Challenges to Historical Method Posed by Electronic Records

The insights of postmodernist history pose a philosophical challenge to modernist historical methods for assessing the reliability and authenticity of records. Changes in the technologies for creating and maintaining records pose a more practical challenge. As bureaucracies rely increasingly on new information and communication technologies to create and maintain records, the question that presents itself is whether the techniques of external and internal criticism are adequate to the task of verifying the authenticity and degree of reliability of electronic records whose most salient feature is the ease with which they can be invisibly altered and manipulated. As Jean Samuels points out in connection with electronic mail messages:

A problem for ownership identification can occur when messages are forwarded or circulated to others. If the original heading (showing source, date, etc.) is removed from the message or if the body of the text is edited (both of which are easily done on most systems) then the original temper or content of the message can be radically or subtly altered. So what may appear as the forwarded message of X is, in fact, the forwarded message of X with additions and changes by Y. Likewise, a message from X may be forwarded, without the original heading, by Y to Z. To Z the message will appears as Y's own thoughts and message.[72]

Attributing authorship represents one dimension of the problem. Another dimension is that of identifying provenance. According to Charles Dollar:

The challenge of identifying and maintaining the provenance of electronic records is much more severe where there is a network or corporate-wide database, because computer to computer linkages dissolve the traditional boundaries between organizations, sub-operating units, and offices that in the past provided much of the provenance based information. In a network or corporate-wide database, the database management system determines where and how information is stored. A user may retrieve information from a corporate database or a distributed database without knowing where the information is stored, which unit created it, whether the information has been updated, or who uses it, because the database information is not self-referential.[73]

As Dibble and others have shown, for records generated by organisations, the administrative-procedural context in which a record has been created is crucial to an assessment of its authenticity and degree of reliability. That context includes where a document was created, the purpose for its creation, the procedural framework in which it was created, the audience for whom it was intended, when and how it was received by the addressee, how it relates to other records dealing with the same matter, and how it was transmitted and preserved over time. In traditional paper recordkeeping systems, Dollar observes, such context tends to manifest itself:

in organization charts and manuals, procedures, policies, physical ... arrangement of the records [e.g., in files], media characteristics such as watermarks, formal elements such as letterheads, and in content/context elements such as names of writers and recipients, dates, references to other documents or files, and the like. In addition, individual documents may contain marginalia, initials, and similar contextual information that reveal the information environment in which records were created, used, and maintained.[74]

As electronic record systems replace paper ones, however, the inherent, and visible, links among the physical, formal and contextual components of a record are disappearing. This is because, in electronic record systems, the components are stored and managed independently of one another within a database. An illustration of the way in which electronic systems separate the various components of a record is provided by Dollar in his description of an electronic health care application case file containing:

> demographic data, medical examinations results and diagnostics, and hospital care records for individuals. The electronic case file for an individual does not exist as a physical entity but rather as chunks of electronic data stored in different parts of the health care application system. These chunks of electronic data become a case file or view of the case file when they manifest a logical structure as a result of being displayed on a monitor or printed. This manifestation is the result of software that joins disparate data and reconstructs them so the whole looks like a document. A manifested electronic case file (or view), therefore, will display sequential logical relations that may not be inherent in the chunks of data that were retrieved. The physical relations of this case file are stored electronically independently of the data.[75]

Some of the identifying components of an electronic record, e.g., those that place it within its administrative, procedural, and documentary context are generated by database or system software that is inaccessible to the user. Moreover, because the components are managed separately, there is no guarantee that they will be preserved in a manner that will permit the reconstruction of the record over time. In many instances, such data will not be preserved at all.

A starting point for historians in their efforts to verify the authenticity of a record is the determination of its status as an original or copy. Since an original record contains all the original markings (e.g., the signature, the seal), traditionally it has been easier to authenticate an original than a copy. Determining an electronic record's status as an original or copy is complicated, not only by the absence of coherent criteria for distinguishing between the two in an electronic environment, but also by the fact that an electronic record cannot survive in the form in which it was originally created for any substantial length of time given the fragility of storage media and the rapidity, to date, of technology obsolescence. The form of an electronic record is substantially determined by hardware and software functionality. Its original integrity may be lost, therefore, when records are migrated from one system to another, transferred to a different character set, or printed to paper. As David Bearman explains:

> As long as the information created in the course of work in an electronic environment remains in the software and hardware system in which it was created, it loses none of the contextual information which is critical to its meaning, but the transition, or

"migration" of data to a new environment threatens to change the
way the information looks, feels or operates, and hence what it
means.[76]

The erosion of an original record over time is not a uniquely
contemporary phenomenon. Over the centuries, ancient texts have suffered
similar erosion as a consequence of "scientific" manipulations:

> A document, and particularly a text, may over the course of time
> undergo apparently scientific manipulations that have in reality
> obliterated the original. For example, it has been brilliantly
> demonstrated that the letter from Epicurus to Herodotus that is
> preserved in Diogenes Laertius' *Lives, Teachings, and
> Apophthegms of the Famous Philosophers* was reworked by a
> secular tradition that buried the letter of the text under the
> annotations and corrections which, whether intentionally or not,
> finally stifled and distorted the letter of the text through "a reading
> that was uncomprehending, indifferent, or partisan."[77]

The original text of the Justinian Code suffered similar indignities at the hands of
medieval commentators and glossators. The main difference between the
ancient and contemporary examples is that with the ancient texts, the
annotations and corrections over time disfigured the original document's content;
with electronic records, the migration of the document over time threatens to
disfigure aspects of its original appearance or presentation elements, such as
colours, original fonts, letterhead, the organisation of the elements of the
discourse. Such disfiguration, equally, may alter or distort its content.

Recent historical literature addressing the implications of information
technology on historical methodology reflects historians' concern that the
complexity and volatility of electronic records may defeat their efforts to establish
the authenticity of such records.[78] On the other hand, many historians also
believe that the computer may actually enhance both the authenticity and the
reliability of records because electronic systems are capable of capturing more of
the context in which electronic records are created and used within organisations
than was possible with traditional recordkeeping systems. Ronald Zweig
maintains that:

> The more sophisticated electronic office systems record an
> additional level of information about documents beyond their
> textual content, their appearance and structure. These systems
> also record how documents are used. In this context, "usage"
> has many possible meanings. Office systems track the creation
> of a document, its evolution through various drafts by various
> authors, and its movement through the organizational hierarchy.
> We can know who received it, who read it, who annotated it. We
> can reconstruct how widely it was distributed amongst decision
> makers. Its system priority, security level and entire life cycle can

be known in ways we can only rarely reconstruct from the extant records of conventional documents. As any contemporary historian will appreciate, extraneous pieces of evidence such as distribution lists, and signed receipts for a document can give valuable additional information about the significance of the documents to which they are attached. ... the electronic version of a document can be designed to retain these usage attributes in a complete form.[79]

Zweig likens these attributes to "fingerprints" on a document, which are capable of establishing the reliability, authenticity, and meaning of records generated within an electronic system.

In Zweig's view, records generated by new technologies transcend the traditional boundaries of paper records and provide a more complete view of the past:

Electronic records can be more comprehensive than any paper document, and modern documents will be compound things that cannot be expressed on paper. They will contain graphics, images, voice, video, animations. ... Documents can contain links and pointers to many other (interlinked) files of 'documents' so that the hypertext links are part of the information that the document contains. Alternatively, the electronic document can be continually updated by links to databases. Historians will not work with documents that have traditional boundaries at all, but with 'entities' that are really pieces of links to other materials which are stored throughout a computer network and are constantly being updated.[80]

There is no question that compound, hypertext, and hypermedia documents offer dramatic possibilities for providing a more detailed picture of the past. On the other hand, the multiplication of sources from which a document can be constructed, which may not be visible to the user, and the dynamic nature of the databases from which the data are drawn, will also exacerbate the already difficult task of establishing the reliability and authenticity of those sources.

Zweig's enthusiasm for the potential of electronic records systems to provide historians with a more complete picture of the past than previously has been possible is tempered by a concern that the potential of electronic office systems to retain contextual information on usage, such as permissions, views, and audit trails may not be realised:

... many such systems ignore the usage information, in favour of mimicking as closely as possible existing office practices. Other systems abandon the systems management information on usage as soon as a copy of the document has been unaltered for a given period of time and it is archived. There are no agreed standards of what sort of usage information should be preserved, or how to do so.[81]

The lack of agreed standards is attributable, in part, to the fact that many electronic systems have been designed to function as *information* systems, rather than as *recordkeeping* systems. Bearman explains the difference between the two in the following way:

> Record-keeping systems keep and support retrieval of records, while information systems store and provide access to information. Record-keeping systems are distinguished from information systems within organizations by the role that they play in providing organizations with evidence of business transactions (by which is meant actions taken in the course of conducting their business, rather than 'commercial' transactions). Non-record information systems, on the other hand, store information in discrete chunks that can be recombined and reused without reference to their documentary context.[82]

In many information systems, the usage context in particular cannot be preserved because the systems have not been designed to capture all the inputs and outputs in an auditable trail.[83] Zweig believes that existing policies and practices governing organisational recordkeeping need to be re-examined and revised to exploit the potential of electronic systems and that historians have a vital role to play in that re-examination and revision. Since records managers and archivists "are not necessarily aware of the special needs of historians, ... it is up to the [historical] profession to define which attributes of electronic documents should be preserved to facilitate our work in reconstructing the past."[84]

Other historians, such as Peter Denley, question the desirability of historians striking an alliance with record creators to determine how, and in what form, electronic records will be preserved:

> The rationale behind data creation is immensely broad, but might perhaps be categorised as 1) the need for a smooth flow of information to make corporate activity possible, 2) the need for proof of activity or entitlement, 3) the presentation of the 'public face' of that activity. When it comes to data storage, the second and third of these categories predominate, indeed take over from the first (to the extent that it becomes important to the data creators that records which challenge or compromise them are destroyed). By contrast, historians want to unpick the public face that is presented. They want to read between the lines, to worm their way into the subtext and assumptions behind the presented image, and to discover the practices that are accidentally or deliberately hidden to view. It was ever thus. All that has changed is the nature and volume of the data, and the way it is created and accessed. That historians are increasingly being involved in the process at an

earlier stage ... is good news, and helps the two sides to better
mutual understanding. It would be illusory, and dangerous, though,
to imagine that there could or should be real partnership. That is
not the function of the historian.[85]

In Denley's view, the interests of the protagonists and interpreters of history are,
inevitably, in conflict with each other. Given those conflicting interests, the
historian's position in relation to record creators must, of necessity, remain an
adversarial one.

3.4.1 COURT CASES INVOLVING HISTORIANS AND ELECTRONIC RECORDS

A forum in which historians have adopted such an adversarial position and, in the
process, raised the issue of what constitutes a trustworthy record in an electronic
environment, is the American courts. In two recent cases: *Armstrong v. Executive
Office of the President* and *Public Citizen v. John Carlin,* historians, journalists,
and other researchers challenged the right of the government to destroy
electronic records generated by federal agencies. Neither *Armstrong* nor *Public
Citizen* was launched explicitly for the purpose of answering the question
whether the techniques of external and internal criticism are adequate for
verifying the authenticity and degree of reliability of electronic records.
Nevertheless, each raises a number of issues concerning what historians and other
researchers consider to be the essential characteristics of such records, and those
issues have a direct bearing on the question of what constitutes record reliability
and authenticity in an electronic environment.

In 1989, Scott Armstrong – who was then executive director of the
National Security Archive – and others sought an injunction prohibiting the
destruction of backup tapes from the electronic mail systems which served the
agencies of the Executive Office of the President (EOP), including the National
Security Council (NSC). The electronic mail was created by the Reagan White
House and government officials intended to erase all the data on the EOP and
NSC systems at the end of the Reagan administration.[86] The lawsuit filed by
Armstrong and others made three claims: first, that some information in the
system qualified either as federal records under the Federal Records Act or as
presidential records under the Presidential Records Act; that the Executive Office
of the President failed to formulate and implement guidelines for the
management of its electronic mail consistent with law and regulation; and that the
Archivist of the United States neglected to carry out his statutory responsibilities
with respect to the electronic records on the systems.

The case was decided in favour of the plaintiffs and the decision was
upheld on appeal. In 1993, the U.S. Court of Appeals for the District of Columbia
in *Armstrong v. Executive Office of the President* ("*Armstrong II*")[87] held that
electronic versions of electronic mail qualify as records that must be created,
managed and disposed under the rules set out in the Federal Records Act
(FRA).[88] The Act prohibits agencies from destroying records without the prior

approval of the Archivist of the United States. In making its ruling, the court rejected the government's claim that the computer system used by the EOP and NSC (the IBM Professional Office System or PROFS[89]) was not a recordkeeping system and that therefore the information contained within it did not qualify as records. The court observed that, while PROFS was not designed as a recordkeeping system, it was nevertheless used "to relay substantive – even classified – 'notes' that, in content, are often indistinguishable from letters or memoranda."[90]

The court also rejected the government's argument that electronic versions of electronic mail messages, once copied to paper, are no longer "records" under the FRA.[91] The court maintained that, unless an electronic message is an *identical* extra copy of a paper printout, it is considered a record whose disposition must be determined in accordance with the FRA. Moreover, the court argued, paper printouts of electronic mail are not exact duplicates of the electronic versions because they do not generally contain all the information found in the electronic original. For example, the paper printout might not include the names of recipients and senders, the date and time of receipt, links to previous messages and complete distribution lists. Speaking for the court, Judge Wald stated that paper printouts that do not include "all significant material" contained in the electronic records "cannot accurately be termed 'copies' – identical twins – but are, at most, 'kissing cousins.'"[92] Although the reliability and authenticity of electronic records were not explicitly addressed in *Armstrong*, the court's ruling nevertheless carries implications for both. The elements of an electronic record identified by the court as "significant" convey information about the administrative-procedural context in which an electronic mail message has been sent or received and thus are key determinants of reliability for this type of record. The court's assertion that a paper printout of an electronic mail message cannot be characterised as a copy of the electronic version is another way of stating that a paper printout is not an authentic copy if it lacks critical elements present in the original electronic record.

In *Armstrong*, electronic mail messages provided a focal point for the court's consideration of what constitutes a record in an electronic environment, what constitutes a complete (and, by implication, reliable) record in that environment, and what does and does not constitute an identical (or authentic) copy of an electronic record. In a subsequent court case, *Public Citizen v. Carlin*, the court was asked to consider the same questions in relation to a broader range of electronic records.

The ruling in *Armstrong* did not affect the ability of federal agencies to destroy incidental electronic records that, in the opinion of the Archivist of the United States, lacked sufficient administrative, legal, research or other value to justify their continued preservation.[93] In 1995, the National Archives and Records Administration (NARA) issued revisions to General Records Schedule 20 (GRS 20)[94] that authorised the destruction of electronic records in fifteen enumerated categories, including electronic records created by computer operators, programmers, analysts and systems administrators, as well as records existing on "live" desktop computer applications. A group of historians, journalists, and other researchers responded by launching a lawsuit, charging that the regulation was "arbitrary and capricious, irrational and contrary to law."[95] According to the plaintiffs in *Public Citizen*,[96] the Archivist had no authority to use a General Records Schedule to authorise the blanket destruction of electronic records, without first determining whether they were housekeeping records of short-term value or program records of long-term value.

The most contentious provisions in the revisions to GRS 20 relate to records created on electronic mail and word processing systems or applications. Items 13 and 14 of GRS 20 permit agencies to delete such records from the original system on which they were created "after they have been copied to an electronic recordkeeping system, paper, or microform for recordkeeping purposes."[97] The plaintiffs maintained that the promulgation of the revisions to GRS 20 allowed agencies to adopt a "print and delete" policy with regard to these types of electronic records.

NARA's defence of the revised GRS 20 was based on its assertion that, far from authorising the destruction of valuable records created by office automation, GRS 20, along with NARA regulations and guidelines, aimed to preserve such records by requiring agencies to transfer them to an appropriate recordkeeping system. According to NARA, electronic mail messages and word processing records typically were stored in disparate electronic files maintained by individuals rather than in centrally controlled files maintained by and for the agency as a whole. As a consequence, these records lacked the circumstantial guarantee of reliability and authenticity that such control provides. NARA believed that instituting procedures directed toward re-asserting centralised control over bureaucratic recordkeeping and bringing electronic records within the scope of that control offered the most appropriate solution to the problem of ensuring the trustworthiness of records and, hence, their value as evidence.

Under GRS 20, agencies were not authorised to delete the versions on the electronic mail and word processing systems until the records had been properly preserved in an agency-controlled recordkeeping system, i.e., a system with the "capability to group similar records and provide the necessary context to connect the record with the relevant agency function or transaction."[98] For word processing records, such context included, among other things, the office of origin, file classification code, key words for retrieval, addressee, author, signer, date and security classification. If the records were maintained in an electronic recordkeeping system, NARA regulations required that they be correlated with related records on paper, microform, or other media.[99] To meet the specific concerns raised in *Armstrong II* with regard to electronic mail messages, item 14 of GRS 20 required agencies to copy the names of sender and recipients and dates of transmission and receipt, where appropriate, along with the message text, to the recordkeeping system before the message was destroyed.[100] According to NARA, the reason agencies were printing electronic records to paper was simply that their electronic systems were incapable of meeting the recordkeeping requirements. Therefore, agencies had little choice but to print the electronic records out and incorporate them into a traditional paper recordkeeping system that was capable of maintaining the records in their appropriate administrative, procedural, and documentary context. NARA pointed out that, as the technology progresses, "agencies will be able to consider converting to electronic recordkeeping systems for their records."[101]

In *Armstrong II*, the government had argued that the process of printing out an electronic record takes away its status as a record. In *Public Citizen*, it argued that the creation of a paper version of an electronic record under GRS 20 takes away the electronic version's long-term value and, in turn, its status as a program record. The view taken by the district court in *Public Citizen* was that the government's argument was "no more persuasive than the one rejected by the Court of Appeals in *Armstrong II*. While an *exact* duplicate of a particular record might be discardable, electronic records cannot categorically be regarded as valueless "'extra copies' of paper versions. ... Simply put, electronic communications are rarely identical to their paper counterparts; they are records unique and distinct from printed versions of the same record."[102] The district court also accepted the plaintiffs' argument that, for electronic records to be complete, the original functionality of the "live" system in which they were created must be preserved. In the opinion of the court, word processing records and electronic spreadsheets, like electronic mail messages,

> contain information that is not preserved in a print-out record or even in other computerized systems of records. For example, print-outs of computer spreadsheets only display the results of calculations made on the spreadsheet, while the actual electronic version of the spreadsheet will show the formula used to make the calculations. ... Some word processing systems allow users to annotate a document with a "summary" or "comments" that contain information on the author of the document, its purpose, the date that it was drafted or revised, and annotations by authors or reviewers. ... These comments, however, usually do not appear on a printed copy of the record. ... Electronic records, therefore do not become valueless duplicates ... once they have been printed on paper; rather they retain features unique to their medium.[103]

The case was originally decided in favour of the plaintiffs in 1997. The court concluded that, in promulgating the 1995 revisions to GRS 20, the Archivist had exceeded his authority and failed to carry out his statutory duty to determine whether the records scheduled for disposal possessed sufficient administrative, legal, research, or other value to warrant their continued preservation. Accordingly, the court declared the regulation "null and void" and ordered it to be withdrawn.

The court's decision was reversed in August 1999 when the Court of Appeals held that GRS 20 was valid.[104] In its ruling, the Court of Appeals rejected Public Citizen's claim that GRS 20 did not require all relevant information contained in an electronic record to be transferred to a paper recordkeeping system. The appeals court agreed with the Archivist that GRS 20 did in fact require that such information be preserved, explicitly in the case of electronic mail records[105] and implicitly in the case of word-processing records. With respect to the latter, the Court stated:

> Although the Archivist claims in his brief that GRS 20, properly interpreted, does require the preservation of ... hidden items in word processing records, he did not make that point express in promulgating GRS 20. The Archivist explains that GRS 20 requires retention of all such information, for the preamble to the schedule requires that a recordkeeping system "preserve the content, structure, and context" of a record. ... In other words, ... if the information is part of a record ... then it must be preserved. ... That the Archivist's interpretation comes for the first time in litigation does not make it unworthy of deference, as "[t]here is simply no reason to suspect that the interpretation does not reflect the agency's fair and considered judgement on the matter in question." ... Considering the substance of that interpretation, we trust that Public Citizen is not aggrieved by this indulgence.[106]

In November 1999, the plaintiffs filed a petition asking the Supreme Court to review the Court of Appeals decision. [107] The petition was denied, bringing legal closure to the case.

There is no doubt that the plaintiffs in *Armstrong* and *Public Citizen* were motivated by a sincere concern that the government's recordkeeping practices posed a threat to the public interest. Nor is there any doubt that there is a public interest in ensuring that an adequate record is preserved for reasons of administrative, political, and historical accountability. There is considerable doubt, however, whether the plaintiffs' arguments concerning the essential characteristics and potential value of an electronic record have advanced our understanding of what constitutes a complete, reliable, and authentic record.

In *Armstrong*, the plaintiffs asserted, and the courts concurred, that an electronic mail message possesses unique characteristics that are lost when it is printed to paper and that such characteristics are relevant to a consideration of its historical value. Speaking for the district court, Judge Richey concluded that a paper copy of an electronic mail message:

> does not contain all of the information included in the electronic version. ... Such information can be of tremendous historical value in demonstrating what agency personnel were involved in making a particular policy decision and what officials knew, and when they knew it. ... Requiring the preservation of such information is consistent with the legislative history of the FRA, which clearly shows that "Congress intended, expected, and positively desired private researchers and private parties whose

rights may have been affected by government actions to have access to the documentary history of the federal government."[108]

The value of electronic mail messages to a determination of "who knew what when" is underscored by the plaintiffs in their appeal brief where they state: "Studies of electronic mail suggest that electronic communications are often the first, most candid, and most crucial communication of the information, ... and, as Iran-Contra investigators found, are particularly valuable because they provide a 'first-hand, contemporaneous account of events.'"[109]

In making these assertions, the plaintiffs (and the courts) are ascribing a unique truth-value to electronic mail messages based on their superior candour and immediacy. Such ascription is perfectly consistent with the "rule of immediacy" underpinning the selection of historical sources and with the "ground-zero" theory underpinning the assessment of legal evidence. According to both the rule and the theory, a record is deemed to be true if it was produced close to the events that are in question.[110] However, as Wittgenstein, Barthes, and other postmodern theorists have shown, the first version of events is not innocent of interpretation. Inevitably, it has a perspective embedded in it, as does any version of events. The argument that electronic mail messages ought to be privileged as sources on the grounds that they provide immediate and unmediated access to events, therefore, is more akin to wishful thinking than demonstrable fact.

Many of the plaintiffs' arguments in *Armstrong* and *Public Citizen* focus on the essential characteristics of a "complete" record in an electronic environment, particularly in light of the FRA's goal to ensure the "accurate and complete documentation of the policies and transactions of the Federal Government."[111] The plaintiffs maintained that "the practice of retaining only the amputated paper print outs is flatly inconsistent with Congress' evident concern with preserving a complete record of government activity for historical and other uses."[112] But how is "complete" being interpreted here? Webster's Dictionary defines complete as "having all necessary parts, elements, or steps."[113] In the view of the plaintiffs, the electronic record in its "live" desktop application constitutes the complete record because it alone allows researchers to see the record through the eyes of its original creator and users. Such interpretation of completeness is alarmingly broad given that it encompasses, potentially, the entire hardware and software environment in which electronic records reside. At the same time, it is surprisingly narrow because it excludes the broader documentary, procedural, and administrative context in which those records are created and used. In that respect such records hardly can be considered complete in the sense of possessing "all their necessary parts, elements, or steps."

In fact, as NARA pointed out, "leaving electronic mail messages and word processing documents on "live" applications results in a "dismembered" collection of documents. For instance, it is impossible to determine from the word processing version of a letter whether the letter was in fact signed and sent to the recipient.

Moreover, electronic mail messages that are not filed in a recordkeeping system with associated records lack the essential administrative-procedural context that explains how such records fit into the agency's decisionmaking process.[114] The plaintiff's interpretation of completeness is, thus, a partial one, failing as it does to take into account the connection between records and their relationship to the actions in which they participate as well as their relationship to other records participating in the same action.

In asserting the unique value of a record in its electronic form, the plaintiffs emphasised its superior candour, completeness, and accessibility relative to its paper counterpart. But they betrayed little if any interest in the accuracy of an electronic record, a surprising lacuna since presumably accuracy is relevant to a consideration of the record's historical value. The explicit goal of the FRA, after all, is to ensure *accurate* as well as complete documentation of federal government policies and transactions. On those grounds, NARA was perfectly correct to insist that procedures directed toward re-asserting centralised agency-wide control over recordkeeping and bringing electronic records within the scope of that control constitute the best means of ensuring the accuracy of records and, hence, their value as evidence. Such position is perfectly consistent with common law assumptions concerning the circumstantial probability of trustworthiness accorded to records created in bureaucratic environments; assumptions that draw specifically on the integral connection between procedural controls exercised over recordkeeping, and record accuracy.

The plaintiffs arguments also fail to take into account the fact that certain aspects of the live system's functionality, the capacity to manipulate records for instance, potentially compromises their integrity as records (i.e., their authenticity). Nor did the plaintiffs consider that, practically speaking, preservation of electronic records in the live system cannot be implemented because media fragility and technology obsolescence necessitate the eventual migration of records from one system to another. Even before migration, records that are no longer active need to be removed from the live system; otherwise the system will eventually collapse under the weight of the accumulated data.

At the same time, the government's position underestimates the extent to which the technological context in which electronic records are originally created and used may contribute to their completeness. Since the presentation elements of an electronic record, such as colours, original fonts, letterhead, and other special signs, are shaped by the software used to create it, the transfer of that record into a different system (whether electronic or paper) could result in the elimination or distortion of these elements. To the extent that the elements contribute to, and influence, the content of the record, their elimination or distortion is relevant to a consideration of their authenticity. While it may not be possible or feasible to maintain electronic records in their original technological context, it is both possible and feasible to preserve evidence of that context by means of annotations to the record or by preserving supplementary documentation about the record's original hardware and software environment.

The failure of the two court cases to advance our understanding of what constitutes a complete, reliable, and authentic electronic record is attributable not only to the inherent weaknesses in the arguments presented but, also, to the forum in which the issues were debated. *Armstrong* and *Public Citizen* provide persuasive evidence of Mirjan Damaška's contention that the adversarial system can be antithetical to meaningful dialogue. The facts of the two cases were provided to the fact finders (the district and appeals court judges) in the form of two alternating one-sided accounts. In each account, complex issues were reduced to black and white positions. Neither of the litigating parties had any interest in conceding the legitimacy of the other's argument or acknowledging grey areas in its own. In fact, the parties' interests were precisely the opposite. As a consequence, valid arguments were made to look debatable, and clear information became obfuscated and confused through the inadvertent and, sometimes, deliberate, misrepresentation or incomplete presentation of facts.

A clear example of obfuscation occurs in *Public Citizen* with the blurring of an essential distinction between what a given software application is capable of and how it is actually used. In its brief to the district court, the plaintiffs cite the "summary" or "comment" fields that are included as a feature of some proprietary word processing packages as substantial evidence of their assertion that word processing documents contain critical information that is not retained in paper print-outs.[115] However, as NARA points out in its reply memorandum, the plaintiffs do not claim to have any actual knowledge of whether and to what extent this feature is used in the regular carrying out of business in any federal agency and so any assertion about the "historical and research value" the information entered in these fields might have is pure speculation.[116] Moreover, such summaries and comments, in fact, are capable of being printed out, and, under the provisions of GRS 20, would be preserved as an essential part of the recordkeeping copy. Thus, in addition to being purely hypothetical, the plaintiffs' example is inaccurate. The inaccuracy is perpetuated by the district court in *Public Citizen* which, in its judgement favouring the plaintiffs, specifically cites summary and content annotations as examples of the kind of information found in electronic records that are not preserved in a paper print-out.[117]

The district court's judgement in *Public Citizen* also reveals a certain amount of confusion about the critical difference between an electronic information system and an electronic recordkeeping system. In support of the plaintiffs' argument that electronic records have a number of "unique and valuable features not found in paper print-outs of the records", the court pointed out that "records in electronic recordkeeping systems have searching, manipulating and indexing capabilities not found in paper records, an advantage recognized by NARA itself."[118] Such observation equates, erroneously, the very limited search capabilities of electronic records that are maintained in disparate locations on live office automation systems with the search capabilities of records maintained in an agency-controlled recordkeeping system. In drawing that equation, the court betrayed its own failure to understand the fundamental difference between the kind of electronic system the plaintiffs are advocating and the kind being advocated by NARA. The Court's efforts to understand the difference between paper and electronic records appear to have blinded it to the equally important distinction between two kinds of electronic systems.

3.5 Conclusion

It is clear that further analysis of the technological, administrative, procedural, and documentary context in which electronic records are created, maintained, and used is essential to determining their reliability and authenticity. In *Armstrong* and *Public Citizen* the essential characteristics of electronic records were discussed in relation to a few specific types and cannot be generalised to all types. Moreover, these cases were motivated by a concern to ensure that potentially valuable electronic records were not destroyed without proper authorisation, rather than by a desire to characterise in any definitive way what constitutes a reliable and authentic record. It is hardly surprising then that the cases failed to provide a coherent and comprehensive assessment of what constitutes a record, what constitutes a complete record, and what constitutes a reliable and authentic record in an electronic environment.

The historian R.J. Morris believes that the economic and social imperatives of bureaucracies, rather than the interests of historians, are likely to drive efforts to define and ensure record reliability and authenticity:

> Many of the problems anticipated by historians are already being experienced by users and information managers. Like historians those responsible for records within a company or government department want to know who saw what when and who was responsible for ideas and changes. In the initial stages of the shift to the electronic record, there has been a temporary solution to the problems of access, attribution and what is a document. Most users still make valiant efforts to mimic the old technology of paper. We all need our printer and still file 'hard copy'. In the long term the solution is likely to come from the inherent needs of capitalist and bureaucratic structures. Bureaucracies need to be able to attribute responsibility and capitalism depends upon the verifiability of contracts.[119]

While there is not general agreement on what elements will provide a circumstantial probability of trustworthiness, it is generally agreed that the capacity to capture those elements needs to be built into the design of electronic record systems. Such need is a recurring theme in the archival literature since archivists have been struggling with these issues for more than a decade. In recent years, some archivists have turned to the centuries old discipline of diplomatics to address this need. The next chapter will explore the way in which diplomatic methodology has been adapted to meet the needs of contemporary recordkeeping. In that adaptation, it has been transformed from a tool for retrospectively assessing the trustworthiness of medieval records into a standard for the creation and maintenance of reliable and authentic electronic records.

Chapter Four

Creating and Maintaining Trustworthy Records in Electronic Systems: Archival Diplomatic Methods

Diplomatics was born in the seventeenth century as an analytical technique for determining the authenticity of records issued by sovereign authorities in previous centuries. Its primary purpose was to ascertain "the reality of the rights or truthfulness of the facts"[1] contained in such documents. In the nineteenth century, historians adopted diplomatics as a tool of documentary criticism for assessing the authority of medieval records as historical sources. At the end of the twentieth century, archivists have discovered new uses for this old science, based on its potential as a standard for ensuring the trustworthiness of modern records generally and electronic records specifically.

4.1 Modern Diplomatics

The first diplomatist, Mabillon, defined diplomatics as "the establishment of certain and accurate terms and rules by which authentic instruments can be distinguished from spurious [ones]."[2] Modern diplomatists define it more broadly as "the discipline which studies the genesis, forms and transmission of archival documents, and their relationship with the facts represented in them and with their creator, in order to identify, evaluate, and communicate their true nature."[3] Within that broader framework, historians have continued to use diplomatics as a tool for the retrospective understanding of historical sources. At the same time, archivists have begun to use it as an aid to understanding current records and records-related technologies. The historian's use of diplomatics is a particularising one, whereas the archivist's new use of it is a universalising one.

As a tool for understanding historical sources, diplomatics continues to evolve as a discipline in its own right and as an auxiliary discipline of history. While it has not abandoned its earlier aim (to distinguish the false document from the genuine one), historical diplomatics has enlarged its territory in the twentieth century. New streams of study, labelled "qualitative" and "quantitative" diplomatics, have emerged, resulting in a significant expansion in the spatial and temporal dimensions of medieval diplomatic analysis.[4] Qualitative diplomatics applies new themes to traditional documents (notably the theme of *document as monument* described in the previous chapter). Quantitative diplomatics, on the other hand, applies traditional themes to a broader range of documentation, postulating that, "the methods of diplomatics, initially founded on sovereign acts of an historical époque, are universally applicable, not only to the ensemble of acts (in German *Urkunden*), but also to all the larger documentation within archives (in German *Akten*)."[5] Though published studies remain rare, there also have been efforts to extend diplomatic analysis to archival documents created in the modern period.[6]

4.2 The Application of Diplomatics to the Records of Twentieth-Century Bureaucracies

Meanwhile, in the field of archival science, diplomatics has been reinvented as a tool for understanding the records-creation processes of twentieth century bureaucracies. The archival interest in diplomatics is not surprising given that the discipline of archival science was born in the nineteenth century as an extension of diplomatics.[7] Even as archival science evolved into an autonomous discipline in the twentieth century, diplomatics remained an integral part of the formation of European archivists and continues to be so to this day. The intuition that diplomatics might be adopted for the purpose of analysing modern records, however, is a relatively recent one. In 1970, Christopher Brooke called on British archivists to develop "a modern diplomatic."[8] It was not until the 1980s, however, when archival science broadened its field to include the control of active and semiactive records, that archivists paid any heed to his call. At the 1989 International Council on Archives' Second European Conference on Archives, Francis Blouin commented on the growing convergence of interest amongst European and North American archivists in reviving and adapting the European tradition of diplomatics "to modern records to cope with the mass and complexity of institutional records, especially those in electronic form." He anticipated that the recordkeeping practices of modern bureaucracies "will become the diplomatics of the 21st century."[9] Blouin's remarks drew support from the delegates to that conference who recommended "that the development of the discipline of modern diplomatics be promoted through research in the typology of contemporary records and in the records-creating procedures of contemporary institutions."[10]

In Europe, the most comprehensive response to the call for archivists to construct a diplomatic suitable for twentieth-century records has come from the Netherlands[11] and Italy.[12] In North America, it has come from Canada where, in a series of articles written between 1989 and 1992,[13] Luciana Duranti examined the principles and concepts developed by diplomatic theorists to evaluate the authenticity of medieval documents to determine whether they could be adapted to deal with records generated by modern bureaucracies. She found that the necessary elements of documentary creation identified by the early diplomatists, i.e., the *juridical system*[14] (the necessary context of document-creation), the *act* (its determinant cause), the *persons* (its agents and factors), the *procedures* (which guide its course), and the *documentary form* (which pulls together all the relevant elements and shows their relationships) are as relevant to an understanding of the nature of records generated by modern bureaucracies as they were to an understanding of records issued by medieval chanceries. The main difference is that, in modern recordkeeping environments, the same elements manifest themselves in different ways. Over the course of the six articles, Duranti refined, reinterpreted, and extended the classical concepts, and introduced new ones to take into account the variety and complexity of bureaucratic recordkeeping environments.

Duranti found that what most clearly distinguishes medieval and modern recordkeeping practices are the volume and complexity of documentary production. In the medieval period, most of the documents "resulted from juridical acts for which the written form was required either *ad probationem* or *ad substantiam*. Furthermore, whether the will determining the act belonged to one or more persons, only one document was issued which referred to the act or put it into effect, although it could be copied or re-issued many times."[15] This situation began to change around the sixteenth century.

> With the diffusion of education, the growing accessibility of writing instruments and materials, the development of communication systems, the increase of business activity, and the rise of complex bureaucracies, two things happened. First, people began to create documents for the purpose of communicating facts, feelings, and thoughts, asking for or providing opinions, preserving memories, elaborating data, and so on. Therefore, an ever increasing proportion of written documentation came to originate from juridical acts and presented a required form. Today, most documents are about facts, often juridically irrelevant, and their written form is discretionary. Secondly, juridical acts, and specifically those defined as transactions, began to result from a combination of related acts, juridical and non-juridical, each of which produced documents. As a corollary, many documents came to refer to the same act."[16]

These two conditions have specific consequences for the diplomatic analysis of modern and contemporary records. The first consequence relates to the categorisation of records in relation to the function they serve. Medieval diplomatists identified two categories of record whose written form was required by the juridical system: *dispositive records* (i.e., records constituting a juridical act) and *probative records* (i.e., records constituting written evidence of a juridical act which was completed before being documented). Although these two categories continue to be relevant, their scope is too narrow to accommodate the diversity of records generated within modern bureaucracies. To accommodate that diversity, it is necessary for modern diplomatists to identify two further categories of record whose written form is discretionary, rather than required: *supporting records* (i.e., records constituting written evidence of a juridically relevant activity which does not result in a juridical act) and *narrative records* (i.e., records constituting written evidence of a juridically irrelevant activity which does not result in a juridical act).[17]

The second condition characterising modern documentary production "is the fragmentation of juridical acts in many related but autonomous juridical and non-juridical acts, each resulting in written documents."[18] This condition is largely attributable to the rise of bureaucracy, which has exercised an enormous influence on documentary production in both the public and the private sphere. A consequence of this circumstance is that the direct, bilateral relationship between the document and the act it embodies is no longer the rule, but the exception.

Duranti explains this new situation in the following way:

> Early diplomatists believed it was possible to go directly from the document to the entire fact or act generating it. "Their methodology presupposed that there is a bilateral relationship between each document and the fact it is about, so that if a fact, (A), is manifested in written form, the document resulting from it, (B), will guide us directly to the fact: A-B-A. This direct, exclusive bilateral relationship exists only for a limited number of documents in a modern bureaucracy. ... Therefore, applying diplomatic methodology to modern and contemporary documents we will find ourselves faced with multilateral relationships, in which each single fact manifests itself in a fragmented documentary form, and each document guides us not only to a small portion of the fact it is about, but, possibly, to a chain of other documents and/or facts. The bond that links the document to the act producing it is still unique but it is not the only relationship that such a document has.[19]

With modern documents, in addition to the bond linking the document to the act producing it, there is an essential bond linking each document to every other document participating in the same matter. That bond is embodied in the dossier which, in modern bureaucracies, has replaced the individual document as the basic unit of administrative activity.[20]

This condition implies that any meaningful application of diplomatics to modern and contemporary records requires an integration of its concepts, principles, and methods with those of archival science. This requirement derives from the fact that, unlike the early diplomatists who dealt only with isolated records, contemporary diplomatists deal with record aggregates. Archival science specifically studies records as aggregations and comprises a body of concepts and methods directed toward the study of records in terms of their documentary and functional relationships and the ways in which they are controlled and communicated.

4.3 Contemporary Archival Diplomatics: The University of British Columbia Project

Duranti's series of articles resulted in the preliminary elaboration of a hybrid discourse on what might be termed *contemporary archival diplomatics*, one that integrates diplomatic and archival principles, concepts, and methods. The articles inspired numerous theses[21], journal articles[22], and an international seminar[23] focusing on the application of diplomatic concepts and methods to twentieth-century record forms. They also laid the groundwork for a three year project carried out between 1994 and 1997 by faculty in the Master of Archival Studies Program at the University of British Columbia (UBC), and funded by the Social Sciences and Humanities Research Council of Canada.[24] The project was entitled "The Preservation of the Integrity of Electronic Records," and its goal was to identify and define conceptually the nature of an electronic record and the conditions necessary to ensure its integrity, meaning its reliability and authenticity, during its active and semiactive life.[25] The research resulted in a set of standards and rules for developing and implementing a trustworthy electronic recordkeeping system.

The researchers began their work by articulating a set of general premises concerning the nature of a record in a modern (and predominantly paper) recordkeeping environment and the conditions necessary to ensure its reliability and authenticity. Those premises were then interpreted within the framework of electronic systems. This interpretation generated a number of hypotheses expressing the necessary and sufficient components of a complete, reliable, and authentic electronic record. The hypotheses constituted the conceptual basis for establishing first, whether a given electronic system contains records and secondly, whether such records are reliable and authentic. The hypotheses were subsequently translated into detailed rules for the creation and maintenance of reliable and authentic records.[26]

The project's findings are relevant to the issues raised in the previous two chapters for a couple of reasons. They provide a substantial foundation on which record creators can build electronic recordkeeping systems capable of satisfying the rebuttable presumption of record integrity required by the Canadian Uniform Electronic Evidence Act and a comprehensive response to some of the concerns raised by the plaintiffs in *Armstrong* and *Public Citizen*.[27] What follows is a summary of the project's analysis and findings[28] as well as an examination of its limits.

4.3.1 THE NATURE OF AN ELECTRONIC RECORD

Definition of an Electronic Record
The first step in analysing the nature of an electronic record is to define it. In archival science, a record is any document created (meaning made or received, and set aside either for action or reference), by a physical or juridical person in the course of practical activity as an instrument and by-product of it. It follows that an *electronic* record is a record created in electronic form. In this definition, electronic records constitute a particular species of recorded information; one that is related to, but distinct from other information species such as *documents* (i.e., information affixed to a medium in an objectified and organised way, according to specific rules of representation), *information* (i.e., meaningful group of data intended for communication, either across space or through time), and *data* (i.e., the smallest meaningful recorded facts).

Components of an Electronic Record
The diplomatic analysis of the components of a record is a process of abstraction and systematisation, the aim of which is to identify the essential or "ideal" attributes of a record and make them transportable to different historical and documentary contexts. By decontextualising and universalising the attributes of

an "ideal" record, the original diplomatists were able to recognise and evaluate records created over several centuries and across different, and sometimes bewildering juridical systems. In the same way, it allows contemporary archivists to recognise and identify electronic records generated within many different and equally bewildering hardware and software environments.

The diplomatic analysis of a record, like its legal and historical analyses, is posited on a direct connection between word and world, i.e., between the record and the event or act it represents. The early diplomatists realised that to gain an understanding of the world through the record, it was necessary to look at a record conceptually as embodying a system of both external and internal elements. As Duranti elaborates:

> In doing so they discovered that [a record] is a whole composed of interrelated but very different groups of elements, and isolated those groups in order to analyze them. Some of the elements belonged to what the document was about, which was termed *fact*, others to the physical and intellectual makeup of the document, which was termed *form*, and still others to the procedure which brought the fact into the document, which was termed *documentation*.[29]

These same groups of elements can still be found in modern and electronic record forms; they tend, however, to manifest themselves differently, and certain of the elements require further elaboration. In an electronic environment, the external and internal elements translate into eight fundamental components of an electronic record, i.e., *medium, content, physical form, intellectual form, action, persons, archival bond*, and *context*.

Medium. The medium is the physical carrier of the content and it is a necessary component because a record does not exist until it is affixed to a medium. With more traditional forms of records, the medium (e.g., parchment, paper) and the message are inextricably linked to each other. With electronic records, the medium (e.g., disk, magnetic tape) exists as a separate physical part of the record. This difference does not carry significant implications with respect to the record's reliability and authenticity because, in literate modern societies, the medium is not intended to convey meaning, but simply to provide a physical carrier for the message. Therefore, each record reproduction in which the only component that changes is the medium can be taken to be a complete and effective record identical to the one that it reproduces.

Content. The content refers to the message the record is intended to convey. As suggested above, for a record to exist at all, it must be fixed and stable, i.e., its message must be affixed to a medium. By this criterion, an electronic document that consists solely of pointers to data residing in different locations within a database, or in multiple databases (sometimes referred to as a "virtual document"), cannot be considered a record in an electronic environment. Although it is possible to see on a computer monitor the document resulting from the assembly of those data in a meaningful form, this document does not exist as such until its components are actually joined together in an inextricable way, i.e., until its content is explicitly articulated in a fixed form. With traditional records, a document that consists of pointers to information contained in other documentary sources is itself a record (it is a record of the sources to be used to make another record). With electronic documents of the kind described above, the pointers lead to data which – being contained in databases that, by their nature, are dynamic – change over time. Thus, such a document lacks stability and, within a period of thirty minutes, may be ten different documents. For this kind of document to become a record it must be set aside, meaning that all the information to which the pointers point must be saved with a unitary identification in the electronic recordkeeping system of the record creator.

Physical Form. The content of a record is transmitted by means of rules of representation that are embodied in its physical and intellectual form. Physical form consists of the formal attributes of the electronic record that, in traditional diplomatics, are called "extrinsic elements"[30] and which determine its external appearance. It includes, among other things, script (e.g., type font, format, inserts, colours, etc.), language, special signs (e.g., symbols indicating the existence of attachments or comments, mottoes, emblems, time-stamps, etc.), seals of any kind (including digital signatures), the configuration and architecture of the electronic operating system, the architecture of the electronic records, and the software. In other words, it includes all those parts of the technological context that determine what the document will look like and how it will be accessed, and that, in electronic systems, are usually invisible to the user. Unlike the medium, the elements of physical form are intended to convey meaning; therefore, any change in them generates a new and different record.

Intellectual Form. The intellectual form of a record comprises the formal attributes that represent and communicate the elements of the action in which the record is involved as well as its immediate documentary and administrative context. In relation to electronic records, intellectual form may be subdivided into three parts: the "information configuration," which refers to the type of representation of the content, whether text, graphic, image, sound, or a combination thereof; the "content articulation," which refers to the elements of the discourse and their arrangement, such as date, salutation, exposition, etc.; and "annotations," which refer to the additions made to the record either in the execution phase of the procedure (e.g., authentication of signatures), in the handling of the matter (e.g., indication of "urgent" or "bring forward," date and name of action taken), in the development of the procedure (e.g., mention of subsequent actions or their outcome), or in the management of the record (e.g., classification code, registry number).

Content articulation includes primarily elements that, in traditional documents, are called "intrinsic elements."[31] The most important are the elements referring to the persons concurring in the formation of the record, its administrative context, and the action to which it relates. These include the superscription,[32] inscription,[33] date of document, date of transmission, and subject. With electronic records that are transmitted across electronic boundaries, such elements are found in the header of the record, which constitutes most of the record's protocol.[34]

Action. The core component of any record is the act or action that gave rise to it. An action is any exercise of will that aims to create, change, maintain or extinguish situations. Accordingly, diplomatics categorises records in terms of their relationship (or proximity) to actions. A *dispositive* record is one whose written form is required by the juridical system as the essence and substance of the act, i.e., the act comes into existence with the creation of the record (e.g., a written contract, a hospital admission record). A *probative* record is one whose written form is required by the juridical system as proof that an act has taken place (e.g., a birth, marriage, or death certificate, or a research laboratory notebook). A *supporting* record is one on which an action is based, but which is not necessary for the action to occur and does not constitute proof of its occurrence. Supporting records are created in the course of carrying out a specific business activity and are intended to provide support for that activity. Most electronic records have a supporting function with respect to the action in which they take part. For example, a geographical informational system, a database-dependant system that presents data in a geographic arrangement, typically contains documents, information, and data, rather than records. However, the system as a whole can be considered a record, if its function is to support the decision-making in a specific business activity (when regarded as a unit it possesses all the necessary components of a record). It can also produce documents that, once extracted from it and linked to other records of action, become records, (e.g., a representation of the density of population in a given location that is attached or linked to a report containing recommendations for the development of new housing). A *narrative* record serves as memory of an action, but does not participate in its formal development: in other words, it is not procedurally linked to an action. Many electronic records have a narrative function, i.e., they simply reflect the various and informal motions individuals go through in order to organise themselves to carry out activities and make decisions. An employee's electronic daybook or journal are typical examples of narrative records, because they are individualistic expressions of intent.

Persons. The agents and factors of the action that originates the record are persons, i.e., the physical and juridical entities acting by means of the record.[35] Traditional diplomatic doctrine maintains that, while many persons may take part in the creation of a record, only three persons are necessary to its existence, that is, the *author* (i.e., the person having the authority and capacity to issue the record or in whose name or by whose command the record has been issued), the *addressee* (i.e., the person to whom the record is directed or for whom the record is intended), and the *writer* (i.e., the person having the authority and capacity to articulate the content of the record).[36] With electronic records, it is necessary to identify two other persons: the record's *creator* (i.e., the person to whose archival fonds[37] the record in question belongs), and the *originator* (i.e., the person owning the electronic address or space from which the record is transmitted or in which it is compiled and saved). Traditional diplomatics does not require that the creator of the record or Its originator be specifically identified because those persons are usually obvious from the location of the record. With electronic records, however, their identities are not so self-evident.

The identification of the creator in connection with each electronic record is necessary to the preservation of its provenance over time. While a record resides in the electronic system in which it is made or received, its creator is easily identifiable as the person having jurisdiction over the system for making, receiving and accumulating records in the conduct of business. But, once the record is taken out of the system, its location on a storage medium and in a given storage facility is no longer meaningful for the purpose of identifying its creator. In an ideal system, the identity of the creator of an electronic record would be revealed by a visual representation such as a logo or a crest which would be attached as an annotation to each record just as, in the past, the stamp of a receiving or registering office was imprinted on each record.

The identification of the originator in connection with each electronic record is necessitated by the fact that such person may be different from the author or writer of the record: the issue here relates primarily to responsibility and accountability. For records that are electronically transmitted, the name of the record's originator is found in the header of the electronic mail message, for records that do not cross electronic boundaries, the originator's name is stored either in the data dictionary or in a document profile and corresponds to the name of the owner of the electronic space in which the record is saved.

Archival Bond. It is a fundamental tenet of classical archival theory that records are necessarily composed of documents and the complex of their relationships. For that reason, the archival bond is an essential component of a record. The archival bond is the relationship that links each record to the previous and subsequent one and to all those which participate in the same activity. It is "originary (i.e., it comes into existence when the record is made or received), necessary (i.e., it exists for every record), and determined (i.e., it is characterised by the purpose of the record)."[38] It is also incremental because, as the connective tissue that joins a record to those surrounding it, it is in continuing formation and growth until the activity is completed.

In a traditional recordkeeping environment, the archival bond – which conceptually arises at the moment a record is set aside, and therefore determines the moment of the record's creation – manifests itself in a number of ways: in the physical arrangement of the records within a file, in annotations made to the record, such as a classification code, which connects it to other records belonging to the same class, and, in the case of incoming and outgoing records, in the registration number assigned to the record, which connects it to previous and subsequent records made or received by the creator and dealing with the same matter. The purpose of classification is to make explicit the relationship between records and the actions in which they participate, to authenticate and perpetuate that relationship, and to make sure that as long as the records exist, such relationship will not be altered. The purpose of registration is to provide evidence of the recorded interactions between the creating body and the external world by recording pertinent data concerning each record that enters and exits the agency, e.g., name and address of sender, name and address of addressee, date and time of receipt, date and time of transmission, action or matter, handling office, classification code, and action taken.[39] As an instrument of documentary control, the "protocol" register (so-called because the information recorded is drawn from the top portion of the record, i.e., its protocol) is designed to serve both records management and accountability purposes. At the same time, it is a valuable instrument for capturing documentary context, since it reflects the relations among all the records that have entered and exited the agency. Because the physical arrangement of electronic records is random, their classification and registration are essential methods for making explicit the archival bond. Since such methods are not typical features of electronic record systems, they need to be defined as requirements, codified in administrative procedures, and embedded within a record system as part of its workflow rules.[40]

Context. The final component of a record is its context, which refers to the framework of action in which the record participates. Four contexts are relevant to non-electronic and electronic records alike: the *juridical-administrative context* (i.e., the legal and organisational system in which the creating body belongs), the *provenancial context* (i.e., the creating body, its mandate, structure, and functions), the *procedural context* (i.e., the procedure in the course of which the record is generated), and the *documentary context* (i.e., the internal structure of the archival fonds of which the record forms a part). This last context represents the totality of all the archival bonds existing within a creator's fonds. While it is clearly impossible for any single record to fully communicate these contexts, it is possible to provide clues and pointers to them through the other identified components. For example, the name of the creator (identified under *persons*) is a pointer to the record's provenancial context; an annotation, such as the classification code (identified under *archival bond*), is a kind of shorthand for the record's administrative, procedural and documentary context.

A conspicuous omission from these categories is the technological context of an electronic record. From the point of view of the trial courts in both *Armstrong* and *Public Citizen*, the technological context of an electronic record (understood as the original hardware and software environment in which an electronic mail message, word processing record, or spreadsheet is generated, including its manipulability, searchability, and auditability) must be captured and preserved because it contributes essential structural and contextual data to such record, and uniquely defines it. However, if technological context refers to the technology generating determined groups of records, this conditions and penetrates their physical form and is, therefore, a component of the records rather than their context. For example, the architecture of electronic records and of their operating system, the word processing or other software used to create them, and the method by which they are encoded, are all attributes of their physical form. Moreover, identifying technological context as a distinct category is potentially misleading. A typical technological context of record creation is a database that is shared by more than one agency. Although the technological context (the shared database) implies that the records within the database are also shared, this is not, in fact, the case. While a "shared database" contains documents, information, or data accessible to many persons, that database is the responsibility of only one juridical person (which may be a consortium of persons), and each person who uses the documents, information or data contained in that shared database in the course of its own activity generates with them, in its own electronic system, its own records.

On the basis of diplomatic analysis, it appears that electronic records possess essentially the same components as traditional records. However, with electronic records, those components are not inextricably joined to one another as they are in traditional records. Instead, they are stored and managed separately as metadata, which are "data describing data and data systems; that is, the structure of databases, their characteristics, locale, and usage."[41]

Metadata may be classed into two main categories. The first category, *metadata of the electronic system*, consists of data that describe the operating system, the program generating the records, the physical location of the records in the electronic system, which are stored in the system's data directory, and the value of each data element, which is stored in the system's data dictionary. The second category, *metadata of the records*, on the other hand, consists of data that place the record within its documentary and administrative context at the moment of its creation, e.g., the name of the sender, receiver, and creator. In some electronic systems, such data are stored in the data dictionary; in others they are assembled into a document profile[42] attached to the record.

An adapted version of this profile (i.e., a record profile) constitutes the best means of bringing together the components of a record and, specifically, those components that establish the record's administrative and documentary context. A record profile is an electronic form generated when the order is given to the system to send or to save an electronic record. It is contemporaneous with the moment of setting aside a record, thereby establishing its moment of creation. Its purpose is to identify a record uniquely and place it in relation to other records belonging in the same aggregation. The profile is considered an annotation to the record and is, therefore, inextricably linked to it for as long as the record exists.

Depending on whether a record is made or received, the profile includes the following elements:[43]

- registration number
- date of receipt
- time of receipt
- date of transmission
- registration number of sending office
- originator's address
- author's name
- time of transmission
- date of record
- archival date (date on which the record becomes part of a dossier or class)
- originator's name
- medium
- handling office

- author's address
- writer`s name
- writer's address
- action or matter
- number of attachments
- type of file of attachment (e.g., WordPerfect, Microsoft Word, Excel, MIME encoded)
- record item identifier
- mode of transmission

- action taken
- addressee's name
- addressee's address
- receiver's name
- receiver's address
- class code
- dossier identifier
- status of transmission (i.e., original, draft, copy)
- draft number

This proposed record profile contains more contextual elements and thus reveals more of the record's administrative, procedural, and documentary context than the one articulated by NARA in the *Public Citizen* case, which limited itself to the identification of the office of origin, file classification code, key words for retrieval, addressee, author, signer, date, and security classification (in the case of word processing records); and to the names of sender and recipients and dates of transmission or receipt (in the case of electronic mail messages).

4.3.2 METHODS FOR ENSURING THE RELIABILITY AND AUTHENTICITY OF AN ELECTRONIC RECORD

The identification of the components of a record and the way in which they manifest themselves in an electronic system provides a basis on which to recognise, capture, and stabilise records created within dynamic electronic record systems. It also provides a foundation on which to build methods for establishing the reliability and authenticity of such records. Before the specific concepts and methods associated with record reliability and authenticity can be considered, however, it is necessary first to identify and elaborate the overarching procedural framework in which those concepts and methods are situated. In other words, it is necessary to identify the salient features of an agency-wide electronic recordkeeping system capable of creating and maintaining reliable and authentic records.

The need for such identification was established in *Public Citizen*. In that case, NARA maintained that the reason agencies were printing electronic records to paper was simply because their electronic systems lacked the capacity to maintain records in their administrative and documentary context and to implement the procedural controls necessary to ensure their reliability and authenticity. Agencies, therefore, had little choice but to print the electronic records out and incorporate them into a traditional paper recordkeeping system that met those requirements. Although it was not formulated with the *Public Citizen* case in mind, the procedural framework articulated by the UBC researchers is an attempt to incorporate agency-wide recordkeeping requirements into the design of electronic systems. The requirements are intended to preserve not only the administrative context of electronic records creation demanded by NARA, but also certain aspects of the technological context demanded by the plaintiffs in the same case.

Procedural Framework
An essential first step to ensure the reliability and authenticity of electronic records is to embed procedural rules for creating, handling, and maintaining such records in an agency-wide records system, and to integrate documentary procedures with business processes. The *records system* comprises the creator's records, along with the procedural rules of its recordkeeping and record-preservation systems. Both systems are controlled by the creator's records management function. The purpose of the recordkeeping and record-preservation system[44] is to control the creation, handling, and maintenance of all the active and semiactive records of an agency, both electronic and non-electronic, with the integrated control of all the records taking place within the electronic system. Integrated control is required by the fact that in most bureaucracies a significant proportion of records continue to be created and maintained in non-electronic form as textual, graphic, cartographic, and architectural records. To maintain the archival bond between records created to carry out the same activity but generated and/or stored on different media in different physical locations, it is necessary to connect those records intellectually.[45]

Control over the electronic records is accomplished by establishing record management domains within the electronic system that define the boundaries of *individual space*, (corresponding to the jurisdiction of the officer to whom it is assigned by the agency); *group space* (corresponding to the jurisdiction of the office, program, team, committee, working group, etc., to which a specific competence, charge, responsibility, task, etc., has been assigned by the agency); and *general space* (corresponding to the jurisdiction of the records office, which is responsible for the records system of the agency). The procedural rules define, on the basis of these boundaries, the space in which records can be made, received, revised, modified or otherwise altered; the space in which they can be individually destroyed; the space in which they will be classified and registered; the space in which originals are stored; the space in which specific elements of the record profile must be filled in; the space in which the retention schedule is implemented; the right of access to each space; and the way in which records will move inside and outside the agency. For non-electronic records, a similar degree of control is established by assigning exclusive competence to the records office for the classification, profiling, registration (when applicable), and consignment to the central records system (the non-electronic equivalent of the general space) of all incoming, outgoing, and internal non-electronic records.

The recordkeeping and record-preservation system establishes agency-wide control over the creation and handling of both electronic and non-electronic records. The integration of business processes and documentary procedures strengthens this control, thereby enhancing reliability, by embedding it within specific business processes. As part of its analysis of the procedures governing medieval documentary production, traditional diplomatic doctrine posited a distinction between the *actio* or "moment of action" and the *conscriptio*, or "moment of documentation" and identified two distinct procedures, with distinct phases, in relation to each of these moments. In her series of articles exploring diplomatics, Duranti found that

> The most obvious fact which differentiates the genesis of medieval documents from that of modern documents ... [is that] [e]ach medieval document contained the whole transaction generating it, and its creation, as the apex of the transaction, was either sequential to it (probative documents) or parallel (dispositive documents), that is, perfectly distinguishable from the transaction as an exercise of will. On the contrary, each modern document incorporates only one phase of the transaction, or even less, and its creation, as a means of carrying out the transaction, is integrated in each of the phases through which the transaction develops, and is not distinguishable from the action of the will. This fact invalidates the definition of the moment of the action and the moment of documentation as two separate sets of routines, or two distinct procedures. They are still two *conceptually distinct moments* ... [however] they are considered integral parts of one procedure.[46]

Duranti's analysis of the ideal structure of the integrated procedure that creates records provides the foundation for the integration of business and documentary procedures. The "ideal" integrated procedure consists of the following steps: (1) identifying all the business procedures within each agency function; (2) for each procedure within each function, determining the category into which it fits,[47] i.e., whether the procedure is constitutive,[48] executive,[49] instrumental[50] or organisational;[51] (3) breaking each procedure down into six phases,[52] i.e., initiative,[53] inquiry,[54] consultation,[55] deliberation,[56] deliberation control,[57] and execution;[58] (4) determining, for each phase of each procedure, its component actions, the records that must be used in relation to each action, the records that must be made, received, and handled in the course of each action[59] and by whom; and (5) deciding the manner in which the records are to be classified, audited, and disposed; their level of confidentiality; and the specific methods for ensuring their reliability and authenticity. The integration of business and documentary procedures results in a description of the records associated with each phase of each procedure and the specific requirements linked to them in relation to access privileges, classification, registration, authentication, auditing, and so on.

It is understood that different kinds of records created in an agency require different levels of control depending on their purpose. The reason for determining the category for each procedure is to assess which procedures, and the records generated from them, require the most control. Because constitutive procedures create, extinguish, or modify the powers of persons with whom an agency interacts, the records generated in carrying out these procedures require the most control aimed at ensuring their reliability and authenticity. Instrumental procedures, on the other hand, which are connected to the giving and receiving of opinions and advice within the agency, do not directly result in any action, and the records generated from those procedures are most effective when they are least controlled.

Specific Methods for Ensuring Reliability

The procedural framework for creating and maintaining reliable and authentic records on an agency-wide basis underpins and informs the analysis of the more specific concepts and methods associated with reliability and authenticity.[60] Reliability (i.e., the capacity of a record to stand for the facts to which it attests) is associated with the creation of a record and refers to the completeness of its intellectual form and the degree of control exercised over its creation procedures. The completeness of the form of the record refers to the fact that the record possesses all the elements of intellectual form necessary for it to be capable of generating consequences. Traditionally, no record is considered complete if its intellectual form does not contain the date of the record's creation, which expresses the relationship between its author and the act it documents, and the signature, which assigns responsibility for the record and its content.

With an electronic record, the date given to the record by its author does not make it complete: the date and time of transmission to either an external or internal addressee or the date and time of transmission to the dossier or class to which the record belongs is necessary. Moreover, because a handwritten or typewritten signature can be attached to an electronic record by anyone, it cannot serve its traditional function and therefore cannot contribute to the record's completeness. Instead, the function of the signature is accomplished by the name contained in the header of an electronic mail message, or in the profile in the case of other record types (both of which are automatically assigned by the system), by an electronic signature or, in specific circumstances (usually those involving legal transactions), by a digital signature. An electronic signature is "a computer data compilation of any symbol or series of symbols executed, adopted, or authorised by an individual to be the legally binding equivalent of the individual's hand-written signature." A digital signature is a special type of electronic signature, one "based upon cryptographic methods of originator authentication, computed by using a set of rules and a set of parameters such that the identity of the signer and the integrity of the data can be verified."[61]

In sum, an electronic record must possess the following elements of intellectual form to be capable of generating consequences: date of record; time and place of creation, transmission, and receipt; identification of names of author addressee, originator and writer (if either or both are different from the author), name (or crest) of creator, title or subject line, classification code, and any other element required by the creator's procedures and/or juridical system. These elements constitute a subset of the total number of elements identified in the record profile.

The diplomatic conception of completeness is somewhat different from the one implied by the plaintiffs in *Armstrong* and *Public Citizen*. There, completeness was linked to the original functionality of the live system in which the record resided. However, certain aspects of that functionality (e.g., a system's auditability), while relevant to an assessment of record reliability and authenticity, are part of the metadata of the system as a whole rather than an integral part of the individual record's intellectual form. Other aspects are either irrelevant to a consideration of record reliability or authenticity (e.g., the searchability and indexability of the system, which relates purely to record retrieval), or actually detrimental to such consideration (e.g., the manipulability of the system which potentially undermines record authenticity).

Identification of a record's physical form is not required to make an electronic record complete, notwithstanding the centrality of physical form to the plaintiffs' arguments in both *Armstrong* and *Public Citizen*. Physical form refers to the formal attributes of a record that shape its external appearance which, in electronic systems, are largely determined by system software. Although it is an essential component of an electronic record, the physical form of any given type of electronic record (i.e., its status as a particular kind of spreadsheet, word-processing record, or electronic mail message and the presence of special features, such as colours, annotations, emblems, and other special signs), is self-evident so long as the record resides in the electronic records system (as that system has been defined in the project). The need to identify and preserve an electronic record's original physical form, or evidence of it, only becomes an issue at the point at which the record is copied or migrated and, therefore, is more appropriately addressed in the context of preserving a record's authenticity rather than in the context of establishing its reliability.

Reliability is also determined in relation to the procedure of the record's creation, i.e., the body of rules governing the making, receiving, and setting aside of records. Some of these rules refer to recordmakers by establishing who is competent to create, modify, and annotate records, others refer to how records must be handled in the course of their compilation, and others still refer to how records must be routed and filed. According to Duranti, "[t]he more rigorous and detailed the rules, the more established the routine, the more reliable the records resulting from their application will be."[62]

There are two kinds of methods in electronic record systems – the first directed to prevention, the second, to verification – for ensuring that such rules are respected and that the reliability of record makers is ensured. Preventative methods include limiting physical access to the technology or to parts of it, establishing and embedding access privileges in the system, and defining and automating workflow rules. Limiting physical access is accomplished by means of magnetic cards, passwords, fingerprints, and so on. Access privileges refer to the authority to compile, classify, modify, annotate, read, retrieve, transfer, and destroy records granted to any officer within an agency who has access to the electronic system. Access to the system for any of these purposes is determined on the basis of the officer's competence.[63] For example, the action officer who makes or receives a record is permitted unrestricted access to it; no officer is permitted to modify a record once it has been transmitted to the general space; and only the records officer is allowed to transfer or destroy records in the general space.[64]

Workflow rules define the various steps, the persons involved, the required input and output information, and the tools needed for each step in a business procedure. The definition of workflow rules is accomplished by integrating business and documentary procedures as described above. When workflow rules are automated, the electronic system permits only the person competent for each action to access the specific records needed to carry out that action and solicits the compilation, annotation, or transmission of the appropriate record at the proper time in accordance with the logical sequence of steps in the procedure. [65]

Verification methods include verification procedures, or an "audit trail," a means of recording all the interactions with records within the system so that any access to the record can be documented as it occurs. Such a procedure may also identify whether the record has been modified, deleted, added to, or simply viewed.[66] In this respect it supports authenticity as well as reliability.

Specific Methods for Ensuring Authenticity
From a diplomatic perspective, reliability and the methods for guaranteeing it are linked to record creation. Authenticity (i.e., the capacity to prove that a record is what it claims to be) is linked, on the other hand, to the record's *mode, form* and *state* of transmission, and to the manner of its preservation and custody. Authenticity is protected through the adoption of methods that ensure that the record is not manipulated, altered, or otherwise falsified after its creation and that it is precisely as reliable as it was when first created. It follows that an authentic electronic record is one that is transmitted in a secure way, whose state of transmission can be ascertained, that it is preserved in a secure way, and whose provenance can be verified.

Methods of ensuring the security of an electronic record's transmission include maintaining an audit trail of every transmission, encrypting records, appending digital signatures to records, and establishing the status of transmission of records. In diplomatic terms, the *mode of transmission* of a record is the method by which a record is communicated over space or time. The more secure the method of transmission, the higher the probability that the record received is what it purports to be. The *form of transmission* of a record is the physical and intellectual form that the record has when the addressee receives it. One means of protecting the integrity of an electronic record's physical and intellectual form from the time it is sent to the time it is received is by affixing to it a digital signature before transmitting it. A digital signature is a kind of electronic seal which allows the recipient to verify the origin of the record (thereby authenticating the record) and to confirm that the record has not been altered (thereby verifying the record's integrity). In fulfilling these two purposes, the digital signature serves a non-repudiation function analogous to the non-disputability function served by the sovereign's seal in the medieval period.

In relation to transmission, the main difference between non-electronic and electronic records resides in the *state of transmission*.[67] The state of transmission of a record refers to its degree of development and authority when it is set aside; in other words, its status as a *draft, copy,* or *original.* A *draft* is a temporary compilation of a document intended for correction; drafts may be in various stages of completion. A *copy* is a reproduction of a record made either from an original, a draft or another copy. It may take the form of an authentic copy,[68] an imitative copy,[69] a copy in the form of an original,[70] a simple copy,[71] a *vidimus,*[72] or a conformed copy.[73] An *original* is the first complete and effective record. For a record to be original, it must be complete (i.e., its form must be the one intended by its author and/or required by the juridical system), primitive (i.e., it must be the first to be produced in its complete form), and effective (i.e., it must be capable of reaching the effects for which it was produced).

With electronic records, the state of transmission is assessed in relation to their routing in the electronic system. Any record that is neither transmitted to an addressee nor consigned to the general space of the electronic records system, but that is saved in the electronic space in which it is made, is considered a draft because it is incomplete. This is because the act of transmitting a record across either external or internal electronic boundaries necessarily adds components to the record, which make it complete (e.g., the date of transmission and the name of the originator and/or author). Any record that is transmitted across electronic boundaries is received at the other end as an original, but it is saved in the space of the originator as a final draft because it is not capable of reaching its purpose and therefore lacks effectiveness.

Each time a person retrieves a record from the general space, he or she has a view of the original (in the case of a record received or an internal record) or of the last draft (in the case of a record sent). If the person copies the record to his or her own electronic space, the result is an imitative copy rather than a copy in the form of original, because some of the record's metadata (i.e., the data that place the record within its documentary and administrative context at the moment of its creation) will change. Each time a person forwards a record to another person, he or she creates an insert of the type of a *vidimus*, and so on.

All of this suggests that, with electronic records, the state of transmission is assessed on the basis of the way in which electronic transmission affects the physical and intellectual form of the records. The analysis also demonstrates that it is possible to identify an original record in an electronic environment despite the fact that courts and commentators have all but abandoned the concept because of the difficulty of establishing the state of transmission retrospectively. However, an electronic system can be designed to specify the record's status as an original, draft, or copy at the point of its creation, making such identification relatively straightforward.[74]

Ensuring the authenticity of electronic records in the manner of their preservation and custody requires the preservation of semiactive records in a climatically suitable and physically secure environment, well documented procedures for the reproduction and migration of both active and semiactive records,[75] and an uninterrupted line of physical custody. In relation to preservation and custody, the main difference between electronic records and traditional records is that the latter are kept authentic by maintaining them in the same form and state of transmission in which they were when made or received and set aside, while the former are kept authentic by continuous copying and periodic migration. All media designed to carry magnetically or optically affixed signals have more limited longevity than paper of reasonable quality, due to the deterioration of the material and, more significantly, the obsolescence of the technology required to read it. An electronic record is unlikely to survive[76] for more than a decade in its original form and all records generated in an obsolescent environment must be copied or migrated to a new one, otherwise they will become inaccessible and, for all intents and purposes, nonexistent.

Copying and migration have different consequences for a record's authenticity. Because copying is a complete reproduction of both the content and formal elements of the records (e.g., microfilming, or transferring the same strings of bits from one magnetic tape to another), the resulting records may be considered faithful reproductions of the original records' physical and intellectual form. Migration, on the other hand, is a reproduction of the content of the record, with changes in configuration and structure (e.g., the imaging of analogue records, or the transfer of hypertext records from one database to another having a different configuration).[77] While, after migration, the resulting records may look like the ones that have been migrated, their physical form has substantially changed, with probable loss of data on the one hand, and the certain addition of new data on the other hand.

This is why self-authenticating and clearly documented processes of reproduction and migration, and uninterrupted custody are so important.[78] If the records are still needed by the record creator for the usual and ordinary conduct of its business, the continuing reliance of the creator on the products of the migration process in itself authenticates them. However, once the records are no longer needed by the record creator to conduct its business, the migration process must be carried out by a neutral party and its products verified and authenticated. The resulting records become authentic copies of the records in the obsolescent environment.

4.4 Limits to Ensuring Record Trustworthiness in a Bureaucracy

The findings of the UBC project are a substantial contribution to an understanding of the nature of a record in an electronic environment and the specific methods necessary to ensure their reliability and authenticity during their active and semiactive life. At the same time, the project demonstrates the inevitable limits of bureaucratic methods for ensuring reliability and authenticity. To explain those limits it is necessary to elaborate the bureaucratic model on which the project implicitly rests. The UBC model is strikingly consistent with Weber's *ideal-type* of bureaucracy, many aspects of which can be traced back to medieval chancery procedures. Medieval chanceries exercised an exclusive competence over the creation of records issued by sovereign authorities and because the records granted privileges, elaborate and rigorous procedures were required to ensure their trustworthiness. The structure and functioning of medieval chanceries reflect, in embryonic form, five salient features of Weber's "ideal" modern bureaucracy: (1) an unambiguous hierarchical authority structure; (2) a rationalisation of offices; (3) the specialisation of labour and specification of competencies; (4) the existence of rules, policies and procedures; and (5) the formalisation of activities by means of written documentation.

The first feature, an unambiguous hierarchy, is reflected in the structure of chanceries, each of which had a nominal chief at the top (the archicancellarius), followed by an effective chief (cancellarius), scribes (scriptores), and clerks at the bottom. The second, a rationalisation of offices, is implicit in the organisation of chanceries into four branches, each assuming responsibility for one stage in the preparation of the document: the compilation of the draft, the preparation of the original, the registration of the document, and the affixing of the seal. This organisation helped to prevent fraud at each step in the documentary process. The third feature, specialised labour and specific competencies, is reflected in a number of ways. Virtually all the chancery staff were required to be notaries because only notaries possessed the special training of ars dictaminis. Among the chancery staff there was further specialisation: the datarii dated (thus validating) the document; the dictatores compiled the drafts; the scriptores prepared the original; the sigillatores had custody of the seals; and the registratores transcribed the documents. The fourth feature, the existence of rules, policies and procedures, is apparent in the requirement that documents be prepared in strict accordance with formularies, which were manuals that provided samples of specific types of documents. The formularies ensured that strict standards for ensuring that every documentary form issued by the chancery was complete and effective, with the correct seal affixed, the correct date attached, the appropriate clauses inserted, and the necessary signatures included. The final feature of Weber's ideal-type bureaucracy is the formalisation of activities by means of written documentation. In modern organisational theory, formalisation includes not only the existence of policies and procedures but, also, documentary memory which is associated with the obligation of the agency to account for its actions through its records. In the Middle Ages, the memory function is implicit in chancery procedures for registering important outgoing documents. The registration of such documents was important for at least three reasons: it served a pure memory function, it could be referred to if necessary to check precedents, and it provided an overview of sovereign policy on various matters.[79]

While Weber's ideal-type is discernible in medieval chancery procedures, it finds its full expression in the structure and functioning of modern bureaucracies. Eugene Kamenka characterises its guiding spirit in the following terms:

> Pure or 'ideal-type' bureaucracy, for Weber ... is depersonalized, rationalistic, rule-bound behaviour ordered by laws and administrative regulations. It separates the bureau from the private domicile of the official; it divorces official activity from the

sphere of private pursuits and attitudes ... [it] takes place on the basis of an *impersonal, hierarchical structure of authority* and a *centrally controlled and supervised delegation of functions.* ... For in bureaucracy, the command structure is unified, not fragmented. A true bureaucrat is free to act only in so far as he is empowered to do so and in the light of bureaucratic procedures and specified goals.[80]

Centralised control and supervision are essential because bureaucrats are obliged to account for their actions through records. Jane Parkinson explains the intimate link between record trustworthiness and bureaucratic accountability in the following way:

> The principle that underlies the concept of accountability ... is linked to the conveying and evaluation of information. ... For ongoing bodies, accountability required the development and refinement of procedures for carrying out actions and documenting them, "to ensure that everything was done according to rule and in proper sequence, so that administrators could account ... at any time precisely for anything that had been done." Effective institutional accountability has therefore depended on record-making, recordkeeping and access to records, and it has influenced the procedures and timing of their creation, their form, their maintenance, their accessibility and their centralization.[81]

To ensure record trustworthiness, bureaucracy has developed essentially two approaches, both of which attempt to compensate for the fact that bureaucrats must rely on records that report events they have not personally witnessed or participated in. In the first approach, bureaucrats assess the reliability of records indirectly by focusing on the reliability of the observers of the events, i.e., the recordkeepers.[82] According to Stanley Raffel:

> Instead of evaluating *records*, administrators can concentrate their efforts on attempting to ensure the reliability of record-*keepers*. Administrators can use the following logic: although the truth of records cannot be directly determined, records are true to the extent that record-keepers are reliable. Therefore, by attempting to make record-keepers reliable, they are indirectly attempting to make records truthful. They can assert their supervisory prerogative, not by watching over records but by watching over observers.[83]

Control over recordkeepers is typically exercised by issuing commands and by close supervision. However as Raffel cogently observes in relation to hospital records close supervision is just as likely to reduce candour in recordkeeping as it is to increase it:

> Supervising now looks not like controlling, guiding, or watching over us but seeking to overhear us. ... Hence, the fact ... that all records about topics that are touchy from a supervisory point of view are defensive. It is always patients who die never doctors who kill them. 'Proper' procedures, even those that self-respecting doctors would never stoop to perform, are always reported to have been followed.[84]

The use of computers to support the carrying out of bureaucratic procedures has resulted in personal supervision being replaced by impersonal technological control systems.[85] In the UBC project, for example, the reliability of recordkeepers is ensured primarily by embedding access privileges within the electronic system, registering every record that enters or exits the system, and by maintaining an audit trail of all the activity that takes place within it. Viewed from this perspective, the computer, which impassively witnesses and captures every interaction and stores it in its indefinitely expandable memory, appears to be the ideal observer of observers. It is present at all the recordkeeping events that take place within it but its recording of those events is not contaminated by human self-interest. Of course, here too, as technology is used more and more for the purposes of controlling humans, the line separating observation, supervision, and surveillance becomes increasingly thin and recordkeepers are likely to experience a corresponding reluctance to communicate freely.

The second approach bureaucrats adopt to compensate for their non-participation in the events the records report is to conceive of the record itself as the event. As Raffel explains:

> Administrators can gain presence and hence make possible their non-participation by re-conceiving of the record as the event. If the record itself can be conceived of as the event, then the administrator, who obviously can be present with the record, is no longer necessarily in a state of ignorance.[86]

In this approach, records are evaluated, not in terms of their effectiveness in mirroring events, but rather in terms of their completeness in accordance with bureaucratic standards. In the UBC project, completeness refers to the fact that a record possesses all the elements of intellectual form necessary for it to be capable of generating consequences. To be considered complete, a number of specific elements of intellectual form must be present in the record profile, among them, the date of the record and the signature of the author. A record's reliability is then assessed in relation to the presence or absence of any of these elements: a reliable record will be one that appears to be reliable by anyone looking at it.

In diplomatic terms, the signature carries special resonance as an indicator of a record's reliability. The requirement that recordkeepers sign their records is the commonest means by which bureaucrats evaluate a record's reliability and is associated both with record completeness and with the accountability of recordkeepers. As Jack Goody observes, the signature "is not only a card of identity, as individual as the print of the finger or the hand, but also an assertion of truth or of consent."[87] Because the bureaucracy needs to be able to treat a record's contents as knowledgeable and definite, rather than uncertain, it requires recordkeepers to sign their records, thus making them responsible for the records' contents. The bureaucracy thus removes from itself the responsibility for knowing the event. According to Raffel:

> By getting the writer to sign the record the administration has gotten the writer to declare or say (by signing) that the record is adequate. His declaration is then treated by the bureaucrat as that which is showing itself to him. He does not know whether the record mirrors the event but he does know that someone *says* that the record mirrors the event. That someone has said that the record is adequate becomes the fact (event) which is presenting itself to the administrator. The administration can therefore point to the declaration as its reason for saying what it says about the record or, better, as its reason for not having to say anything about the record. ... The record appears to be adequate in that the writer has declared it to be adequate. [88]

The signature provides the bureaucrat with two options: "If he decides to rely on the observer, he can know about the event. If he does not rely on the observer, then he can at least know whom he finds unreliable."[89] The signature's sanctioning function is reinforced by the requirement that certain records be signed by more than one person.

Clearly, the presence of a signature does not rule out unreliability. As Raffel points out, "the fact that records must be signed makes some recordkeepers even less inclined to be accurate when, as so often, the truth would incriminate them."[90] The point of the signature, from the bureaucrat's perspective, is to avoid questions about the recordkeeper's intent. To overcome the problem of intent, the bureaucracy requires the recordkeeper "to *declare* his intent, in this case his intent to have spoken the truth. The declaration is supposed to solve the problem of intent by making intent into something that can be spoken rather than that which any speech leaves unsaid."[91] Technological efforts to adapt the signature to an electronic environment reinforce the traditional purpose served by the signature in a bureaucracy. It was mentioned earlier that one of the central functions of the digital signature is its "non-repudiation function." In this respect it bears more than a passing resemblance to the medieval sovereign's seal and presumed indisputability. Both kinds of seals are symbols of authority and responsibility intended to foreclose any further speech concerning the truth-value of the object to which they are attached. With medieval seals, the sovereign's status gave the seal its authority. With electronic signatures, the complexity of the technology confers authority on them.

Weber's *ideal-type* bureaucracy emphasises efficiency, functionality, formalisation, and routinisation. It tends to underestimate the human dimension of any organisation and, in fact, aspires to a dehumanised ideal as Weber himself is the first to concede:

> Its specific nature, which is welcomed by capitalism, develops the more perfectly the more the bureaucracy is 'dehumanized,' the more completely it succeeds in eliminating from official business love, hatred, and all purely personal irrational elements which escape calculation. ... [Moreover] the individual bureaucrat cannot squirm out of the apparatus in which he is harnessed. ... the professional bureaucrat is chained to his activity by his entire material and ideal existence. In the great majority of cases, he is only a single cog in an ever-moving mechanism which prescribes to him an essentially fixed route of march.[92]

Critics of Weberian style bureaucracy point out that if it is to accomplish its objectives, a bureaucracy must take into account a range of variables, including human ones. As Kamenka, among others, points out:

> Weber's emphasis on precision and reliability in administration, on its rule-bound character, has to be supplemented by recognition that human attitudes and relationships are involved. The norms of impersonality may bring administration into conflict with citizens and thus make them 'inefficient'. Functional sub-divisions will set up sub-group loyalties in the bureaucracy vital to the successful functioning of the sub-division, yet leading to conflicts within the whole. ... That which is 'functional', 'efficient', is not always a coherent logical structure – efficiency may depend, and usually does, on a delicate balancing, in concrete contexts, of competing and conflicting trends and *desiderata*. A bureaucracy needs impersonality and 'good relations', predictability and flexibility, rules and discretions, central control and local initiative.[93]

Kamenka's observation reinforces the point that Weber's model of bureaucracy is just that – a model – and that actual bureaucracies tend to be complex beasts that rarely fit the "ideal-type" at all points. Weber himself did not intend the *ideal-type* to mirror real-world bureaucracies. As he explains:

> An *ideal-type* is formed by the one-sided *accentuation* of one or more points of view and by the synthesis of a great many diffuse, discrete, more or less present and occasionally absent *concrete individual* phenomena, which are arranged according to those one-sidedly emphasized viewpoints into a unified *analytical* construct. ... In its conceptual purity, this mental construct ... cannot be found empirically anywhere in reality. It is a *utopia*. Historical research faces the task of determining in each individual case, the extent to which this ideal-construct approximates to or diverges from reality.[94]

The *ideal type* thus should be seen as a general description of the characteristic structural features of modern bureaucracy rather than as a detailed prescription for organisational practice. As David Beetham observes: "Like all models ... it provides a useful starting point, rather than a final resting place, for analysis."[95]

Moreover, in different cultures, the bureaucratic ideal will be interpreted differently, being determined to a considerable extent by cultural priorities. Not all cultures attach the same value to formalisation and centralised control nor do they all share a need to ensure predictability and reduce uncertainty. Geert Hofstede has explored some of the differences among national cultures in a study of work-related values.[96] Using data obtained by comparing the beliefs and values of employees within the subsidiaries of the same multinational corporation in forty countries around the world, he identified four main criteria by which these national cultures differ. These criteria have been labelled "dimensions" and are as follows: *Power Distance, Uncertainty Avoidance, Individualism-Collectivism,* and *Masculinity-Femininity.*

The first two dimensions are the most relevant to understanding how bureaucracies function in different cultures. *Power Distance* "indicates the extent to which a society accepts the fact that power in institutions and organisations is distributed unequally." People in large Power Distance cultures prefer centralised decision-making and control while people in small Power Distance cultures prefer such control to be decentralised. *Uncertainty Avoidance* "indicates the extent to which a society feels threatened by uncertain and ambiguous situations and tries to avoid these situations by providing greater career stability, establishing more formal rules, not tolerating deviant ideas and behaviours, and believing in absolute truths and the attainment of expertise."[97] While Power Distance relates to centralisation, Uncertainty Avoidance relates to formalisation. People in strong Uncertainty Avoidance cultures need written rules and regulations while people in weak Uncertainty Avoidance cultures believe there should be as few rules as possible.

Richard Mead has translated these four dimensions into four distinct styles of bureaucracy: *Full Bureaucracy,* which comes closest to Weber's *ideal-type* bureaucracy, is characterised by large power distance and strong uncertainty avoidance; *Market Bureaucracy* is characterised by small power distance and weak uncertainty avoidance; *Workflow Bureaucracy* is characterised by small power distance and strong uncertainty avoidance; and *Personnel Bureaucracy* is characterised by large power distance and weak uncertainty avoidance.[98]

Hofstede's research shows that cultural differences will yield different attitudes toward the value of record trustworthiness relative to other organisational goals, and will result in different strategies for ensuring it. Commenting on Hofstede's research, Bearman observes that, in American organisations (which tend, in general, to be market bureaucracies),

Technologies [i.e., computer-based methods] have been acquired in order to enhance the ability of individuals throughout the organisation to do their jobs rather than in order to further corporate control or norms. European organizations [which tend, with the exception of Scandinavia and the Netherlands, to fall into the category of full or workflow bureaucracies] have been much more hesitant to introduce these technologies, and when they do so they usually develop substantial administrative controls surrounding their use.[99]

Similarly, in Bearman's view, American organisations are more likely to rely on technological intervention rather than on administrative rules and regulations to ensure the trustworthiness of electronic records. The perceived advantage of a technology-oriented approach is that the control exerted over recordkeeping and recordkeepers is automatic and invisible to the users of the system. On the other hand, the very invisibility of technological control mechanisms is precisely what makes them more insidious than traditional mechanisms of bureaucratic control. While the extent of technological surveillance is unknown to the user, the fact of such surveillance is not. Over the long term, uncertainty over its precise extent is bound to translate into a generalised atmosphere of distrust within an organisation. In an ironic reversal, technological remedies to the problem of ensuring record trustworthiness may themselves become the next problem requiring a solution.

Ultimately, the limits of contemporary archival diplomatics as a body of concepts and methods for ensuring the trustworthiness of electronic records are inseparable from the limits of the Weberian model of bureaucracy on which those concepts and methods are built. As Mary Douglas points out, bureaucracies "systematically direct individual memory and channel our perceptions into forms compatible with the relations they authorise."[100] Records are the most visible manifestation of that directing and channelling function and the procedural and technological methods for creating and controlling them the primary means of accomplishing it.

4.5 Conclusion

The UBC project's findings offer a fairly precise answer to the question of what constitutes a complete, reliable, and authentic record in an electronic environment. That answer is relevant not only to record creators but also to lawyers and historians for a number of reasons. First, the diplomatic analysis of a record's status of transmission in an electronic environment demonstrates why the concept of an original continues to be relevant. Secondly, the methods advocated by the project for ensuring record reliability and authenticity provide a substantial foundation on which record creators can build electronic recordkeeping systems capable of satisfying the rebuttable presumption of record integrity required by Canada's Uniform Electronic Evidence Act. Thirdly, the project's findings take into account the significance of the technological context of electronic record creation in assessing record trustworthiness, thereby addressing some of the concerns raised by the plaintiffs in *Armstrong* and *Public Citizen*. At the same time, the findings acknowledge the continuing relevance of the broader documentary, procedural, and administrative contexts of electronic record creation to such assessment. Finally, the primary products of the research are in the form of standards and rules for identifying electronic records and for evaluating their reliability and authenticity. As a result, they are also capable of serving as a tool for *retrospectively* assessing record trustworthiness and for identifying gaps in the security and verification procedures operative in electronic recordkeeping systems. Such capacity is of particular relevance to historians who will be looking at electronic records long after they have exhausted their original administrative purpose.

Notwithstanding the fact that the relationship between records and reality – between the word and the world – is at times an ambiguous and problematic one, there is no question that the pursuit of record reliability and authenticity is valid and necessary and requires the imposition of standards. Standards, of necessity, organise reality into universalistic rather than particularistic categories and prescribe, rather than describe the features of that reality in order to control and evaluate specific manifestations of it. This underlying purpose connects the concepts and methods developed by the UBC project to those that have been developed by the disciplines of law and history. Contemporary archival diplomatics aims primarily to control concrete manifestations of recordkeeping reality, while the legal and historical principles and rules of evidence aim to evaluate those manifestations.

Conclusion

This book has explored the concepts and methods associated with record trustworthiness from the perspectives of law, history, and diplomatics, and traced their evolution from antiquity to the digital age. A number of interconnected themes have emerged. The first theme has been the extent to which legal, historical, and diplomatic methods for assessing and ensuring the trustworthiness of records operate within a framework of inferences, generalisations, and probabilities. Inferences about record trustworthiness rest on generalisations which, in turn, are furnished primarily by common sense experience and logic. In his discussion of the theories of relevancy on which legal rules of evidence rely, Peter Tillers neatly summarises the limits of such generalisations:

> Our conceptual knowledge of tendencies in the world is such that it is always necessary for the fact-finder or actor to determine whether the complex and varied features of a particular event are sufficient to distinguish that situation, either partially or entirely, from the types of events to which the generalization speaks. ... The thesis that all generalizations, when applied, have this sort of range of potential indeterminacy seems to rest on the twin metaphysical assumptions (which we find quite plausible) that (1) actual events are always inherently distinctive in the sense that they have a large complex of features that may, in principle, affect the appropriateness of regarding them as being within the domain of any particular generalization, and that (2) any generalization, however complex, is in principle only a partial description of tendencies of nature since no generalization that we presently possess describes the significance of all features and characteristics that are to be found in the world of existence.[1]

Given these limits, the methods for assessing and ensuring record trustworthiness are more accurately characterised as a hedge against uncertainty concerning our knowledge about past events, than as a guarantor of certainty about it.

The "range of potential indeterminacy" inherent in all generalisations about the nature of reality is not ignored in analyses of legal, historical, and diplomatic methods. As one textbook on legal evidence explains:

> Because one cannot usually return in a time machine to show a trier of fact "what really happened," investigations do not produce "facts." They produce evidence, from which the trier of fact will resolve the parties' factual dispute(s) by deciding the *probable* facts.[2]

In his book *Historical Knowing*, Goldstein describes the process of historical research as a construction of an historical past, rather than the reconstruction of a real past: "it involves treatment of evidence and thinking about evidence and is preoccupied with the determination of what conception of the historical past makes the best sense given the character of the evidence in hand."[3] The documentary universe described by diplomatic methods is, similarly, less a representation than it is a construction of the real world. As Duranti explains:

> Diplomatics saw the documentary world as a system and built a system to understand and explain it. Early diplomatists rationalised, formalised and universalised document-creation by identifying within it the relevant elements, extending their relevance in time and space, eliminating their particularities, and relating the elements to each other and to their ultimate purpose.[4]

Implicit in these observations is a recognition that law, history, and diplomatics operate within a coherence, rather than a correspondence, theory of fact-finding.[5] Within a coherence theory of fact-finding, the truth of a proposition is assessed in relation to its coherence with other propositions that we accept as true, rather than in relation to its correspondence with an external, verifiable reality. The Rationalist tradition of legal evidence, the Modernist tradition of historical scholarship, and the Weberian model of bureaucracy on which contemporary archival diplomatics is built all constitute particular constructions of the world, rather than demonstrably accurate reflections of it. They represent ideal types and, as such, are normative and aspirational. The Rationalist tradition aspires to the ideal of justice, the Modernist tradition to that of historical truth and the Weberian model to that of accountability. To realise these aspirations, reality has been organised into universalistic rather than particularistic categories that prescribe, rather than describe, its features in order to control and evaluate specific manifestations of it. The validity and strength of each discipline's methods for assessing and ensuring record trustworthiness can only be judged, therefore, in relation to the integrity and internal coherence of its procedures, rather than in relation to any verifiable standard of correspondence with the past as it actually happened, simply because such a standard is unattainable. In this context, the limits of assessing record trustworthiness are attributable, ultimately, not to defects in method, but to "well-founded ambiguities" that defy resolution.[6]

This is not to suggest that the methods for assessing record trustworthiness are necessarily untrustworthy, or that a correspondence theory of truth has no place in the fact-finding process. Dorothy Haecker maintains, in relation to historical ways of knowing, "that the concept of coherence is an indispensable part of the analysis of historical verification, that the concept of correspondence is indispensable to the understanding of historical reference, and that both are involved in the notion of historical meaningfulness."[7] The same may be said in relation to legal ways of knowing. Peter Tillers argues eloquently that it is a mistake to suppose that we can trust nothing whose validity or reliability is not subject to a logically compelling demonstration. The fact is that nothing in this cosmos is susceptible to a logically compelling demonstration (except upon arbitrary premises), and yet it is plain enough that we do not distrust everything we believe merely because the validity of our beliefs is not in that sense logically demonstrable. ... The supposition that it is irrational to believe anything that cannot be proved rests on a basic misapprehension of what it means to be rational. Reason is not an instrument that can establish *anything* with certainty; but it is nonetheless certain that we can and do use reason and thought in wending our way through life and the cosmos. ... In our daily life, we draw innumerable inferences upon which we rely and upon which we stake our lives and fortunes and we will not be easily persuaded that the inferences we have drawn are untrustworthy.[8]

Tillers' argument suggests that, while we cannot defend foundationalist standards, at the same time, we cannot avoid them. Common sense dictates a certain leap of faith in accepting that the propositions we make about the nature of reality are valid, if not ultimately verifiable. Moreover, the pursuit of justice, historical truth, and accountability are important and socially necessary endeavours and the pursuit of all three requires a commitment to the value of accurate fact-finding.[9] At the same time, the realisation that the methods for assessing record trustworthiness, and the generalisations on which they are built, are human constructs, rather than transcendent verities, leads to the conclusion that those methods need continually to be reassessed and re-evaluated as new ways of looking at the world present themselves.[10]

The second theme that has emerged in the course of this exploration concerns the specific generalisations on which the legal, historical, and diplomatic methods discussed are based. In all three disciplines, the methods for assessing and ensuring record trustworthiness in general, and record reliability in particular, are rooted in observational principles.[11] Records are viewed as a source of information that permit us to make inferences about the real world. Because they are assumed to reflect events in the real world, records depend for their reliability on the claim of the recordkeeper to have been present at those events. Accordingly, the methods for assessing record trustworthiness aim to ensure that the record accurately reflects those events, and that it is uncontaminated by the distorting influence of bias, interpretation, or unwarranted opinion on the part of the recordkeeper.

For records created by bureaucracies, the organisational context simply enlarges the traditional conception of the recordkeeper's presence in time and place. The bureaucratic controls exercised over recordkeepers and recordkeeping constitute a further dimension of observation whereby the bureaucracy itself becomes a watcher over recordkeepers. The reliability of bureaucratic records is thus ensured, not only because the recordkeeper is close to the event recorded but also because the recording itself takes place within a framework of bureaucratic observation and surveillance. The degree of reliability of the records can then be measured in relation to the degree to which the bureaucracy shapes and constrains the speech of recordkeepers.

The gradual replacement of traditional mechanisms of bureaucratic supervision by impersonal technological control systems has not resulted in an abandonment of bureaucratic observational principles as a means of assessing and ensuring record trustworthiness. It has tended, rather, to perpetuate and reinforce them. The computer has become the perfect observer, with its capacity to witness and capture the actions and interactions of recordkeepers on a microscopic scale. It is present at all the record-creating events that take place within it but its recording of those events is not contaminated by human self-interest. The computer's homunculus eye view is, nevertheless, a narrow one, since it is confined to the electronic environment and fails to capture the broader documentary and administrative context in which electronic records are created, used, and made meaningful.

The observational principles on which methods for assessing and ensuring record trustworthiness are based reflect a conception of records as witnesses to events and a corresponding view of the world as one that is capable of being witnessed. As Raffel explains:

> It becomes possible for a record to correspond to the world only when 'the world' is formulated as itself revealing the things which must be said about it. This is not to say that the world *does* disclose itself. Rather: in so far as one can formulate the world as made up of things which present or fail to present themselves, it thereby becomes possible for a record to 'represent' the world. It is neither correct nor incorrect then to treat records as corresponding to the world. The proper statement of the relationship of records to the world is that, in so far as one wants to see records as corresponding to the world, one *must* treat the world as revealing or presenting what must be said about it.[12]

Raffel's comments underline the fact that the legal, historical, and diplomatic methods are all rooted in a particular way of looking at the world and in a particular conception of records as a kind of testimony about that world. His comments also reinforce the point that the methods reflect a particular mode of instantiation, one that is shaped by each discipline's procedures of investigation and, therefore, does not exhaust all the possible ways of looking at the world or at the relationship between records and the world.

Mark Cousins observes, for example, that the practice of both legal and historical investigation pivots around the same questions: Did an event occur or not? Do reports or allegations that an event has occurred correspond to the best evidence of the existence of such an event? Into which class of event does the event fall? Who and what are responsible for it? What are the lines of causality to be drawn in respect of the event? What degrees of responsibility do or can particular persons bear? As a consequence, the past that is of concern to legal and historical inquiry, "is not the past in general, but only the past as it concerned the event and the questions of responsibility, which such events raise." While the truth uncovered by a court of law or by an historian is subject to appeal, "such an appeal will merely extend reasoning about the event and responsibility for the event. The production of new evidence will permit a representation which was not [previously] available. ... Arguments concerning failures of [previous] reasoning ... will seek to overthrow its representation of the event."[13] Grounded in a view of the world that is witnessable and event-full, legal and historical procedures thus tend to focus on actions and their agents and are better equipped to assess responsibility than to expose intentionality. In the same way, bureaucratic methods for ensuring record trustworthiness are directed largely at foreclosing questions about the intentionality of recordkeepers, preferring to focus instead on ensuring that recordkeepers are made responsible for the statements made in the records.

The third theme that has emerged is the continuing validity of a best evidence principle to the assessment of record trustworthiness. As espoused by Nance, that principle refers to the obligation of litigating parties to present the "epistemically best," meaning the logically most probative, evidence. It has been suggested that adherence to such principle, in the more specific context of the rule governing documentary originals, might manifest itself in an obligation of the litigating parties to produce the most complete record, i.e., the record containing all the essential elements of physical and intellectual form present in the original. It has been shown that the dimension of completeness is particularly pertinent to electronic records, given that their structural, contextual, and discursive components may exist in separate parts of a database and can be managed separately unless they are purposefully brought together. The foundation evidence that supports a presumption of record integrity, therefore, should be capable of demonstrating not only the reliability of an electronic record system's input and verification procedures, but also the completeness of procedures for reproducing the original structure of the record and any original annotations, to the extent that these are relevant to an understanding of the record's content. This implies that courts will have to come to terms with the question of what constitutes a complete record and be capable of assessing the significance of missing elements with respect to the record's reliability and authenticity.

The best evidence principle may also be extended, by analogy, to the historian's use of documentary evidence. The adherence to the principle in an historical context might manifest itself in the historians' obligation to ensure that the electronic records on which they base their stories about the past are also the most complete. In fact, in the two American court cases that have been discussed, historians have already demonstrated their concern to ensure the preservation of the most complete version of federal government records, notwithstanding some disagreement concerning how best to interpret completeness.

Understood broadly, the best evidence principle implies that judges and litigants, as well as historians, need to educate themselves about the nature of electronic records and how they manifest themselves in various electronic record systems in order to be capable of assessing record completeness and to ensure that the epistemically best evidence is presented. For all their limitations, the standards for ensuring record trustworthiness, based on contemporary archival diplomatics, that have emerged in the course of the UBC research project are an invaluable means of facilitating that understanding. The standards provide a precise and detailed answer to the question of what constitutes a complete, reliable, and authentic record in an electronic environment, one that is relevant to lawyers, judges, and historians, as well as to record creators. The standards not only provide a substantial foundation on which to build trustworthy electronic recordkeeping systems, they are also capable of serving as a tool for retrospectively assessing record trustworthiness and for identifying gaps in the security and verification procedures operative in electronic recordkeeping systems.

Historians, in particular, need to understand information technology, not simply because it soon will be the primary vehicle through which stories about the human past are told but also because technology, and the tension between empowerment and surveillance it embodies, are an essential part of that story. R.J. Morris speculates that:

> Historians will seek to understand the late twentieth century in order to relate it to collective identities and experiences of their own period. If the current analysis of 'post modernism' is any guide to this, that experience will be complex and fragmented. ... The archives of IT, the e-data, will be one base from which that complexity and fragmentation can be recreated and interrogated. Even the current fragmentation of historical practice should warn us that historians will want to tell many stories. IT and e-data will not only be a source of these stories but part of the story itself. [14]

Historians need to understand the products of the digital age, both to comprehend it and to assess its effect on late twentieth-century culture.

A final theme that has emerged concerns if and where a line should be drawn between observation and surveillance in designing technological mechanisms for ensuring record trustworthiness. Recent research in the history and sociology of technology, Margaret Hedstrom points out, emphasises the "social construction of technology" and the significance of human choices in shaping it. This perspective

> considers technology to be the embodiment of human choices that influence how a machine is designed, what it is designed to accomplish, and how it is intended to accomplish its objectives. The design, development, marketing, acceptance or rejection, and interpretation of a technology are social processes shaped by rich interaction between cultural norms, economic and

political power, social values, and the potential of a new machine or process.[15]

Electronic record systems are still in their infancy and there is time yet to explore and debate questions concerning the appropriate balance to be struck between the social value of trustworthy records and the social costs of increased surveillance. Such exploration needs, however, to take place sooner rather than later. As Hedstrom cautions, the "social construction of technology" perspective also suggests that "technologies ultimately reach 'closure' – a point at which debate over the features of the technology ceases and the artefact or process stabilises. Upon reaching closure, technical features alone may limit or eliminate possibilities, require adjustments in social and political systems, undermine deeply held cultural values, and alter power relations."[16] This suggests the need to weigh the social value of record trustworthiness against other social values in order to ensure that the technological mechanisms we develop and implement reflect an equitable balance among those values and do not simply shore up the worst excesses of bureaucratic surveillance.

The societal need to ensure record trustworthiness has been recognised since antiquity and continues to be recognised at the end of the twentieth century. While the technological means of assessing and ensuring record trustworthiness have changed fundamentally over time as the sovereign's seal has given way to the electronic seal, the underlying principles guiding those means have remained remarkably consistent. The conceptual adjustments that have been made constitute incremental, rather than radical, change. It seems safe to predict that the pattern of technological transformation and incremental conceptual change which has characterised the evolution of methods for assessing and ensuring record trustworthiness since antiquity will survive into the coming century and into the next age of recordkeeping.

Notes

Introduction

[1] *Oxford English Dictionary* (New York: Oxford University Press, 1971), vol. 2, s.v. "trust."
[2] Barbara J. Shapiro, *Probability and Certainty in Seventeenth Century England: A Study of the Relationships between Natural Science, Religion, History, Law and Literature* (Princeton, N.J.: Princeton University Press, 1983), 164.
[3] *Ibid.*
[4] Mark A. Johnson, "Computer Printouts as Evidence: Stricter Foundation or Presumption of Reliability?" *Marquette Law Review* 75 (Winter 1992): 439.
[5] [Canada], *Dishonoured Legacy: The Lessons of the Somalia Affair. Report of the Commission of Inquiry into the Deployment of Canadian Forces to Somalia* (Ottawa: Minister of Public Works and Government Services Canada, 1997), vol. 1, xxx.
[6] *Ibid.*, vol. 5, 1218.
[7] *Ibid.*
[8] *Ibid.*, 1219.
[9] *Ibid.*, 1244.
[10] *Ibid.*, 1245.

Chapter One

[1] The Justinian Code, or *Corpus Juris Civilis*, comprises four sections. The core of the Code is constituted by the first three sections, i.e., the Codex, which was issued in 529, the Digest, which was issued in 533, and the Institutes, which were issued in 534. The final section was added to the Code in 565 after the death of Justinian and is constituted by the Novellae Constitutiones, i.e., the legislation issued by Justinian himself which was published posthumously.
[2] Luciana Duranti, "The Concept of Appraisal and Archival Theory," *American Archivist* 57 (Spring 1994): 331.
[3] *Ibid.*
[4] *Ibid.*
[5] Luciana Duranti, "Medieval Universities and Archives," *Archivaria* 38 (Fall 1994): 41.
[6] Luciana Duranti, "Archives as a Place," *Archives and Manuscripts* 24 (Nov. 1996): 246-47.
[7] Duranti, "Concept of Appraisal," 332. In Roman times and during the early Middle Ages, sovereignty was owned exclusively by the emperor and the pope and by persons to whom they endowed that right, such as notaries. In the thirteenth century, however, sovereignty was extended to monasteries and city-states. Thereafter, continuing custody by a monastery or city-state could endow a document with public faith.
[8] J.T. Abdy, *A Historical Sketch of Civil Procedure Among the Romans* (Cambridge: Macmillan and Co., 1857), 120.
[9] M. Carr Ferguson, "A Day in Court in Justinian's Rome: Some Problems of Evidence, Proof, and Justice in Roman Law," *Iowa Law Review* 46 (1961): 753.
[10] The titles are as follows: the authentication of documents (C.4.21.20; Nov. 73), attestation (C.4.21.20; Nov. 73), signatures (C.4.21.17, 20), seals (C.6.22.8), registration (C.4.21.17; Nov. 73.8), comparison of handwriting (C.4.21; Nov. 49.2; Nov. 73), the requirement to produce documentary originals (D.22.4.2), the protocols necessary in notarial documents, and the regulations affecting notaries (Nov. 44), the faith reposing in public and quasi public documents (D.22.3.10; C.2.1.2, 6; C.4.21.4, 17, 20; C.7.52.6; C.8.18.11; Nov. 17.47.1; Nov. 49.2), and forgery (C.9.22; Nov. 80.7). Cited by C.A. Morrison, "Some Features of the Roman and the English Law of Evidence," *Tulane Law Review* 33 (1956): 579-80.
[11] Luciana Duranti, "Diplomatics: New Uses for an Old Science [Part I]," *Archivaria* 28 (Summer 1989): 12 (hereafter cited as "Diplomatics I").
[12] Ferguson, "Day in Court," 755-56.
[13] *Ibid.*, 755-56; see also *ibid.*, 770.
[14] Duranti, "Concept of Appraisal," 332-33.

[15] Thomas F.X. Noble, "Literacy and the Papal Government in Late Antiquity and the Early Middle Ages," in *The Uses of Literacy in Early Medieval Europe*, ed. Rosamund McKitterick (Cambridge: Cambridge University Press, 1990), 89

[16] *Ibid.*

[17] Wendy Davies and Paul Fouracre, eds., *The Settlement of Disputes in Early Medieval Europe* (Cambridge: Cambridge University Press, 1986), 210.

[18] Peter Burke, "The Uses of Literacy in Early Modern Italy," in *The Social History of Language*, ed. Peter Burke and Roy Porter (Cambridge: Cambridge University Press, 1987), 23.

[19] Armando Petrucci, "The Illusion of Authentic History," in *Writers and Readers in Medieval Italy: Studies in the History of Written Culture*, ed. and trans. Charles M. Radding (New Haven: Yale University Press, 1995), 243.

[20] Clanchy, *From Memory to Written Record: England, 1066-1307*, 2nd ed. (Oxford: Blackwell, 1993), 304-5.

[21] *Ibid.*, 305.

[22] For a detailed study of the role of notaries in England during the thirteenth and fourteenth centuries, see C.R. Cheney, *Notaries Public in England in the Thirteenth and Fourteenth Centuries* (Oxford: Clarendon Press, 1972). For their role in England since the reformation, see C.W. Brooks, R.H. Hemholz and P.G. Stein, *Notaries Public in England Since the Reformation* (London: Erskine Press, 1991).

[23] Arthur Giry, *Manuel de Diplomatique*, trans. and quoted in John Henry Wigmore, *Evidence in Trials at Common Law*, ed. and rev. by James H. Chadbourn (Boston: Little, Brown, 1978), vol. 7, para. 2161.

[24] *Ibid.* For a more detailed history of the seal, see Thomas Frederick Tout, "The King's Seal and Sealing as a Means of Authentication," in *Chapters in the Administrative History of Mediaeval England: the Wardrobe, the Chamber and the Small Seals* (New York: Barnes & Noble, 1967).

[25] *Ibid.*

[26] *Ibid.*

[27] Wigmore, *Evidence in Trials at Common Law*, ed. and rev. by James H. Chadbourn (Boston: Little, Brown, 1978), vol. 9, para. 2426.

[28] *Ibid.*

[29] Barbara J. Shapiro, *Beyond Reasonable Doubt and Probable Cause: Historical Perspectives on the Anglo-American Law of Evidence* (Berkeley, Calif.: University of California Press, 1991), 3-4.

[30] Jean-Phillipe Levy, "The Evolution of Written Proof," *American University Law Review* 13 (1964): 146.

[31] *Ibid.*, 145.

[32] *Ibid.*, 147-48.

[33] Clanchy, *Memory to Written Record*, 146-49.

[34] *Ibid*, 322, 149.

[35] *Ibid.*, 323.

[36] *Ibid.*, 323-4. Innocent III's measures for the prevention and detection of forgery are described in Reginald L. Poole, *Lectures on the History of the Papal Chancery Down to the Time of Innocent III* (Cambridge: The University Press, 1915), 151-60.

[37] Clanchy, *Memory to Written Record*, 324.

[38] *Ibid.*

[39] *Ibid.*

[40] *Ibid.*, 325

[41] *Ibid.*

[42] Donald R. Kelley, *Foundations of Modern Historical Scholarship: Language, Law and History in the French Renaissance* (New York: Columbia University Press, 1970), 23-24.

[43] *Ibid.*, 24.

[44] A noteworthy example from the fourteenth century is Francesco Petrarch's analysis of the authenticity of a privilege granted by Caesar Augustus and Nero in the first century, exempting Austria from the jurisdiction of Emperor Charles IV. Petrarch identified a number of anachronisms in the document that proved it was a forgery. See Peter Burke, *The Renaissance Sense of the Past* (New York: St. Martin's Press, 1970), 50-54.

[45] Olga Zorzi Pugliese, "Introduction," in Lorenzo Valla, *The Profession of the Religious and Selections from The Falsely Believed and Forged Donation of Constantine*, ed. and trans. Olga Zorzi Pugliese, 2nd ed. (Toronto: Centre for Reformation Studies, 1994), 23.

[46] Cited in "Introduction," 24-25.

[47] Valla, *The Falsely Believed and Forged Donation of Constantine*, 103, XI, 35.

[48] *Ibid.*, 101, IX, 31.

[49] *Ibid.*, 101-2, IX, 32.

[50] *Ibid.*, 99, VIII, 28.

[51] Kelley, *Foundations of Modern Scholarship*, 45-46.

[52] Ernst Breisach, *Historiography Ancient, Medieval, and Modern*, 2nd ed. (Chicago: University of Chicago Press, 1994), 161.

[53] Interestingly, Valla's treatise was not itself viewed as an historical controversy but rather as a legal one. According to Julian Franklin, "the issue was less narration of the past as such than the present jurisdiction of the Church." Julian H. Franklin, *Jean Bodin and the Sixteenth-Century Revolution in the Methodology of Law and History* (New York: Columbia University Press, 1963), 121.

[54] *Ibid.*, 2

[55] *Ibid.*, 4.

[56] Shapiro, *Probability and Certainty*, 164.

[57] Franklin traces the roots of historical Pyrrhonism back to the sixteenth century and the writings of Cornelius Agrippa and Francesco Patrizzi. Arnaldo Momigliano situates it in the seventeenth and eighteenth centuries and the writings of La Mothe Le Vayer, Pierre Bayle and Daniel Huet. See Franklin, *Jean Bodin and the Sixteenth Century Revolution*, 89-102; Arnaldo Momigliano, "Ancient History and the Antiquarian," *Studies in Historiography* (London: Weidenfeld and Nicolson, 1966), 10-13. Accounts of historical Pyrrhonism and its influence may also be found in Paul Hazard, *The European Mind*, trans. J. Lewis May (Cleveland: World Publishing Co., [1963]), chapter 2, *passim* and J.G.A. Pocock, *The Ancient Constitution and the Feudal Law: English Historical Thought in the Seventeenth Century*, 2nd ed. (Cambridge: Cambridge University Press, 1986), 6-8.

[58] Jacques Le Goff, *History and Memory*, trans. Steven Rendall and Elizabeth Claman. (New York: Columbia University Press, 1992), 185,186.

[59] Quoted by Kelley, *Foundations of Modern Scholarship*, 116.

[60] Franklin, *Jean Bodin and the Sixteenth Century Revolution*, 126

[61] Quoted in *ibid.*, 128.

[62] *Ibid.*

[63] *Ibid.*, 129.

[64] *Ibid.*, 130.

[65] *Ibid.*, 130-31. Franklin points out in a footnote that "in the sixteenth century public records are normally regarded as perpetual annals in which the recording of all significant occurrences is the official charge of special commissioners, preferably priests. The official, sometimes sacerdotal, status, together with the fact that they are 'open to inspection,' is what gives them special authority." (Franklin, 141, n. 48). In *De Institutione Historiae Universae*, Baudouin refers approvingly to the Roman and early Church custom of preserving monuments of "uncorrupted faith" in archives as a means of ensuring their trustworthiness.

[66] Assertions of the continuing validity of the preferential rule for public documents can be found throughout the previous centuries. One of the strongest statements is found, ironically, in a book of forgeries published in 1498 by Annius of Viterbo. Annius published a series of annotated texts on the earliest periods of ancient history. The texts, which included annals of the Babylonian and Persian monarchies, as well as of the Greek and Roman empires, were soon exposed as forgeries. In his accompanying commentary on the texts, Annius claimed to have discovered infallible criteria for discriminating between true and false documents based on his assertion of the annals' authenticity. In *De locis theologicis*, Cano summarises Annius' rules as follows: "The first rule ... is this. All those are to be accepted without argument who have written in public and attested faith (*qui publica et probata fide scripserunt*). Second, the acts and annals of the four monarchies can be rejected or denied by no one, because they were noted down exclusively in public faith, and were preserved in libraries and archives. ... The third rule is that those who write only from hearsay or opinion are to be rejected as mere private persons unless they are not in disagreement with the public attestation. From which it follows that no one is to be accepted as a chronicler unless he is in harmony with the annals of the four monarchies." Cano, *De locis theologicis*, quoted by Franklin, *Bodin and the Sixteenth Century Revolution*, 122, n. 21. As Franklin points out, Annius claimed to have acquired his texts from two Armenian monks and may have believed the texts to be authentic.

[67] Franklin, *Bodin and the Sixteenth Century Revolution*, 132-33.

[68] *Ibid.*, 133.

[69] *Ibid.*, 140.

[70] *Ibid.*

[71] *Ibid.*, 147.

[72] *Ibid.*, 148-51.

[73] *Ibid.*, 11.

[74] *Ibid.*, 152.

[75] Momigliano, "Ancient History and the Antiquarian," 2.

[76] R.G. Collingwood, *The Idea of History*, ed. by Jan Van Der Dussen, rev. ed. (New York: Oxford University Press, 1994), 258-59.

[77] The prevalence of this theme is apparent in Allen Johnson's summary of several works of historical criticism that appeared in the seventeenth and eighteenth centuries. Two examples are worth mentioning. The first is the criticism of Jean Mabillon. His *Traité des études monastiques*, which was printed in 1691, includes a chapter containing advice to readers of history on how to determine whether an historian is trustworthy. Mabillon advises readers to avoid any historian who is a mere copyist rather than an original, contemporary authority, unless he has corrected or explained an original authority, or if the original authority has been lost. He also counsels readers to look for a certain honesty, judgement, and accuracy on the part of the historian (though Mabillon does not provide clues as to how these are to be determined). Finally, he advises readers to trust historians whom the church has approved and reject all others. The second example is the criticism of Henri Griffet. According to Johnson, Griffet, who published *Traité des différentes sortes de preuves qui servent à établir la vérité de l'histoire* in 1769, is the first writer to compare the historian to "a judge in court who must confront witnesses, examine them, and ascertain the truth by painstaking study and comparison of the evidence. He must ever carry in his hand the torch of criticism in order to determine the trustworthiness of witnesses". Griffet also recommends the use of original and authentic records, by which he means state papers or official records. He regards the authority of such records to be superior to all other historical sources, including the testimony of a contemporary writer. On the other hand, "the agreement of contemporary testimony and authentic records ... constitutes complete historical proof and establishes the truth of the facts in question." See Allen Johnson, *The Historian and Historical Evidence* (New York: Scribner's, 1926), 101-40.

[78] Anthony Grafton, "The Footnote from De Thou to Ranke," *History and Theory* 33 (1994): 63-64.

[79] *Ibid.*, 53. For a detailed study of the history of the footnote see Grafton's subsequent book-length study, *The Footnote: A Curious History* (Cambridge, Mass.: Harvard University Press, 1997).

[80] Grafton, "Footnote from De Thou," 73.

[81] *Ibid.*

[82] *Ibid.*, 71-72.

[83] *Ibid.*, 62-63.

[84] George Huppert, *The Idea of Perfect History: Historical Erudition and Historical Philosophy in Renaissance France* (Urbana: University of Illinois Press, 1970), 159.

[85] *Ibid.*, 160.

[86] Duranti, "Diplomatics I," *Archivaria*, 13.

[87] *De re diplomatica* (Paris, 1681), 1, quoted by C.R. Cheney, *The Papacy and England 12th - 14th Centuries* (London: Variorum Reprints, 1982), 8.

[88] James Westfall Thompson, *A History of Historical Writing* (New York: The Macmillan Co., 1942), vol. 2, 19. Since Mabillon devoted an entire section of his treatise to the analysis of different kinds of script, *De re diplomatica* is also considered the first treatise on paleography. Since the eighteenth century, however, diplomatics and paleography have been regarded as separate disciplines.

[89] Leonard E. Boyle, "Diplomatics," in *Medieval Studies: An Introduction*, ed. James M. Powell (Syracuse, N.Y.: Syracuse University Press, 1992), 84.

[90] Marc Bloch, *The Historian's Craft*, trans. Peter Putnam (New York: Alfred A. Knopf, 1963), 81.

[91] Le Goff, *History and Memory*, 193-94. The quotations Le Goff inserts in his text are taken from Georges Tessier, "Diplomatique," in *L'Histoire et ses méthodes*, ed. Charles Samaran (Paris: Gallimard, 1961), 641.

[92] Ian Hacking, *The Emergence of Probability: A Philosophical Study of Early Ideas About Probability, Induction and Statistical Inference* (Cambridge: Cambridge University Press, 1974), 34.

[93] *Ibid.*, 33-34.

[94] For the connection between the emergence of the concept of evidence as induction and the emergence of probability theory specifically, see *ibid.*, 31-48.

[95] John Locke, *An Essay Concerning Human Understanding*, ed. A.D. Woozley (New York: New American Library, 1974).

[96] Shapiro, *Probability and Certainty*, 37.

[97] Locke, *Essay Concerning Human Understanding*, 403.

[98] *Ibid.*, 403-4.

[99] *Ibid.*, 405.

[100] *Cambridge Dictionary of Philosophy* (Cambridge: Cambridge University Press, 1995), s.v. "Locke, John."

[101] One of the more unusual and obscure results of that influence is Joannis Craig's "Rules of Historical Evidence," which appears as two chapters in his book *Theologiae Christianae Principia Mathematica*. The book, which was published in 1699, purported to validate scientifically certain Christian truths against agnostics. The chapters relating to evidence were an attempt to establish rules of historical evidence on the basis of mathematical principles. Craig defined historical probability as "probability which is deduced from the testimonies of others who are affirming their own observation or experience." He used algebraic equations, based on propositions and problems, which purported to establish the reliability of historical evidence. Examples of propositions for which he produced elaborate algebraic equations include: "suspicions of historical probability transmitted through single successive witnesses (other things being equal) increase in proportion to the numbers of witnesses through whom the history is handed down" and "velocities of suspicion produced in equal periods of time increase in arithmetical progression." See *Craig's Rules of Historical Evidence* from Joannis Craig, *Theologiae Christianae Principia Mathematica* (1699), in *History and Theory* Beiheft 4 ('s-Gravenhage: Mouton and Co., 1964).

[102] Shapiro, *Probability and Certainty*, 179.

[103] Lord Chief Baron Gilbert, *The Law of Evidence*, 6th ed. (London: W. Clarke and Sons, 1801), 1

[104] *Ibid.*, 5.

[105] William Twining, "The Rationalist Tradition of Evidence Scholarship," in *Rethinking Evidence: Exploratory Essays* (Oxford: Blackwell, 1990), 36. Gilbert's treatise was not formally published until 28 years after his death and his work reflects an understanding of evidence formed in the opening decade of the eighteenth century. See Stephan Landsman, "The Rise of the Contentious Spirit: Adversary Procedure in Eighteenth Century England," *Cornell Law Review* 75 (March 1990): 592.

[106] Jeremy Bentham, "False Theory of Evidence (Gilbert's)," Appendix C of *An Introductory View of the Rationale of Judicial Evidence*, in *The Works of Jeremy Bentham*, ed. John Bowering (New York: Russell and Russell, 1962), vol. 6, 186-87.

[107] Although he identifies a wide range of documents in his hierarchy, among them, writs, affidavits, depositions, bills in chancery, and wills, Gilbert appears to have based his assertion of the superior trustworthiness of written evidence on the authority accorded to a much narrower range of documents by Common law courts in earlier times. According to James Bradley Thayer, "the vast majority of documents used in trials in early times were no doubt of the solemn, constitutive, and dispositive kind, instruments under seal, records, certificates of high officials, public registers, and the like. Such documents, if the authenticity of them were not denied, 'imported verity,' as the phrase was, fixed liability and determined rights." See James Bradley Thayer, "The Best Evidence," in *A Preliminary Treatise on Evidence at the Common Law* (Boston: Little, Brown, 1898), 504.

[108] Bentham's discussion of makeshift evidence may be found in chapters XIII of *An Introductory View of the Rationale of Judicial Evidence* and in Books V and VI of the *Rationale of Judicial Evidence*. See *Works of Jeremy Bentham*, vol. 6, 57-60; vol. 7, 118-73. His discussion of pre-appointed evidence may be found in Chapter XIV of *An Introductory View of the Rationale of Judicial Evidence* and in Book IV of the *Rationale of Judicial Evidence*. See *Works of Jeremy Bentham*, vol. 6, 60-67; vol. 7, 508-85.

[109] Bentham, "False Theory of Evidence," 184.

[110] *Ibid.*, 186.

[111] *Works of Bentham*, vol. 6, 593.

[112] The major treatises on the law of evidence written during the nineteenth century, and their contribution to the Rationalist tradition of evidence scholarship are discussed at length in Twining, "Rationalist Tradition," 35-59.

[113] *Ibid.*, 73 (model II).

[114] Common law, in this context, refers to "the body of those principles and rules of action, relating to the government and security of persons and property, which derive their authority solely from usages and customs of immemorial antiquity, or from the judgements and decrees of the courts recognizing, affirming, and enforcing such usages and customs; and, in this sense, particularly the ancient unwritten law of England." *Black's Law Dictionary*, 6th ed. (St. Paul, Minn.: West Publishing, 1990), s.v. "common law". This definition of Common law, as 'judge-made', or case law should not be confused with the European Common law, or *jus commune*, which refers to the Roman Civil law and, specifically, the *Justinian Code* as it was revived and interpreted by medieval scholars. According to R.C. van Caenegem, this *jus commune* (also known as the 'common written laws')" was so called

because it was shared by learned lawyers and law faculties all over Europe (including England). It contrasted with the *jus proprium* or *municipale*, i.e., the 'own' laws and customs of innumerable countries, provinces and towns throughout Europe." R.C. van Caenegem, *Judges, Legislators and Professors: Chapters in European Legal History* (Cambridge: Cambridge University Press, 1987), 44. With the rise of sovereign states, national legal systems began to replace the *jus commune*, which became a subordinate or supplementary law. In the nineteenth century, the principal states of Western Europe adopted civil codes. According to John Merryman, "the subject matter of these civil codes was almost identical with the subject matter of the first three books of the *Institutes* of Justinian and the Roman Civil law component of the *jus commune* of medieval Europe." John Henry Merryman, *The Civil Law Tradition: An Introduction to the Legal Systems of Western Europe and Latin America*, 2nd ed. (Stanford, Calif.: Stanford University Press, 1085), 10.

[115] For a more detailed history of the best evidence rule relating to documents, see Wigmore, *Evidence in Trials at Common Law*, ed. and rev. by James H. Chadbourn (Boston: Little, Brown, 1972), vol. 4, para. 1177 (hereafter cited as *Wigmore on Evidence*, followed by name of reviser, and year of revision in parentheses, volume number, and paragraph number); Thayer, "Best Evidence," 503-5; W.S. Holdsworth, "Documentary Evidence," in *A History of English Law*, vol. 9 (London: Methuen, 1926), 163-77.

[116] For a more detailed history of the exception, see *Wigmore on Evidence* (Chadbourn revision, 1974), vol. 5, para. 1518.

[117] Ch. V. Langlois and Ch. Seignobos, *Introduction to the Study of History*, trans. G.G. Berry (London: Duckworth & Co., 1898).

[118] Earlier nineteenth century efforts include Johann Gustav Droysen, *Outline of the Principles of History (Grundriss der Historik)*, trans. E. Benjamin Andrews (Boston: Ginn and Co., 1893) and Ernst Bernheim, *Lehrbuch der historischen Methode* (Leipzig: Duncker & Humblot, 1889). Other manuals of historical method that appeared during the nineteenth century are discussed in Allen Johnson's *The Historian and Historical Evidence*, 126-40.

[119] Felix Gilbert, *History: Politics or Culture? Reflections on Ranke and Burckhardt* (Princeton, N.J.: Princeton University Press, 1990), 18.

[120] *Ibid.*, 32, 18.

[121] Leonard Krieger, *Time's Reasons: Philosophies of History Old and New* (Chicago: University of Chicago Press, 1989), 98.

[122] Langlois and Seignobos, *Introduction to Study*, 64. Their observation echoes one made by Gustav Droysen thirty-one years earlier in his manual of historical method: "The science of history is the result of empirical perception, experience and investigation. ... All empirical investigation governs itself according to the data to which it is directed, and it can only direct itself to such data as are immediately present to it and susceptible of being cognized through the senses. The data for historical investigation are not past things, for these have disappeared, but things which are still present, here and now, whether recollections of what was done, or remnants of things that have existed and of events that have occurred." Droysen also refers to documents as "traces". See Droysen, *Outline of Principles*, 10-11, para. 4-5.

[123] Langlois and Seignobos, *Introduction to Study*, 159.

[124] Olivier Guyotjeannin, "The Expansion of Diplomatics as a Discipline,"" *American Archivist* 59 (Fall 1996): 416. Originally published as "La diplomatique médiévale et L'élargissement de son champ," *La Gazette des Archives* 172 (1996): 13-18. The original French text reads as follows: " ... de convoyer sur le chantier historique un matériau dûment édité, daté, critiqué. Il mettait en œuvre une critique négative, si l'on peut dire, décelant les falsifications; ivraie de sa moisson de documents; dont il était aussi chargé de trier la paille (le formulaire) du grain (les faits attestés); ou, pour prendre une autre métaphore, qui a eu son heure de gloire, de faire sauter la gangue de formules, où le minerai des données restait captif sans son intervention experte."

[125] Harry Bresslau, *Handbuch der Urkundenlehre für Deutschland und Italien*, 2 vols. (1889; reprint, Berlin: W. de Gruyter, 1968.).

[126] Arthur Giry, *Manuel de diplomatique: Diplomes et chartes Chronologie technique: Éléments critiques et parties constitutives de la teneur des chartes Les chancelleries; Les actes privés* (1893; reprint, New York: Burt Franklin, 1964).

[127] Cesare Paoli, *Programma scolastico di paleografia latina e di diplomatica*, 3 vols. (Firenze: G.C. Sansoni, 1894-1901).

[128] Théodor von Sickel, *Beiträge zur Diplomatik*, 3 vols. (Vienna: K.K. Hofund Staatsdruckerei, 1864-1865).

[129] Julius Ficker, *Beiträge zur Urkundenlehre*, 2 vols. (Innsbruck: Neudruck der Ausg., 1877; reprint, Aalen: Scientia Verlag, 1966).

[130] Duranti, "Diplomatics I," 14. See also Guyotjeannin, "Expansion of Diplomatics," *American Archivist*, 416-17. For a more detailed history of diplomatics see Georges Tessier, "Diplomatique," *L'Histoire et ses méthodes*, ed. Charles Samarin (Paris: Librarie Gallimard, 1961), 633-76. For a more detailed elaboration of classical diplomatic method see *Encyclopaedia Britannica*, 11th ed. (New York, 1910), s.v. "diplomatics," 300-306; *The New Encyclopaedia Britannica Macropedia*, 15th ed. (Chicago, II., 1974), s.v. "diplomatic," 807-13.

[131] The procedures of internal criticism are elaborated in Langlois and Seignobos, *Introduction to Study*, 141-208.

[132] *Ibid.*, 66-67.

[133] Quoted in Gilbert, *History: Politics or Culture*, 17.

[134] Langlois and Seignobos, *Introduction to Study*, 194.

[135] *Ibid.*, 204. According to Allen Johnson, Langlois' and Seignobos' notion of "collective certainty" is analogous to Ernst Bernheim's notion of "inner probability." See Johnson, *Historian and Historical Evidence*, 144-46.

[136] Carl B. Joynt and Nicholas Rescher, "Evidence in History and the Law," *Journal of Philosophy* 56 (1959): 565.

Chapter Two

[1] The Common law is the dominant legal tradition of Canada, Great Britain, Ireland, the United States, Australia, and New Zealand, and it has had substantial influence on the law of several nations in Asia and Africa.

[2] The Civil law is the dominant legal tradition in most of Western Europe, and of Central and South America, many parts of Asia and Africa and it has also carved out a niche in certain parts of the Common law world (e.g., Québec, Louisiana, Puerto Rico).

[3] For a more detailed examination and comparison of Common law and Civil law approaches to evidence and fact-finding, see Mirjan Damaška, *Evidence Law Adrift* (New Haven.: Yale University Press, 1997).

[4] For the evolution of the jury system see Thomas Andrew Green, *Verdict According to Conscience: Perspectives on the English Criminal Trial 1200-1800* (Chicago: University of Chicago Press, 1985). See also Barbara Shapiro, *Beyond Reasonable Doubt and Probable Cause*.

[5] Damaska, *Evidence Law Adrift*, 28.

[6] Damaška, *Evidence Law Adrift*, 20-21.

[7] Although the main target of Enlightenment philosophers and revolutionary politicians was Roman-canonical criminal procedure which allowed the use of torture to obtain full proof, the principle of free proof also affected civil procedure, though to a lesser degree.

[8] Damaška, *Evidence Law Adrift*, 21.

[9] *Ibid.*, 20.

[10] *Ibid.*, 21-22. The Continental attraction to Common law forms of justice resulted, during the revolutionary period, in a number of Continental countries adopting the jury trial for the adjudication of serious criminal cases. However, Damaška dryly observes, "the Continental love affair with the jury was one of short duration. Country after country instituted reforms requiring jurors to deliberate with a panel of professional judges with the consequence that the jury turned into the lay component of a professionally dominated unitary tribunal." *Ibid.*, 28. Today, Belgium, Denmark, and Switzerland are the only western European countries in which true criminal juries have survived.

[11] Definitions taken from *Black's Law Dictionary*, 6th ed. (St. Paul, Minn.: West Publishing, 1990), s.v. "common law"; "statutory law," "statute."

[12] Gerald L. Gall, *The Canadian Legal System*, 4th ed. (Ottawa: Carswell, 1995), 210.

[13] John Brierley and Roderick A. MacDonald, eds., *Québec Civil Law: An Introduction to Québec Private Law* (Toronto: Emond Montgomery Publications, 1993), par. 91.

[14] For a more detailed discussion of the separation of powers of the legislature and the judiciary and the historical context of that separation, see John Merryman, *Civil law Tradition*, 34-38.

[15] As Damaška points out, however, Civil law adjudicators, "although formally free to disregard legal opinions of their superiors, actually look to higher courts for guidance: opinions of higher-ups are followed as a matter of normal institutional practice, and departures from those opinions entail a sanction – that is, as in common law, reversal on appeal." Damaška, *Evidence Law Adrift*, 9.

[16] Mirjan Damaška, "Presentation of Evidence and Factfinding Precision," *University of Pennsylvania Law Review* 23 (May 1975): 1103-4.

[17] In areas where rights and obligations are at stake, such as the law of contracts and the law of wills, and where the stability of the written word is considered critical to their enforcement, more precise standards are imposed by the Common law. But even in these areas, commentators suggest, the Common law should move towards greater flexibility. Ethan Katsh, for example, suggests that the digital world is transforming the nature of contracts. He argues that the traditional model of paper contracts, with its emphasis on formalism, stability, and clarity, will inevitably give way to to a relational model of contracts, that emphasises fluidity and flexibility; instead of binding parties to an act, the relational model binds parties to a process. See M. Ethan Katsh, "Contracts: Relationships in Cyberspace," in *Law in a Digital World* (New York: Oxford University Press, 1995), 114-32. In the area of wills, John Langbein notes that "what is peculiar to the law of wills is not the prominence of the formalities [e.g., the requirements of writing, witnesses, and signatures] but the judicial insistence that any defect in complying with them automatically and inevitably voids the will." He maintains that the rigid formalism of the Wills Act should be replaced by a substantial compliance doctrine which looks at the question of intent and whether formal defects are actually harmful to the statutory purpose of the Wills Act. See John H. Langbein, "Substantial Compliance with the Wills Act" *Harvard Law Review* 88 (January 1975): 489-531.

[18] Damaška, "Presentation of Evidence," 1104.

[19] In *Evidence Law Adrift*, Damaška points out that in the civil procedure of many Continental countries there are "a considerable number of provisions attributing conclusive weight to specified documentary evidence unless displaced by a specific procedure attacking its validity. Much of this constitutes "preconstituted proof" designed to discourage litigation over certain transactions or to reduce evidentiary difficulties in case of dispute." Damaška, *Evidence Law Adrift*, 21. During the nineteenth century Jeremy Bentham, who was a great admirer of Civil law, attempted with limited success to incorporate the concept of pre-constituted proof into the British legal system for the same purpose. In his legal treatises, Bentham speaks approvingly of the utility of "preappointed evidence" (i.e., evidence specifically created with a view to being used as evidence and thus invested with securities to ensure its trustworthiness) for decreasing litigation in civil cases. His discussion of pre-appointed evidence may be found in Chapter XIV of *An Introductory View of the Rationale of Judicial Evidence* and in Book IV of the *Rationale of Judicial Evidence*. Both are in *Works of Jeremy Bentham*, vol. 6, 60-67; vol. 7, 508-85.

[20] *Wigmore on Evidence*, 11 vols. (Boston: Little, Brown, 1972-1983).

[21] Canada and nine of its provinces are Anglo-American or "Common law" jurisdictions. Québec, on the other hand, is a "Civil law" jurisdiction, possessing a legal tradition rooted in French law. The main source of private law in Québec is the Civil Code. Nevertheless, the law of evidence set out in Book Seven of the 1994 Civil Code of Québec (C.C.Q.) is largely inspired by Common law rules of evidence and the procedural system under which the rules of evidence are enforced is adversarial in nature and therefore belongs to the tradition of English Common law. Reference will be made, therefore, to articles in the C.C.Q. that are analogous to Common law provisions governing the reliability and authenticity of documentary evidence. For a more detailed discussion of the law of evidence in Québec and its relationship to the law of evidence in the rest of Canada see the following: Kathleen Delaney-Beausoleil, "La valeur de preuve des documents d'archives: aspects théoriques," *Les valeurs archivistiques: théorie et pratique. Actes du colloque organisé conjointement par la Division des archives et les Programmes d'archivistique de l'Université Laval, 11 novembre 1993* (Québec: Université Laval, 1994), 25-34; Yves-Marie Morissette, "Title Nine: Proof," *Quebec Civil Law*, eds. Brierley and MacDonald, 687-698; and Léo Ducharme, "The Rules of Evidence in Civil and Commercial Matters in Québec Law," *Essays on the Civil Codes of Québec and St. Lucia*, ed. Raymond A. Landry and Ernest Caparros (Ottawa: University of Ottawa Press, 1984), 75-107.

[22] *Wigmore on Evidence* (Tillers rev., 1983), vol. 1, para. 12.

[23] *Ibid.*, para. 11.

[24] *Black's Law Dictionary*, 6th ed. (St. Paul, Minn.: West Publishing, 1990), s.v. "relevancy."

[25] *Wigmore on Evidence*, (Tillers rev., 1983), vol. 1A, para. 37.4.

[26] *Ibid.*

[27] *Ibid.*

[28] *Wigmore on Evidence*, (Chadbourn rev., 1972), vol. 4, para. 1171.

[29] *Ibid.*, para. 1172.

[30] According to Laurence H. Tribe, such deficiencies, distortions or suppressions "are usually attributed to the four testimonial infirmities of ambiguity, insincerity, faulty perception, and erroneous

memory." For a discussion of these infirmities, see Tribe, "Triangulating Hearsay," *Harvard Law Review* 87 (1974): 957-74.

[31] *Wigmore on Evidence*, vol. 4, para. 1172.

[32] Charles T. McCormick, *McCormick's Handbook of the Law of Evidence*, ed. Edward W. Cleary, 2nd ed. (St. Paul, Minn.: West Publishing, 1972), 584.

[33] J. Douglas Ewart et al., *Documentary Evidence in Canada* (Agincourt, Ont.: Carswell, 1984), 12 (hereafter cited as *Ewart on Documentary Evidence*).

[34] *Ibid.*, 14.

[35] *Wigmore on Evidence*, (Chadbourn rev., 1974), vol. 5, para. 1522.

[36] John Sopinka, et al., *The Law of Evidence in Canada* (Toronto: Butterworths, 1992), 188-189 (hereafter cited as *Sopinka on Evidence*). See also Anthony Sheppard, *Evidence*, rev. ed. (Toronto: Carswell, 1996), para. 783-89 (hereafter cited as *Sheppard on Evidence*).

[37] *Sopinka on Evidence*, 190-92.

[38] [1970] S.C.R. 608, 12 C.R.N.S. 349, 14 D.L.R. (3d) 4, 73 W.W.R. 347.

[39] The arguments for necessity were not based on witness availability since the nurses were present in the courtroom during the trial. Instead necessity was defined in terms of mercantile inconvenience, cost to the parties, and cost to the public in the increased length of trial. See *Sopinka on Evidence*, 192.

[40] The original trial judge in *Ares v Venner* relied on Wigmore's discussion of hospital records in allowing the nurses' notes to be admitted. The Supreme Court's reasons for decision are strikingly similar to the ones Wigmore provides. See *Wigmore on Evidence* (Chadbourn rev., 1976), vol. 6, para. 1707.

[41] *Sopinka on Evidence*, 192. The effect of the nurses' presence in the courtroom on the Court's decision to admit the notes does not appear to be settled. Hall, J. stated that the presence of the nurses in the courtroom eliminated any hearsay dangers posed by faulty perception or inaccuracy since the opponent could have put the nurses on the stand to test their perceptions. In *R. v Khan*, however, McLachlin, J. maintained that the nurses' presence was irrelevant to the decision since any testimony from the nurses probably would have been a futile exercise in terms of testing their memory of the events they recorded. Moreover, since the proponent of the evidence had not called the nurses to testify, the opponent would not be able to cross-examine the nurses; he or she could only lead evidence. See *R. v Khan* [1990] 2 S.C.R. 531, 59 C.C.C. (3d) 92, 79 C.R. (3d) 1, 41, O.A.C. 353, 11 W.C.B. (2d) 10, 113 N.R. 53, cited in *Sopinka on Evidence*, 194.

[42] *Sopinka on Evidence*, 195. With regard to the second change, Ewart disagrees, maintaining that the nurses' statements are more accurately characterised as observations. *Ewart on Documentary Evidence*, 66

[43] Wigmore, *Evidence at Common Law* (Chadbourn rev., 1979), vol. 2, para. 478. But see also *Wigmore*, (Chadbourn rev., 1974), vol. 5, para. 1530, in which he argues that the principle of testimonial assertion does not necessarily exclude all entries made by persons not having personal knowledge of the facts recorded. Wigmore concludes that, "where an entry is made by one person in the regular course of business, recording an oral or written report, made to him by other persons in the regular course of business, of a transaction lying in the personal knowledge of the latter persons, there is no objection to receiving that entry under the present exception, verified by the testimony of the former person only, or of a superior who testifies to the regular course of business, provided the practical inconvenience of producing on the stand the numerous other persons thus concerned would in the particular case outweigh the probable utility of doing so." His conclusion is generally accepted in the business records provision of the Evidence Acts. See also *Ewart on Documentary Evidence*, 61-65, in which Ewart argues for an expansion of the common-law exception to allow for the admissibility of declarations made by a person without personal knowledge of the facts recorded on the grounds of "transmitted duty."

[44] In *Setak Computer Services Corp. v Burroughs Business Machines, Ltd.*, (1977), 15 O.R. (2d) 750, 76 D.L.R. (3d) 641 (H.C.J.) at 755 (O.R.), Griffiths, J., stated, "in my opinion, the common law exception applies only to writings or records made by a person speaking from personal observation or knowledge of the facts recorded." Cited in *Sopinka on Evidence*, 197.

[45] In *R. v Laverty* ((1979), 47 C.C.C. (2d) 60, 9 C.R. (3d) 288 (Ont. C.A.)), an arson case, the Ontario Court of Appeal ruled that notes prepared by a deceased fire investigator were inadmissible as hearsay because they were merely an aide-memoire which the investigator kept for himself and which he was not under a duty to make. Cited in *Sopinka on Evidence*, 197-98.

[46] *Ewart on Documentary Evidence*, 54. In Québec, the presumed reliability of business records is expressed in the C.C.Q., article 2870. According to that article, "the reliability of documents drawn up

in the ordinary course of business or an enterprise, of documents entered in a register kept as required by law and of spontaneous and contemporaneous statements concerning the occurrence of facts is, in particular, presumed to be sufficiently guaranteed."

[47] *Ewart on Documentary* Evidence, 54.

[48] *Cargil Grain Ltd., v Davie Ship Building Ltd.*, [1977] 1 S.C.R. 569, 10 N.R. 347 (S.C.C.); *Setak Computer Services Corp. v Burroughs Business Machines, Ltd.*, (1977), 15 O.R. (2d) 750, 76 D.L.R. (3d) 641 (H.C.J.); but see also *Woods v Elias*, (1978), 21 O.R. (2d) 840 (Co. Ct.), where Court held that application of the *Ares* principle was restricted to hospital records. All cases above cited in *Sopinka on Evidence*, 196.

[49] Canada Evidence Act, R.S.C. 1985, c. C-5, s. 30 [am. 1994, c. 44, s. 91]; Evidence Act, R.S.B.C. 1979, C. 116, s. 48; Manitoba Evidence Act, R.S.M. 1987, c. E150 (also C.C.S.M., c. E150), s. 49; Saskatchewan Evidence Act, R.S.S. 1978, c. S-16, s. 31; Evidence Act, R.S.O. 1990, c.E.23, s. 35; Evidence Act, R.S.Y.T. 1986, c. 57, s. 37; Evidence Act, R.S.N.W.T. 1988, c. E-8, s. 47; Evidence Act, R.S.P.E.I. 1988, c. E-11, s. 32; see also Alberta Evidence Act, R.S.A. 1980, c. A-21, s. 36(1). Citations drawn from *Sheppard on Evidence*, para. 783, fn. 3.

[50] Canada Evidence Act, s. 30(1). For the purposes of this provision, "business" is defined as "any business, profession, trade, calling, manufacture or undertaking of any kind carried on in Canada or elsewhere whether for profit or otherwise, including any activity or operation carried on or performed in Canada or elsewhere by any government, by any department, branch, board, commission or agency of any government, by any court or other tribunal or by any other body or authority performing a function of government". S.30(12), "business". The definition of "business" in the provincial and territorial business record provisions is similarly broad.

[51] 318 U.S. 109, 63 S. Ct. 477 (1943), cited in *Sopinka on Evidence*, 200, n. 139. Sopinka points out that, although it is an American case, the two criteria were included in a Federal provision worded similarly to the Canadian provincial enactments. The summary of the case that follows is based on Sopinka's discussion in *Sopinka on Evidence*, 200-1.

[52] *Ibid.*, 201.

[53] *Ibid.* See also *ibid.*, 210-12 for further discussion of the implied requirement of an absence of a motive to misrepresent in court interpretations of the business record provisions.

[54] *Ibid.*, 203.

[55] Canada Evidence Act, s. 30(6).

[56] *Setak Computer Services Corp. v Burroughs Business Machines Ltd.*, (1977), 15 O.R. (2d) 750, 76 D.L.R. (3d) 641 (H.C.J.), at 760-61. Quoted in *Sopinka on Evidence*, 203-4.

[57] According to Wigmore, "the entry should have been made at or near the time of the transaction recorded – not merely because this is necessary in order to assure a fairly accurate recollection of the matter, but because any trustworthy habit of making regular business records will ordinarily involve the making of the record contemporaneously. The rule fixes no precise time; each case must depend on its own circumstances." *Wigmore on Evidence*, vol. 5, para. 1526.

[58] Kim Lane Scheppele, "The Ground-Zero Theory of Evidence," *Hastings Law Journal* 49 (1997-98): 322-23.

[59] British Columbia, s. 48(2); Manitoba, s. 49(4); Saskatchewan, s. 31 (3); Ontario, s. 35(4); *Winnipeg South Child & Family Services v R.S.* (1986), 40 Man. R. (2d) 64 at 68 (Q.B.) (second-hand hearsay not warranting any weight.). All the cases above cited in *Sheppard on* Evidence, para. 801, fn. 4. See also *Sopinka on Evidence*, 204-5.

[60] *Matheson v Barnes*, [1981] 2 W.W.R. 435 (B.C.S.C.); *Setak Computer Services Corp. v Burroughs Business Machines Ltd.* (1977), 15 O.R. (2d) 76 D.L.R. (3d) 641 (Ont. H.C.); *Olyny v Yeo* [1989] 3 W.W.R. 314 (B.C.C.A.); *Can-Dive Services Ltd., v Pacific Coast Energy Corp.* (1994), 32 C.P.C. (3d) 103 (B.C.S.C.); *Hunt v Westbank Irrigation District*, [1991] 6 W.W.R. 549 at 556 (B.C.S.C.); see also *Fox v White* (1990), 39 C.P.C. (2d) 221 (Alta. C.A.); but see Manitoba Evidence Act, s. 58(1)(a)(ii)(b)(2) (record containing second-hand hearsay admissible if maker prepared it as part of continuous record, under duty to record, and person supplying information had personal knowledge; maker called as witness if available); *Reitze v Brusser*, [1979] 1 W.W.R. 27 (Man. Q.B.). All the cases above cited in *Sheppard on Evidence*, para. 802, fn. 1.

[61] 253 N.Y. 124, 170 N.E. 517 (1930, N.Y.C.A.), cited in *Sopinka on Evidence*, 204. The wording of the relevant provision in the New York statute is analogous to that of the provincial business record provisions.

[62] *Sopinka on Evidence*, 205.

[63] Griffiths, J., in *Setak Computer Services Corp. v Burroughs Business Machines Ltd.* (1977), 15 O.R. (2d) 750, 76 D.L.R. (3d) 641 (Ont. H.C.), at 762-63 (O.R.), cited in *Sopinka on Evidence*, 206.

[64] *Adderly v Bremner* (1967), 67 D.L.R. (2d) 274 (Ont. H.C.), cited in *Sopinka on Evidence*, 205-6.

[65] *Sopinka on Evidence*, 206.

[66] Section 30(1) reads "where oral evidence in respect of a matter would be admissible in a legal proceeding." According to Sopinka, "the statute merely provides a method of proof of an admissible fact. It does not make the document admissible when oral testimony of the same fact would be inadmissible. One interpretation that is open is that if the maker of the record took the witness stand he could not testify as to what someone else told him. That would be inadmissible as hearsay and the same limitation applies to business records under s. 30 of the Canada Evidence Act." *Sopinka on Evidence*, 207.

[67] *R. v Grimba* (1977), 38 C.C.C. (2d) 469 (Ont. Co. Ct.), at 471. Quoted in *Sopinka on Evidence*, 208.

[68] *R. v Boles* (1984), 57 A.R. 232 at 235 (C.A.); *R. v Anthes Bus. Forms Ltd.*, 10 O.R. (2d) 153 at 174; affirmed [1978] 1 S.C.R. 970; *R. v Sanghi* (1971), 6 C.C.C. (2d) 123 (N.S.C.A.); *R. v Penno*, [1977] 3 W.W.R. 361 (B.C.C.A.); see also *R. v Monkhouse*, [1988] 1 W.W.R. 725 (Alta., C.A.) (payroll employee transcribing time cards onto payroll sheets not required to give evidence; proper admission of payroll manager's evidence extracted from payroll records); *Apsassin v Can.* (1987), 17 C.P.C. (2d) 187 (Fed. T.D.) (Indian agent reports being hearsay because made through interpreter but still admissible; trustworthiness required of document not demanding that court be absolutely convinced evidence totally devoid of human error; no reason to believe interpreter biased; both parties agreeing to interpreter thus interpreter merely conduit). All cases above cited in *Sheppard on Evidence*, para. 798, n. 1.

[69] *Adderly v Bremner* (1967), 67 D.L.R. (2d) 274 (Ont. H.C.); *Aynsley v Toronto General Hospital* (1967), 66 D.L.R. (2d) 575; varied 7 D.L.R. (3d) 193; affirmed 25 D.L.R. (3d) 241 (*sub nom. Toronto General Hospital Trustees v Matthews*) (S.C.C.) [Ont.]; *de Genova v de Genova* (1971), 5 R.F.L. 22 (Ont. H.C.); see also *Thompson v Toorenburgh* (1973), 50 D.L.R. (3d) 717; affirmed without written reasons 50 D.L.R. (3d) 717n (S.C.C.) [B.C.]. All cases above cited in *Sheppard on Evidence*, para. 801, n. 5.

[70] *Sopinka on Evidence*, 208.

[71] *Ibid.*, 209.

[72] *McCormick on Evidence*, 3rd ed. (St. Paul: West Publishing, 1984), 875, quoted in *Sopinka on Evidence*, 209. See also *Ewart on Documentary Evidence*, 65-66.

[73] At Common law, official statements fall into three categories: a *register* or *record*, which "comprises in a single volume or file a *series* of homogeneous statements, *recorded* by entries made more or less *regularly*." A register or record is kept in official custody. Typical examples of registers and records are birth, marriage, and death registers, vital statistics and records of conveyance. A *return* or *report* "is a single document *made separately* for each transaction as occasion arises." It too is preserved in official custody. A *certificate*, on the other hand, "is not preserved by the official, but is *given out* by him to an applicant for the latter's use." Typical examples of certificates are birth, marriage, and death certificates as well as certified copies of public documents. From *Wigmore on Evidence*, (Chadbourn rev., 1974), vol. 5, para. 1636.

[74] According to Wigmore, "The general experience that a rule of official duty or a requirement of legal conditions is fulfilled by those upon whom it is incumbent has given rise occasionally to a presumption of due *performance of official duty*. This presumption is more often mentioned than enforced; and its scope as a real presumption is indefinite and hardly capable of reduction to rules." *Wigmore on Evidence* (Chadbourn rev., 1981), vol. 9, para. 2534. See also *Sopinka on Evidence*, 119.

[75] *Wigmore on Evidence* (Chadbourn rev., 1974), vol. 5, para. 1632.

[76] *Ibid.*

[77] See *Sheppard on Evidence*, para. 818-22; *Sopinka on Evidence*, 231.

[78] *Wigmore on* Evidence, (Chadbourn rev., 1974), vol. 5, para. 1632.

[79] *Nowlan v Elderkin*, [1950] 3 D.L.R. 773 (N.S.T.D.), cited in *Sheppard on Evidence*, para. 823.

[80] *Finestone v R.*, [1953] 2 S.C.R. 107 at 108 [Que.]; *R v Halpin*, [1975] Q.B. 907 (C.A.), cited in *Sheppard on Evidence*, para. 824.

[81] Section 26(1) states that, "a copy of any entry in any book kept in any office or department of the Government of Canada, or in any commission, board or other branch of the public service of Canada, shall be received as evidence of such entry, and of the matters, transactions and accounts therein recorded, if it is proved by the oath or affidavit of an officer of such department, commission, board or other branch of the public service, that he book was, at the time of the making of the entry, one of the ordinary books kept in such office, department, commission, board or other branch of the public service, that the entry was made in the usual and ordinary course of business of such office,

department, commission, board, or other branch of the public service, and that such copy is a true copy thereof." Canada Evidence Act, R.S.C. 1985, c. C-5.

[82] Stanley Raffel, *Matters of Fact: A Sociological Inquiry* (London: Routledge, 1979), 23, 29.

[83] Marilyn T. MacCrimmon, "Developments in the Law of Evidence: The 1988-89 Term The Process of Proof: Schematic Constraints," *The Supreme Court Law Review*, 2nd ser., vol. 1 (Toronto: Butterworths, 1990): 346-47.

[84] *Ibid.*, 347-48. The analogous argument in history is that the historian's perspective shapes his presentation of the facts. The main points of similarity and difference between historians' concern with the possibility of objectivity or detachment in the writing of history and the legal discipline's concern with the possibility of impartiality or objectivity in adjudication are discussed in William Twining, "Some Scepticism about Some Scepticism," in *Rethinking Evidence: Exploratory Essays* (Oxford: Blackwell, 1990), 103-9.

[85] Scheppele, "The Ground-Zero Theory of Evidence," 333-34.

[86] *Wigmore on Evidence*, (Chadbourn rev., 1972), vol. 4, para. 1172. See also *Sheppard on Evidence*, para. 529.

[87] *Wigmore on Evidence*, (Chadbourn rev., 1978), vol. 7, para. 2130. In Québec, the rules governing the authentication of documents are found in the following articles of the C.C.Q.: 2813-2821 (dealing with "authentic acts", i.e., public documents), 2822-2825 (dealing with "semi-authentic acts", i.e., public documents issued by foreign bodies), 2826-2830 (dealing with "private writings," including writings related to acts carried out in the usual and ordinary course of business), and 2831-2836 (dealing with "other," i.e., unsigned writings).

[88] Benning, J., in *Stamper v Griffin*, 20 Ga. 312, 320 (1856), cited in *ibid*.

[89] See *Wigmore on Evidence*, (Chadbourn rev., 1978), vol. 7, para. 2132; *Sheppard on* Evidence, para. 533; *Sopinka on Evidence*, 949-50.

[90] *Sheppard on Evidence*, para. 531. See also *Sopinka on Evidence*, 950-53, 965; *Wigmore on Evidence*, Chadbourn rev., 1974), vol. 5, para. 2133, 2134, 2153.

[91] *Ewart on Documentary Evidence*, 69.

[92] *Sopinka on Evidence*, 953.

[93] Section 30(6) of the Canada Evidence Act stipulates that "the court may, on production of any record, examine the record, admit any evidence in respect thereof given orally or by affidavit including evidence as to the circumstances in which the information contained in the record was written, recorded, stored or reproduced, and draw any reasonable inference from the form or content of the record." Canada Evidence Act, R.S.C. 1985, c. C-5.

[94] *Ewart on Documentary Evidence*, 105.

[95] *Ibid.*, 105-6.

[96] See *Wigmore on Evidence*, (Chadbourn rev., 1978), vol. 7, para. 2158, 2159; *Sopinka on Evidence*, 941-44; *Ewart on Documentary Evidence*, 173.

[97] *Wigmore on Evidence*, (Chadbourn rev., 1978), vol. 7, para. 2158.

[98] Such records are not, however, presumed to be reliable. As Sheppard points out, "leading writers on the law of evidence disagree about whether or not the Common law recognized an exception to the hearsay rule for a statement in a document at least 30 years old." See Baker, *The Hearsay Rule*, (1950), p. 162; *McMillan v Colford* (1932), 5 M.P.R. 127 at 133 (N.B.C.A.); *Tobias v Nolan* (1985), 71 N.S.R. (2d) 92; affirmed 78 N.S.R. (2d) 271 (C.A.) (ancient document is over 20 years old); *Apsassin v Canada* (1987), 17 C.P.C. (2d) 187 (Fed. T.D.) (documents over 50 years old admissible; makers deceased and documents almost old enough to be termed historical documents); *R. v Zundel* (1987), 56 C.R. (3d) 1; leave to appeal to S.C.C. refused 56 C.R. (3d) xxviii [Ont.]; *Delgamuukw v British Columbia*, [1989] 6 W.W.R. 308; see also [1991] 3 W.W.R. 97 at 166 (B.C.S.C.) reversed on other grounds, [1997] 3 S.C.R. 1010. All the cases above cited in *Sheppard on Evidence*, para. 805, fn. 1. For a detailed examination of the ancient documents rule, see Geoffrey S. Lester, "The Problem of Ancient Documents [Parts I and 2]," *The Advocates Quarterly* 20: 1 and 2 (Jan. and Mar. 1998): 101-31; 133-75.

[99] In some jurisdictions, the court or the legislature has reduced the period to twenty years. See Ontario Evidence Act, s. 59 [am. 1993, c. 27, Sched.] (twenty years); Yukon Evidence Act, s. 56; Northwest Territories Evidence Act, s. 55 (twenty years); *Tobias v Nolan* (1985), 71 N.S.R. (2d) 92 at 99; affirmed 78 N.S.R. (2d) 271 (C.A.) (twenty years at Common law); *Delgamuukw v British Columbia*, [1989] 6 W.W.R. 308 (B.C.S.C), all the cases above cited in *Sheppard on Evidence*, para. 532, fn. 2.

[100] *Sopinka on Evidence*, 955.

[101] *Wigmore on Evidence*, (Chadbourn rev., 1978), vol. 7, para. 2134. Wigmore goes on to point out: "Whether the mere age is itself an evidential circumstance at all has been judiciously doubted, though it may be argued that men would hardly undertake the risk of forgery for the sole use of posterity, and thus the circumstance of age alone is some evidence; but it has never been suggested to be sufficient of itself."

[102] As Sopinka points out: "if, however, there is any suspicious appearance on the face of the document by erasure, interlineation or otherwise, the court will require proof of it in like manner as that of a document of more recent date." *Sopinka on Evidence*, 955.

[103] Ellenborough, L.C.J., in *Roe v Rawlings*, 7 East 279, 291 (1806), cited in *Wigmore on Evidence*, (Chadbourn rev., 1978), vol. 7, para. 2137.

[104] *Croughton v* Blake, 12 M. & W. 205, 208 (1843) Parke, B., cited in Wigmore *on Evidence*, (Chadbourn rev., 1978), vol. 7, para. 2139, n. 2. See also cases cited in *Sopinka on Evidence*, 956, n. 177.

[105] *Sopinka on Evidence*, 956.

[106] *Ibid.*, 956.

[107] *Wigmore on Evidence*, (Chadbourn rev., 1978), vol. 7, para. 2161.

[108] *Ibid.* At Common law, a corporate seal does not carry the same presumption of trustworthiness as an official seal. See *ibid.*, para. 2169. However, Sopinka points out that, "in general, a corporation seal may be proved by anyone familiar with it, without calling a witness who saw it affixed. ... The corporate seal will be presumed to have been affixed by the proper person, although this may be rebutted by the proof of absence of authority." *Sopinka on Evidence*, 967, 954.

[109] *Wigmore on Evidence*, (Chadbourn rev., 1972), vol. 4, para. 1172, p. 396.

[110] *Ibid.*, para. 1178. If a document is being introduced simply to prove its existence, the best evidence rule does not apply. The document must still be authenticated, however. In Québec, the rules governing the production of documentary originals are found in the C.C.Q., articles 2840-2842 (dealing with the reproduction of certain documents) and 2860-2861 (dealing with means of proof).

[111] *Ibid.*, para. 1232.

[112] *Ibid.*, para. 1179.

[113] (1879), 3 S.C.R. 296, at 304, cited in *Sopinka on Evidence*, 932.

[114] *Sopinka on Evidence*, 932; *Sheppard on Evidence*, para. 553; *Wigmore on Evidence*, (Chadbourn rev., 1972), vol. 4, para. 1233.

[115] *Sheppard on Evidence*, para. 554.

[116] Canadian law does not distinguish among the various kinds of secondary evidence. As Sopinka points out, "so far as admissibility is concerned, there are no degrees of secondary evidence, and oral evidence of the contents of a paper from a person who has read it and a copy of the document are put exactly on the same footing. While more weight may be attached to a copy of a document than oral evidence of it, there is no requirement to account for copies before oral evidence can be adduced." *Sopinka on Evidence*, 934.

[117] *Sheppard on Evidence*, para. 564-71; *Sopinka on Evidence*, 933-36.

[118] *Sopinka on Evidence*, 937.

[119] *Sheppard on Evidence*, para. 580.

[120] R.S.C. 1985, c. C-5.

[121] *Sopinka on Evidence*, 939-40. See also Charles T. McCormick et al., *McCormick on Evidence*, ed. John William Strong, 4th ed. (St. Paul, Minn.: West Publishing, 1992), vol. 2, para. 231; *Sheppard on Evidence*, para. 541.

[122] *McCormick on Evidence*, vol. 2, para. 231.

[123] 265 F.2d 418, 76 A.L.R.2d 1344 (2d Circ.1959).

[124] See also *United States v Alexander*, 326 F.2d 736 (4th Cir.1964).

[125] *R. v Sunila*, (1986), 26 C.C.C. (3d) 331 at 337-39 (N.S.S.C.) (data collected mechanically by radar and computer); *Tecoglas Inc. v Domglas Inc.: Domglas Inc., v Tecoglas Inc.* (1985), 3 C.P.C. (2d) 275 (Ont. H.C.) (computer records admissible). Cases cited in *Sheppard on Evidence*, para. 792. In Québec, the rules governing the reliability of computerised business records are found in the C.C.Q., articles 2837-2839.

[126] Under s.30(12), "'record' includes the whole or part of any book, document, paper, card, tape or other thing on or in which information is written, recorded, stored or reproduced". The Court in *R v Vanlerberghe* stated that, "[section 30] clearly covers mechanical as well as manual book-keeping records and the keeping of records, and the flow-out or printout of that bookkeeping system clearly falls within the meaning of "records" in s. 30 and was therefore admissible." Quoted in *Sopinka on Evidence*, 214.

[127] *R. v McMullen* (1979), 100 D.L.R. (3d) 671 at 674-76 (Ont. C.A.); *R. v Bell* (1982), 35 O.R. (2d) 164; affirmed 55 O.R. (2d) 287 (S.C.C.); *R. v Hanlon* (1985), 69 N.S.R. (2d) 266 (Co. Ct.); *R. v Vanlerberghe* (1978), 6 C.R. (3d) 222 (B.C.C.A.); *R. v Burns Foods Ltd.* (1983), 42 A.R. 70 (Prov. Ct.); *R. v Cordell* (1982), 39 A.R. 281 (C.A.); see also *Prism Hospital Software Inc., v Hospital Medical Records Institute*, [1991] 2 W.W.R. 157 (B.C.S.C.) (files on floppy disks and tapes being documents stored on magnetic media). Cases cited in *Sheppard on Evidence*, para. 547.
[128] Uniform Law Conference of Canada, "Uniform Electronic Evidence Act Consultation Paper," March 1997, para. 3, <http://www.law.ualberta.ca/alri/ulc/> (March 1997) (hereafter "ULCC Consultation Paper").
[129] *R. v Vanlerberghe* (1978), 6 C.R. (3d) 222 at 224 (B.C.C.A.).
[130] *R. v Burns Foods Ltd.* (1983), 42 A.R. 70 at 75 (Prov. Ct.).
[131] *Sopinka on Evidence*, 214, alluding to the Court's decision in *R. v McMullen*.
[132] *Sopinka on Evidence*, 214, alluding to the Court's decision in *R. v Vanlerberghe*.
[133] Ken Chasse, "Appendix J: Computer-Produced Records in Court Proceedings," in *Proceedings of the Seventy-Sixth Annual Meeting [of the] Uniform Law Conference of Canada*, Edmonton, Alta, University of Alberta Faculty of Law, 1995, 15, <http://www.law.ualberta.ca/alri/ulc/> (March 1997).
[134] The Uniform Electronic Evidence Act was adopted by the ULCC in 1998. A slightly revised version was introduced to the House of Commons as part 3 ("Amendments to the Canada Evidence Act") of Bill C-6 ("An Act to support and promote electronic commerce by protecting personal information that is collected, used or disclosed in certain circumstances, by providing for the use of electronic means to communicate or record information or transactions and by amending the Canada Evidence Act, the Statutory Instruments Act and the Statute Revision Act") during the Second Session, Thirty-Sixth Parliament (48 Elizabeth II, 1999). Bill C-6 was passed by the House of Commons on October 26, 1999.
[135] Uniform Law Conference of Canada, "Uniform Electronic Evidence Act [and Comments]," n.d. <http://www.law.ualberta.ca/alri/ulc/> (September 1998) (hereafter "ULCC Evidence Act and Comments"). S.1(b) "electronic record". In the model statute, "data" is defined as "representations, in any form, of information or concepts" s.1(a) "data". According to the drafters of the statute, the definition of data "ensures that the Act applies to any form of information in an electronic record, whether figures, facts, or ideas." *Ibid.*, "Section 1: Comment." The printouts excluded from the definition will be discussed below in the context of revisions to the best evidence rule.
[136] "ULCC Consultation Paper," para. 1.
[137] *Ibid.*, para. 31-34. The position taken by the ULCC is opposite to the one taken by the drafters of the 1995 Australian Uniform Evidence Act. Under s.146(3) of the Uniform Evidence Act , electronic records are admissible without foundation evidence. The Australian Law Reform Commission noted: "It is true that errors, accidental and deliberate, occur and can occur at every stage of the process of recordkeeping by computers. The fact is, however, that they are the exception rather than the rule, they tend to occur at the stage when the information is fed into the system, and there are techniques available which can be, and are, employed at each stage of the recordkeeping process to eliminate error. ... To require extensive proof, on each occasion, of the reliability of the computer records is to place a costly burden on the party seeking to tender the evidence, to give the opposing party a substantial tactical weapon and to add to the work of the courts. In many cases there will be no bona fide issue as to the accuracy of the records. It is more efficient to leave the party against whom the evidence is led to raise any queries and make any challenges it may have." Quoted in Stephen Odgers, *Uniform Evidence Law* (Sydney, Australia: The Federation Press, 1995), para. 146.3. The Australian law thus places the tactical burden on the opponent of evidence to *disprove* the trustworthiness of electronic records, rather than on the proponent of the evidence to *prove* trustworthiness as is done in the ULCC statute.
[138] The Common law and statutory business records exceptions to the hearsay rule are unaffected by the Act. The ULCC maintains that the existing law "does not require separate proof of the truth of a record's contents. The making and use of the record in the course of business provides sufficient guarantee of the truth of the record's contents to support admission." See "ULCC Consultation Paper," para. 54. In other words, the reliability of a record's contents is determined in relation to the business context in which the record was created, rather than in relation to the technological context of its creation and can be adequately demonstrated under existing law. The ULCC also takes the position that the existing procedures for authenticating records work equally well for paper or electronic records. Accordingly, the Uniform Act simply confirms the Common law rule by asserting that "the person seeking to introduce an electronic record has the burden of proving its authenticity by evidence capable of supporting a finding that the electronic record is what the person claims it to be."

See "ULCC Evidence Act and Comments," s. 3. As with paper records, the evidence may be given orally or by affidavit and may be challenged by the opponent of the evidence.

[139] "ULCC Consultation Paper," para. 24-26. As the framers of the Act point out, this position is consistent with the C.C.Q., articles 2837-2839, and with recent amendments to the New Brunswick Evidence Act on Electronically Stored Documents, S.N.B. 1996 c. 52. In both cases, the integrity of the records must be demonstrated as a condition of being admitted and this is achieved by requiring evidence of the reliability of the computer system that produced it. See "ULCC Consultation Paper," para. 27.

[140] According to the drafters of the Act, "the Act does not say expressly that the proponent of an electronic record does not have to produce an original, but the displacement of the usual best evidence rule will have that effect. ... Even if there is an original of an electronic record, as in the case of an electronic image of a paper document, the Act does not require the production of the paper. Nor does it require that the original have been destroyed before the electronic image becomes admissible. The Act sets up a rule for admitting electronic records. Records retention policies, for paper or electronic records, are beyond its scope and should not be determined by the law of evidence in any event. Someone who destroys paper originals in the ordinary course of business, ideally in accordance with a rational schedule, should not be prejudiced in using reliable electronic versions of those records." "ULCC Evidence Act and Comments," s. 4(1).

[141] *Ibid.*

[142] "ULCC Evidence Act and Comments," s. 4(2).

[143] *Ibid.*, s1(c) "electronic records system".

[144] The drafters of the Act point out that, "an electronic record is not part of the system that produced it. Section 4 provides that the integrity of a record can be proved by proving the integrity of the system that produced it. If the system included the record itself, section 4 would not work." "ULCC Evidence Act and Comments," s. 1(c).

[145] *Ibid.*, s. 5(a).

[146] The drafters of the Act point out that "This does not mean that a simple computer record needs the support of a sophisticated recordkeeping system in order to be admissible. A small business, for example, may have a computer with off-the-shelf software and no 'records management manual'. The recordkeeping system is implied in the operation of the computer. It should be recognized, however, that the integrity of records in such a system may be exposed to more successful attack in court." "ULCC Evidence Act and Comments," s. 5(a).

[147] *Ibid.*

[148] "ULCC Evidence Act and Comments," s. 7.

[149] "ULCC Evidence Act and Comments," s. 8.

[150] Chasse's list includes the following factors: (1) sources of data and information; (2) contemporaneous recording: (3) routine business data and information; (4) data entry; (5) business reliance; (6) software reliability; and (7) security. See Chasse, "Appendix J: Computer-Produced Records," 20.

[151] For example, the framers of the Act point out, the New Brunswick Evidence Act on Electronically Stored Documents aims at a standard below that of the National Standard but acceptable to the New Brunswick legislature.

[152] "ULCC Consultation Paper," para. 68-72.

[153] "ULCC Evidence Act and Comments," s. 6.

[154] The adversary system is another distinguishing feature of Common law adjudication that has no analogue in the Civil law tradition. In Civil law proceedings party lawyers play a significantly smaller role than they do in Common law proceedings. The pre-trial collection of evidence and the appointment of expert witnesses are both controlled by the judge or another court official. At the trial, although party lawyers are permitted to question witnesses, fact-finding is carried out primarily by the judge. As Damaška summarises it, "the examination of evidence [is] organized as a single integrative enterprise without a formal order of proof on the Common law pattern. The fission of fact-finding into two contrary cases – plaintiff's and defendant's, each orchestrated by the party's lawyer – is unknown or rudimentary." Damaška, *Evidence Law Adrift*, 78.

[155] Dale A. Nance, "The Best Evidence Principle," *Iowa Law Review* 73 (January 1988): 235.

[156] Damaška, "Presentation of Evidence," 1093-94. The epistemological frailties of the Civil law's inquisitorial approach to fact-finding are discussed at 1091-92.

[157] Gilbert, *Law of Evidence*, 6th ed., 3.

[158] Nance, "The Best Evidence Principle," 240.

[159] *Ibid.*, 265.

[160] *Ibid.*, 244.

Chapter Three

[1] James Wilkinson, "A Choice of Fictions: Historians, Memory, and Evidence," *PMLA* 111 (Jan. 1996): 84.

[2] Gertrude Himmelfarb, "Postmodernist History," in *On Looking into the Abyss: Untimely Thoughts on Culture and Society* (New York: Alfred A. Knopf, 1994), 136.

[3] *Ibid.*, 133.

[4] David Hackett Fischer, *Historians' Fallacies: Toward a Logic of Historical Thought* (New York: Harper & Row, 1970), 62.

[5] The following manuals of methodology were consulted: Jacques Barzun and Henry F. Graff, *The Modern Researcher*, 5th ed. (New York: Houghton Mifflin Co., 1992); Louis Gottschalk, "The Historian and the Historical Document," in *The Use of Personal Documents in History, Anthropology, and Sociology*, prepared for the Committee on Appraisal of Research, ed. Louis Gottschalk, Clyde Kluckhohn, et al. (New York: Social Science Research Council, [1945]), 3-78; G.J. Renier, *History: Its Purpose and Method.* (New York: Harper & Row, 1950); Robert Jones Shafer, ed. *A Guide to Historical Method.* 3rd ed. (Belmont, Calif.: Wadsworth Publishing Co., 1980).

[6] The association of authenticity with the trustworthiness of the record as a record (rather than as a statement of facts) is found in all the manuals of historical methodology with one exception. In *The Modern Researcher*, Barzun and Graff make the distinction but reverse the definitions of authenticity and reliability. Barzun and Graff, *Modern Researcher*, 99.

[7] Barzun and Graff do not use these terms, but again they make the same distinction.

[8] G.R. Elton, "Two Kinds of History," in *Which Road to the Past?* (New Haven: Yale University Press, 1983), 101. Elton's comments are echoed by Louis Gottschalk who points out that to say a statement is credible does not mean that the statement reflects what actually happened, "but that it is *as close to* [reflecting] *what actually happened as we can learn from a critical examination of the best available sources.* The historian thus establishes *credibility* or *verisimilitude* (in this special sense of conformity with a critical examination of the sources) rather than *truth.*" See Louis Gottschalk, "The Historian and the Historical Document," 35.

[9] Fischer, *Historians' Fallacies*, 62.

[10] Marc Bloch, *The Historian's Craft* (New York: Alfred A. Knopf, 1963), 62.

[11] Michael Stanford, *A Companion to the Study of History* (Oxford: Blackwell, 1994), 160-61.

[12] The discussion of external criticism is found in Shafer, *Guide*, 127-47; in Gottschalk, "The Historian and the Historical Document," 28-34, in Renier, *History*, 108-10; and in Bloch, *Historian's Craft*, 90-110. External criticism also includes the application of all the auxiliary disciplines of history, e.g., paleography, numismatics, chronology, sigillography, and, of course, diplomatics. However, since their application is traditionally confined to ancient and medieval documents, they will not be discussed here. The application of diplomatics to modern and contemporary records is the subject of the next chapter.

[13] Leon J. Goldstein, "Historical Realism and Skepticism," in *Historical Knowing* (Austin: University of Texas Press, 1976), 43.

[14] Internal Criticism is discussed in Renier, *History*, 162-65; in Gottschalk, "The Historian and the Historical Document," 35-47; and in Shafer, *Guide*, 149-70. Shafer and Gottschalk discuss the topic in very similar terms and in similar depth. The difference is mainly in the way the two authors identify categories. For the most part, my discussion of internal criticism follows Shafer's categories.

[15] Shafer, *Guide*, 153.

[16] *Ibid.*, 16

[17] Most of the reasons cited in modern manuals that support an assumption of bias and, conversely, those supporting an assumption of neutrality, are analogous and, in many cases, identical, to those identified by Langlois and Seignobos in the nineteenth century, and by Baudouin in the sixteenth century. The awareness of cultural bias however, is a twentieth century development.

[18] Shafer, *Guide*, 155.

[19] Le Goff, *History and Memory*, 130. See also Charles A. Beard, "Written History as an Act of Faith," in *The Philosophy of History in Our Time*, ed. Hans Meyerhoff (New York: Doubleday, 1959), 150-51; Carl Becker, "What are Historical Facts?" in *Detachment and the Writing of History: Essays and Letters of Carl Becker*, ed. Phil L. Snyder (Ithaca, N.Y.: Cornell University Press, 1958), 56-59; Collingwood, *Idea of History*, 248. For the main points of similarity and difference between historians' concern with the

possibility of objectivity or detachment in the writing of history and the legal discipline's concern with the possibility of impartiality or objectivity in adjudication see Twining, "Some Skepticism about Some Skepticism," *Re-Thinking Evidence*, 103-9.

[20] The measure of the reliability of historians' accounts of the past goes considerably beyond their treatment of documentary evidence. For the purposes of the present study, however, the treatment of reliability is confined to that of the *record's* reliability. The peer review process is the ultimate arbiter of the reliability of the historian's account of the past.

[21] Gottschalk, "The Historian and the Historical Document," 39.

[22] Bloch, *Historian's Craft*, 64.

[23] Stanford, *Companion to Study of History*, 163.

[24] Le Goff, *History and Memory*, 184.

[25] Elton, "Which Road to the Past," 93.

[26] Vernon K. Dibble, "Four Types of Inference from Documents to Events," *History and Theory* 3 (1964): 204-5.

[27] For example, Dibble points out, "[t]ranscripts of some legal proceedings may be less complete than they would be otherwise because interested parties can have remarks 'stricken from the record'. In contrast, alterations initiated by an interested party to his own advantage are likely to make for a more complete and a more accurate record if the recordkeeper is in a position to make his own independent check on the accuracy of the suggested alteration." *Ibid.*, 207-8.

[28] *Ibid.*, 207-8.

[29] Robert C. Sharman, "Causation in Historical Study," in *Debates and Discourses: Selected Archival Writings on Archival Theory 1951-1990* (Canberra: Australian Society of Archivists, 1995), 102.

[30] *Ibid.*, 110-11.

[31] The relevant case is *Adderly v Bremner*, which is discussed on p. 42 above.

[32] Sharman, "Causation," 111.

[33] *Ibid.*, 111.

[34] Fischer, *Historians' Fallacies*, 62.

[35] Mark Cousins, "The Practice of Historical Investigation," in *Poststructuralism and the Question of History*, ed. Derek Attridge, Geoff Bennington and Robert Young (Cambridge: Cambridge University Press, 1987), 131.

[36] Pierre Braun, "La valeur documentaire des lettres de rémission," cited in Natalie Zemon Davis, *Fiction in the Archives: Pardon Tales and their Tellers in Sixteenth Century France* (Stanford, Calif.: Stanford University Press, 1987), 3.

[37] *Ibid.*, 4.

[38] *Ibid.*, 5. As Davis further explains, "Letters and memoirs from peasants and artisans are rare. Marriage contracts, wills, and other contracts are plentiful and tell us much about the actions, plans, and sensibilities of men and women who could not even sign their names at the bottom, but the documents themselves are dominated by notarial sequences and formulae. Letters of remission were also collaborative efforts ... but they gave much greater scope to the person to whom the notary was listening. Depositions and records of interrogations in criminal cases are extant for certain jurisdictions in the sixteenth century and are valuable indications of the way people recounted events. But witnesses were supposed to confine themselves to what they had seen or heard of a crime, and their stories often lack a beginning and an end ... they ... say little about motive ... and they do not [always] tell how the affair turned out. ... As for the accused ... their testimony was ordinarily directed at every moment by the judge." *Ibid.*, 5-6.

[39] Dibble, "Four Types of Inference," 209.

[40] R.G. Collingwood, *Idea of History*, 260.

[41] An obvious exception are cases involving fraud, e.g., the issuing of forged cheques or fraudulent electronic funds transfer. In such cases, the inauthentic record is admitted for the purposes of proving the fraud.

[42] C.R. Cheney, "The Records of Medieval England," in *Medieval Texts and Studies* (Oxford: Clarendon Press, [1956], 1973), 11.

[43] Le Goff, *History and Memory*, 183.

[44] Shafer, *Guide*, 149.

[45] Davis, *Fiction in the Archives*, 5.

[46] Carlo Ginzburg, "Checking the Evidence: The Judge and the Historian," *Questions of Evidence: Proof, Practice, and Persuasion across the Disciplines*, ed. James Chandler, Arnold I. Davidson, and Harry Harootunian (Chicago: University of Chicago Press, 1994), 294.

[47] Roland Barthes, "Historical Discourse," in *Introduction to Structuralism*, ed. Michael Lane (New York: Basic Books, 1970), 153-54.

[48] This explanation is drawn from John Fiske, "Signifier/signified," *Key Concepts in Communication and Cultural Studies*, 2nd ed. (New York: Routledge, 1994)

[49] Linda Hutcheon, *A Poetics of Postmodernism: History, Theory Fiction* (New York: Routledge, 1988), 122.

[50] Richard J. Evans, *In Defense of History* (New York: Norton, 1997), 81.

[51] Chandler, Davidson, and Harootunian, "Introduction," in *Questions of Evidence*, 5.

[52] This etymology of the terms "document" and "monument" is drawn from Jacques Le Goff, "Documento/Monumento," in *Enciclopedia Einaudi* (Turin: Einaudi, 1978), vol. 5, 38-48.

[53] Michel Foucault, *The Archaeology of Knowledge*, trans. A.M. Sheridan Smith (New York: Harper and Row, 1972), 7.

[54] Le Goff, *History and Memory*, 184.

[55] Quoted in Petrucci, "Illusion of Authentic History," *Writers and Readers in Medieval Italy*, 237.

[56] *Ibid.*

[57] Mario Liverani, quoted in *ibid.*, 238.

[58] For an overview of new directions in the area of "qualitative" or "social" diplomatics, see Olivier Guyotjeannin, "The Expansion of Diplomatics as a Discipline," *American Archivist* 59 (Fall 1996): 417-19. For a sample of new directions in the more specific area of sigillography (the study of seals), see the selection of articles compiled in Brigitte Bedos-Rezak, ed., *Form and Order in Medieval France: Studies in Social and Quantitative Sigillography* (Aldershot: Variorium Reprints, 1993).

[59] Petrucci, "Illusion of Authentic History," 238.

[60] *Ibid.*, 239.

[61] *Ibid.*, 240-46.

[62] Himmelfarb, "Postmodernist History," 132.

[63] J.L. Austin, *How to Do Things with Words*, 2nd ed. (Cambridge, Mass.: Harvard University Press, 1975), 109-10.

[64] Keith Jenkins, *Re-Thinking History* (London: Routledge, 1991), 39.

[65] *Ibid.* The "problem of other minds" is also at the heart of the legal hearsay rule prohibiting the admissibility of testimonial statements that cannot be tested by cross-examination.

[66] Collingwood, *Idea of History*, 282-302.

[67] Himmelfarb, 131, 133.

[68] *Ibid.*, 140. Himmelfarb's comments in this passage are directed at postmodernists in general and at the work of Hayden White in particular, whom she calls "the leading postmodern philosopher of history." For White's views on history as narrative discourse, see White, *Metahistory: The Historical Imagination in Nineteenth-Century Europe* (Baltimore: Johns Hopkins University Press, 1973); *Tropics of Discourse: Essays in Cultural Criticism* (Baltimore: Johns Hopkins University Press, 1978); *The Content of the Form: Narrative Discourse and Historical Representation* (Baltimore: Johns Hopkins University Press, 1987). See also Keith Jenkins, "On Hayden White," in *On 'What is History?': From Carr and Elton to Rorty and White* (London: Routledge, 1995), 134-79.

[69] Raymond Martin, Joan W. Scott, and Cushing Strout, "Forum on *Telling the Truth About History*," *History and Theory* 34 (1995): 320.

[70] Carlo Ginzburg, "Checking the Evidence," *Questions of Evidence*, 294.

[71] *Ibid.*, 295.

[72] Jean Samuel, "Electronic Mail: Information Exchange or Information Loss?" in *Electronic Information Resources and Historians: European Perspectives*, ed. Seamus Ross and Edward Higgs (Göttingen and London: Max-Planck-Institut für Geschichte and the British Library Board, 1993), 61.

[73] Charles M. Dollar, *Archival Theory and Information Technologies: The Impact of Information Technologies on Archival Principles and Methods*, ed. Oddo Bucci (Macerata: University of Macerata, 1992), 50-51.

[74] *Ibid.*, 49.

[75] *Ibid.*, 37. See also *ibid.*, app. C.

[76] David Bearman, "Archival Principles and the Electronic Office," in *Information Handling in Offices and Archives*, ed. Angelika Menne-Haritz (München: K.G. Saur, 1993), 190.

[77] Le Goff, *History and Memory*, 183.

[78] The effect of electronic records on historical research and on the attributability and verifiability of electronic sources of history are discussed, for example, in Ross and Higgs, eds. *Electronic Information Resources* and in R.J. Morris, ed. "Historians and the Electronically Created Record," *History and Computing* 4 (1992).

[79] Ronald Zweig, "Beyond Content: Electronic Fingerprints and the Use of Documents," in *Electronic Information* Resources, 254.

[80] *Ibid.*, 255.

[81] *Ibid.*, 254.

[82] David Bearman, "Record-Keeping Systems," *Archivaria* 36 (Autumn 1993): 17. The electronic records management regulations issued by the U.S. National Archives and Records Administration also draw a distinction between an electronic information system and an electronic recordkeeping system. An electronic information system is defined as: "A system that contains and provides access to computerized Federal records and other information." An electronic recordkeeping system is defined as: "An electronic system in which records are collected, organized, and categorized to facilitate their preservation, retrieval, use, and disposition." 36 C.F.R. [Code of Federal Regulations] Chapter XII, Part 1234.2 subpart A: "Definitions," 1999.

[83] Paul Marsden, "What is the Future? Comparative Notes on the Electronic Record-keeping Projects of the University of Pittsburgh and the University of British Columbia," *Archivaria* 43 (Spring 1997): 162.

[84] Zweig, "Beyond Content," 257.

[85] Peter Denley, "The Flood and the Hunt: Data Creation, Storage and Retrieval in the Electronic Age," in *Electronic Information Resources*, 23.

[86] At the outset of the lawsuit, only Reagan's electronic mail was at issue. By the end of the lawsuit, the electronic mail generated by the Bush and Clinton White House was also at issue.

[87] *Armstrong II*, 1 F.3d 1274, 1287 (D.C. Cir. 1993).

[88] 44 U.S.C. para. 2201 *et seq.*, 2901 *et seq.*, 3101 *et seq.*, and 3301 *et seq.* The FRA requires that each federal agency "make and preserve records containing adequate and proper documentation of the organization, functions, policies, decisions, procedures and essential transactions of the agency." *Ibid.*, at 3101. The term "records" includes "all books, papers, maps, photographs, machine readable materials, or other documentary materials, regardless of physical form or characteristics, made or received by an agency of the United States Government under Federal law or in connection with the transaction of public business and preserved or appropriate for preservation by that agency or its legitimate successor as evidence of the organization, functions, policies, decisions, procedures, operations or other activities of the Government or because of the informational value of the data in them." (44 U.S.C. 3301).

[89] The PROFS system was the original system employed by the EOP. In 1989 the EOP installed the OASIS system as an additional means of transmitting information among employess. The original PROFS system ceased operations in 1992. The NSC has its own PROFS system as well as a similar system known as "All-In-One." *Armstrong II*, at 1279, n. 2.

[90] *Ibid.*, at 1279.

[91] *Ibid.*, at 1285.

[92] *Ibid.*, at 1283.

[93] Ibid., at 1287.

[94] General Records Schedules are authorisations by the Archivist of the United States to destroy records that are of a specific "form or character common to several or all agencies" and that lack, "after a specified period of time" sufficient administrative, legal, research or other value to warrant their continued preservation. 44 U.S.C. para. 3303a(d). General Records Schedule 20, which was first issued in 1972, authorises the destruction of certain forms of electronic records.

[95] *Public Citizen, Inc. v John Carlin* , 2 F. Supp. 2d 1 (D.D.C. 1997).

[96] The plaintiffs included Public Citizen, Inc., the American Historical Association, the American Library Association, the Center for National Security Studies, the National Security Archive, the Organization of American Historians, Scott Armstrong, and Eddie Becker. Public Citizen Inc., is a public interest lobby group founded by Ralph Nader in 1971.

[97] [U.S.] National Archives and Records Administration, "General Records Schedule 20; Disposition of Electronic Records: Notice of Issuance of General Records Schedule," 60 F.R., 28 August 1995, pp. 44643-44650.

[98] *Ibid.*, 44644.

[99] 36 C.F.R. [Code of Federal Regulations] Chapter XII, Part 1234.22 subpart C: "Standards for the Creation, Use, Preservation, and Disposition of Electronic Records: Creation and Use of Text Documents," 1999.

[100] See also *ibid.*, part 1234.24.

[101] 60 F.R., 44644.

[102] *Public Citizen v Carlin*, 2 F. Supp. 2d 1 (D.D.C. 1997), at 12.

[103] *Ibid.*
[104] *Public Citizen v Carlin,* 184 F.3d 900 (D.C. Cir. 1999).
[105] In the opinion of the court, item 14 and its accompanying note satisfy the concerns raised in Armstrong "by requiring the recordkeeping system to capture all relevant transmission data." *Ibid.,* at 910.
[106] Ibid., at 910, 911.
[107] The plaintiffs' petition is available at the Public Citizen web page at <http://www.citizen.org/litigation/briefs/pccar114.htm>.
[108] *Armstrong v Executive Office of the President,* 810 F. Supp. 335 (D.D.C.) at 341; *Armstrong II* at 1285.
[109] Armstrong, Plaintiffs-Appellees v Executive Office of the President, Defendants-
Appellants, "Brief for the Appellees/Cross-Appellants," Civil Action No. 93-5002, 93-5048
(D.C. Cir. May 3, 1993), part II(a),
<http://eff.bilkent.edu.tr/pub/Legal/Cases/PROFS_case/plaintiff.briefs> (March 28, 2000).
[110] The rule of immediacy and the ground-zero theory are discussed at, respectively, pp. 58 and 42 above.
[111] 44 U.S.C. s. 2902(1)
[112] *Armstrong II* at 1285.
[113] *Webster's Ninth New Collegiate Dictionary* (Markham, Ont.: Thomas Allen, 1991), s.v. "complete".
[114] Public Citizen, Plaintiffs-Appellees, v Carlin, Defendants-Appellants, "Brief for Appellants," Civil Action No. 97-5356, 98-5173 (D.C. Cir. 1998), at I A. 2
<http://www.nara.gov/records/grs20/briefapp.html>,(March 3, 2000).
[115] Cited in Public Citizen, Plaintiffs, v Carlin, Defendants, "Reply Memorandum in Support of Defendants' Motion to Dismiss or, in the Alternative, for Summary Judgement and in Opposition to Plaintiffs' Cross-Motion for Summary Judgement," Civil Action No. 96-2840 (D.C. Cir. n.d.), at I.C <http://www.citizen.org/litigation/briefs/grs20gov.htm> (March 3, 2000).
[116] *Ibid.*
[117] *Public Citizen v Carlin* (D.D.C. 1997) at 12. The court's comments are quoted at p. 80 above.
[118] Ibid., at 11.
[119] R.J. Morris, "Back to the Future: Historians and the Electronically Created Record," *History and Computing* 4 (1992): iv.

Chapter Four

[1] Duranti, "Diplomatics I," *Archivaria,* 17.
[2] Quoted in C.R. Cheney, *The Papacy and England 12th - 14th Centuries* (London: Variorum Reprints, 1982), 8.
[3] Duranti, "Diplomatics I," 17.
[4] For an overview and comprehensive bibliography of classical and contemporary studies of medieval diplomatics see Olivier Guyotjeannin, Jacques Pycke et Benoît-Michel Tock, *Diplomatique médiévale* (Paris: Brepols, 1993).
[5] Guyotjeannin, "Expansion of Diplomatics," *American Archivist,* 419
[6] Notable diplomatic studies of historical sources for the modern period (especially from the 16th to the 18th centuries) include Heinrich Otto Meisner, *Archivalienkunde vom 16. Jahrhundert bis 1918* (Leipzig: Koehler & Amelang, 1969), and Georges Tessier, *Diplomatique royale française* (Paris: A et J. Picard, 1962). For an overview of diplomatic research undertaken for the modern period, see Bernard Barbiche, "Diplomatics of Modern Official Documents (Sixteenth – Eighteenth Centuries: Evaluation and Perspectives," *American Archivist* 59 (Fall 1996): 432-36.
[7] For an overview of the historical connection between diplomatics and archival science, see Luciana Duranti, "Archival Science," *Encyclopedia of Library and Information Science,* ed. Allen Kent, vol. 59, supp. 22 (New York: Marcel Dekker, 1997), 3-5.
[8] C.N.L. Brooke, "The Teaching of Diplomatic," *Journal of the Society of Archivists* 4 (April 1970): 8.
[9] Francis X. Blouin, Jr., "Convergences and Divergences in Archival Tradition: A North American Perspective," *Second European Conference on Archives: Proceedings,* ed. Judith A. Koucky (Paris, International Council on Archives, 1989), 29, 28. Other archivists who have advocated the revival of diplomatics for modern records include Tom Nesmith, "Archives from the Bottom Up: Social History and Archival Scholarship," *Archivaria* 14 (Summer 1982): 5-26; Don C. Skemer, "Diplomatics and Archives," *American Archivist* 52 (Summer 1989): 376-82; and Hugh Taylor, "My Very Act and Deed:

Some Reflections on the Role of Textual Records in the Conduct of Affairs," *American Archivist* 51 (Fall 1988): 456-69.

[10] Koucky, ed., *Second European Conference of Archives*, 113.

[11] Dutch archivists have focused on the development of a typology of modern records, undertaking a major project investigating the forms of records created and used by organisations since the nineteenth century. For a summary of this research and its products, see David Bearman and Peter Sigmond, "Explorations of Form of Material Authority Files by Dutch Archivists," *American Archivist* 50 (Spring 1987): 249-53; Peter J. Sigmond, "Form, Function and Archival Value," *Archivaria* 33 (Winter 1991-92): 141-47.

[12] In Italy, Paola Carucci has focused on record-creation procedures, adapting traditional diplomatic concepts and methods to the specific recordkeeping environment of contemporary Italian administration. See *Il Documento Contemporaneo* (Rome: La Nuova Italia Scientifica, 1987).

[13] Duranti. "Diplomatics I," 7-27; "Diplomatics ... (Part II)," *Archivaria* 29 (Winter 1989-90): 4-17; " Diplomatics ... (Part III)," *Archivaria* 30 (Summer 1990): 4-20; "Diplomatics ... (Part IV)," Archivaria 31 (Winter 1990-91): 10-25; "Diplomatics ... (Part V)," *Archivaria* 32 (Summer 1991): 6-24; "Diplomatics ... (Part VI)," *Archivaria* 33 (Winter 1991-92): 6-24.

[14] A juridical system is a social group organised on the basis of a system of rules. It comprises the social group, the organisational principle of the group, and the system of binding rules recognised by the social group.

[15] Duranti, "Diplomatics (Part II)," 8.

[16] *Ibid.* A juridically relevant fact or act is one whose results are taken into consideration by the juridical system in which it takes place. A juridically irrelevant fact or act is one whose occurrence has not been consciously foreseen by the juridical system in which it takes place.

[17] For further explanation of the medieval and modern diplomatic analysis of actions and the categorisation of records in relation to them, see Duranti, "Diplomatics (Part II)," 4-17.

[18] *Ibid.*, 10.

[19] *Ibid.*, 15.

[20] This observation comes from Gérard and Christiane Naud, "L'analyse des archives administratives contemporaines," *Gazette des Archives* 115 (1981): 218.

[21] See, for example, Steven Davidson, "The Registration of a Deed of Land in Ontario: A Study in Special Diplomatics," (Master of Archival Studies thesis, University of British Columbia, 1994); Anthony Gregson, "Records Management Attributes in International Open Document Exchange Standards" (Master of Archival Studies thesis, University of British Columbia, 1995); Joni Mitchell, "Civil Litigation, Probate and Bankruptcy Procedures: A Diplomatic Examination of British Columbia Supreme Court Records" (Master of Archival Studies thesis, University of British Columbia, 1995), Janice Simpson, "Broadcast Archives: A Diplomatic Examination," (Master of Archival Studies thesis, University of British Columbia, 1994); Janet Turner, "Special Diplomatics and the Study of Authority in the United Church of Canada" (Master of Archival Studies thesis, University of British Columbia, 1994).

[22] See, for example, David Bearman, "Diplomatics, Weberian Bureaucracy, and the Management of Electronic Records in Europe and America," *American Archivist* 55 (Winter 1992): 168-81; Tom Belton, "By Whose Warrant? Analysing Documentary Form and Procedure," *Archivaria* 41 (Spring 1996): 206-20; Susan E. Storch, "Diplomatics: Modern Archival Method or Medieval Artifact," *American Archivist* 61 (Fall 1998): 365-83; Janet Turner, "Experimenting with New Tools: Special Diplomatics and the Study of Authority in the United Church of Canada," *Archivaria* 30 (Summer 1990): 91-103.

[23] Subsequent to the publication of Duranti's six articles, a joint seminar exploring the application of diplomatics to contemporary records was held by archivists from the Bentley Historical Library of the University of Michigan and by members of the faculty of the École nationale des chartes in Paris. The seminar took place in two sessions, the first in Paris in 1992, the second in Ann Arbor in 1993 and resulted in a series of articles which were published in French in *La Gazette des Archives* 172 (1996) and in English in *The American Archivist* 59 (Fall 1996). The articles reflect a consensus on the part of the contributors that the discipline of diplomatics can contribute significantly to an understanding of contemporary recordkeeping environments.

[24] The UBC researchers comprised Duranti as principal investigator, Terry Eastwood as co-investigator and the author as research assistant.

[25] The identification and elaboration of methods for ensuring the trustworthiness of inactive electronic records fell outside the scope of the UBC project. It is, however, the focus of a follow-up research project currently being undertaken by an international research team. That project, which builds on

the findings of the UBC project, is entitled International Research on Permanent Authentic Records (InterPARES). An overview of InterPARES is available at <http://www.interpares.org>.

[26] That final step was accomplished with the assistance of the U.S. Department of Defense Records Management Task Force, which approached the researchers one year into the UBC project for the purpose of collaborating with it. The Task Force's mandate was to develop a new departmental records management system for both electronic and non-electronic records and it was actively seeking a theoretical foundation for its reengineering effort. It contributed to the UBC methodology its own standard modelling technique, which was useful for the purposes of analysing and graphically representing the diplomatic and archival concepts, and making their meaning comprehensible and relevant to information system designers. The hypotheses developed at UBC provided the concepts to be represented, while the modelling technique provided the means of translating those concepts into activity and entity models that show the relationships of their components from well identified viewpoints and for determined purposes. On the basis of the activities identified in the models, the UBC researchers developed detailed rules for creating and handling reliable and authentic records, both electronic and non-electronic. The rules were subsequently translated by the Task Force into mandatory functional requirements for records management application software used by the Department of Defense. See Assistant Secretary of Defense for Command, Control, Communications and Intelligence, "Design Criteria Standard for Electronic Records Management Software Applications," DOD 5015.2-STD (November 1997), <http://web7.whs.osd.mil/corres.htm> (December 1999).

[27] In fact, a significant impetus for proposing the project was provided by the decision in the *Armstrong* case, which had underscored the need for a more systematic analysis of the nature and boundaries of a record in an electronic environment. See Luciana Duranti and Terry Eastwood. "Protecting Electronic Evidence: A Progress Report," *Archivi & Computer* 5 (1995): 213

[28] The summary of the UBC project that follows is based on an article co-authored by Duranti and MacNeil at the project's conclusion. See Luciana Duranti and Heather MacNeil. "The Protection of the Integrity of Electronic Records: An Overview of the UBC Research Project," *Archivaria* 42 (Fall 1996): 46-67. The project's hypotheses (articulated in templates), activity and entity models, glossary of terms, rules, and a bibliography of project-related publciations are available for viewing at the project's web site located at <http://www.slais.ubc.ca/users/duranti/>.

[29] Duranti, "Diplomatics (Part II)," 4.

[30] The extrinsic elements of documentary form are discussed in the context of medieval and modern documentary production in Duranti, "Diplomatics (Part V)," 6-10.

[31] The intrinsic elements of documentary form are discussed in the context of medieval and modern documentary production in *ibid.*, 11-16.

[32] The superscription is "the mention of the name of the author of the document and/or the action." See *ibid.*, 12.

[33] The inscription is the mention of "the name, title and address of the addressee of the document and/or action." See *ibid.*, 12.

[34] In diplomatic terms, the protocol is the first of three physical subsections of a document. It "contains the administrative context of the action (i.e., indication of the persons involved, time and place, and subject) and initial formulae". See *ibid.*, 11.

[35] The diplomatic identification of the various persons concurring in the formation of a document in the context of medieval and modern documentary production is discussed in Duranti, "Diplomatics (Part III)," 4-20.

[36] It is important to point out that these are conceptual persons. In fact, the author and writer of a record may be the same physical person.

[37] The archival fonds is the whole of the records created by a physical or juridical person by reason of its activity and preserved for action or reference.

[38] Giorgio Cencetti, *Scritti archivistici* (Rome: Il Centro di Ricerca editore, 1970), 39. Jenkinson uses the term "interrelatedness." See Hilary Jenkinson, "Introductory," in *Public Record Office, Guide to the Public Records, Part I* (London: Public Record Office, 1949), 2.

[39] During the middle ages, registration was an important aspect of papal and royal chancery procedures. It involved the copying of important outgoing documents into a book called a register. Registers served as memory of acts and decisions taken and could be referred to if necessary to check precedents and to establish the authenticity of documents issued by chanceries. For the nature and use of registers in papal and royal chanceries see Maria Luisa Ambrosini and Mary Willis, *The Secret Archives of the Vatican* (Boston: Little, Brown, 1969), *passim*; Robert I. Burns, *Society and Documentation in Crusader Valencia*, vol. 1 of *Diplomatarium of the Crusader Kingdom of Valencia: The Registered Charters of Its Conqueror, Jaume I, 1257-1276* (Princeton, N.J.: Princeton University Press,

1985), 48-57; Alain de Boüard, *Manuel de diplomatique française et pontificale* (Paris: A. Picard, 1929), vol. 1, 190-211; Arthur Giry, *Manuel de Diplomatique* , 687-88, 752-54; Poole, *Lectures on the History of the Papal Chancery*, 123-36. The practice of registration continues to this day in most European countries and consists of making an entry into a register that identifies salient information concerning the administrative and documentary context of every incoming and outgoing document. An illustration of the information captured in a modern protocol register is provided in Elio Lodolini, *Archivistica: Principi e problemi*, 4th ed. (Milano: Franco Angeli, 1987), 92-93.

[40] The UBC researchers have articulated the procedural rules for classifying and registering records in an electronic system. See rules A121 (create classification scheme), A131(l) (establish procedures for registration), under "Rules for Activities Involved in "Manage Archival Framework;" also A23 (classify records), and A24 (register records), under "Rules for Activities Involved in "Create Records," "Handle Records," and "Preserve Records," located at the UBC project's web site.

[41] Lewis J. Bellardo and Lynn Lady Bellardo, *A Glossary for Archivists, Manuscript Curators and Records Managers* (Chicago: Society of American Archivists, 1992), s.v. "metadata".

[42] For an examination of the role of the profile in open document exchange standards and a comparison of the attributes of this type of profile with the intrinsic and extrinsic elements of form identified by diplomatics, see Anthony Gregson, "Records Management Attributes in International Open Document Exchange Standards," (Master of Archival Studies thesis, University of British Columbia, 1995).

[43] The procedural rules developed by the researchers for the creation of a record profile may be found at rules A131(h), (i), (j), (k), under "Rules for Activities Involved in "Manage Archival Framework," located at the project's web site. Some of these fields would be filled in by the system, others by the author or writer, and others still would be filled in by the record office. The fact that all the fields must be included on the form does not mean that every field must be filled in for every record made or received. Only the profiles of the records for which maximum reliability and authenticity are required would have all the fields filled in.

[44] The *recordkeeping system* comprises a set of rules governing the making, receiving, setting aside, and handling of active and semiactive records in the usual and ordinary course of the creator's affairs, and the tools and mechanisms used to implement them. The *record-preservation system* is a set of rules governing the intellectual and physical maintenance by the creator of semiactive records, and the tools and mechanisms necessary to implement them. Although semiactive records are no longer needed for action, they are still required for purposes of reference.

[45] The researchers have attempted to accomplish this (1) by instituting procedures for creating an electronic record profile for every non-electronic record consigned to the central records system as well as for every electronic record set aside, and (2) by establishing a repository of those record profiles. The procedural rules for showing the connection among active records in all media that belong in the same aggregation may be found at A131(q), under "Rules for Activities Involved in "Manage Archival Framework," located at the project's web site.

[46] Duranti, "Diplomatics (Part IV)," 14. "Transaction" is used rather than "action," but the meaning ascribed to it is synonymous with "action," the more appropriate term adopted in the UBC project.

[47] The definitions of the various categories of procedures that follow are from *ibid.*, 19.

[48] Constitutive procedures are those procedures which create, extinguish, or modify the exercise of power of the addressee. Constitutive procedures may be categorised as procedures of concession, of limitation, or of authorisation, and their purpose is to fulfil the agency's mandate.

[49] Executive procedures are those procedures which allow for the regular transaction of affairs according to rules established by a different authority, e.g., personnel, finances.

[50] Instrumental procedures are those procedures which are connected to the expression of opinions and advice.

[51] Organisational procedures are those procedures, the purpose of which is to establish organisational structure and internal procedures and to maintain, modify, or extinguish them.

[52] The definitions of the diplomatic phases of a procedure that follow are from *ibid.*, 14-19.

[53] The initiative phase comprises those acts that start the mechanism of the procedure.

[54] The inquiry phase comprises the collection of the elements necessary to evaluate the situation.

[55] The consultation phase comprises the collection of opinions and advice after the relevant information has been assembled.

[56] The deliberation phase consists of the decision-making.

[57] The deliberation control phase consists of the control exercised by a person or persons different from those making the decision on the substance and/or form of the deliberation.

[58] The execution phase consists of all the actions that give a formal character to the decision, such as the validation, communication, notification, or publication of the related record.

[59] The records are identified not only on the basis of their intellectual form, but also on the basis of their function with respect to the action to which they relate (whether dispositive, probative, supporting, or narrative).

[60] For a more detailed discussion of the concepts as they are understood in diplomatics and archival science, see Luciana Duranti, "Reliability and Authenticity: The Concepts and Their Implications," *Archivaria* 39 (Spring 1995): 5-10.

[61] [U.S.] Department of Health and Human Services. Food and Drug Administration, 21 CFR Part 11, "Electronic Records; Electronic Signatures; Final Rule; Electronic Submissions; Establishment of Public Docket; Notice," March 20, 1997, 13465. In electronic contracting law and a number of other areas of the substantive law, digital signatures are becoming the standard method of ensuring the reliability and authenticity of electronic records. See, for example, [U.S.] Dept. of Health and Human Services. 21 CFR Part 11, 13430-66; European Commission Directorate-General XIII, "Towards a European Framework for Digital Signatures and Encryption: Communication from the Commission to the European Parliament, the Council, the Economic and Social Committee and the Committee of the Regions Ensuring Security and Trust in Electronic Communication," COM (97) 503 [1997]; Bernard D. Reams, Jr., *Electronic Contracting Law: EDI and Business Transactions, 1996-1997 edition* (New York: Clark, Boardman, Callaghan, 1997).

[62] Duranti, "Reliability and Authenticity," 6

[63] Competence is a sphere of functional responsibility entrusted to an office.

[64] The procedural rules for defining access privileges may be found at A123 under "Rules for Activities Involved in "Manage Archival Framework," located at the project's web site.

[65] A demonstration prototype based on an automated work flow process has been developed by the National Archives of Canada. For a description of the prototype, see John McDonald, "Towards Automated Record Keeping, Interfaces for the Capture of Records of Business Processes," *Archives and Museum Informatics* 11 (1997): 277-85.

[66] The procedural rules for auditing may be found at A131(t), under "Rules for Activities Involved in "Manage Archival Framework," located at the project's web site. The Canadian Somalia Inquiry identified as significant failures of the electronic system the absence of audit procedures and the lack of system audits to ensure that the National Defence Operations Centre (NDOC) data logs were being properly maintained. See pp. xii-xiii above.

[67] The state of transmission of a record in the context of medieval and modern documentary production is discussed in Duranti, "Diplomatics I," 18-21.

[68] An authentic copy is "a copy certified by officials authorised to execute such a function, so as to render it legally admissible in evidence." See *ibid.*, 21.

[69] An imitative copy "reproduces, completely or partially, not only the content but also the forms, including the external ones (layout, script, special signs, medium and so on), of the original." See *ibid.*, 20-21.

[70] A copy in the form of an original comes into existence when "two originals of the same document, addressed to the same person and having the same date, are sent to that person in two subsequent deliveries." In such a case, "the oldest document is considered to be the original, the second is qualified as *a copy in the form of an original*." *Ibid.*, 19. While it is as complete and effective as the original, it lacks the quality of primitiveness that the original has.

[71] A simple copy "is constituted by the mere transcription of the content of the original." *Ibid.*, 21.

[72] A vidimus falls within the category of an authentic copy and takes the form of an insert, i.e., a document "entirely quoted (if textual) or reported (if visual, like maps) in subsequent original documents in order to renew [its] effects. ... An authentic copy in general and a vidimus in particular, only guarantees the conformity of the copy to the original text." *Ibid.*, 21, n. 38 and 39.

[73] A conformed copy is "an exact copy of a document on which has been written explanation of things that could not or were not copied, e.g., written signature may be replaced on conformed copy with notation that it was signed by the person whose signature appears on the original." *Black's Law Dictionary*, 5th ed., s.v. "conformed copy."

[74] The procedural rules elaborated by the UBC researchers for establishing the state of transmission of records may be found at A131(m), under "Rules for Activities Involved in "Manage Archival Framework," located at the project's web site.

[75] The procedural rules elaborated by the researchers for copying and migrating active and semiactive electronic records may be found at A131(n), (p), (u), (v), under "Rules for Activities

Involved in "Manage Archival Framework," and at A33 and A43, under "Rules for Activities Involved in "Create Records," "Handle Records," and "Preserve Records," located at the project's web site.

[76] Survival means not only the survival of an electronic record's physical existence, but includes the survival of its readability and intelligibility.

[77] In *Preserving Digital Information: Report of the Task Force on Archiving of Digital Information* (Washington: Commission on Preservation and Access and the Research Libraries Group, 1996), 5, migration is defined as "the periodic transfer of digital materials from one hardware/software configuration to another, or from one generation of computer technology to a subsequent generation." For a contrasting definition of migration as well as an extensive discussion of the consequences of copying, reformatting, conversion, and migration on the preservation of an electronic record's readability, intelligibility, and authenticity, see Charles M. Dollar, *Authentic Electronic Records: Strategies for Long-Term Access (Chicago:* Cohassets Associates, 1999), 11-43. Dollar's discussion of authenticity draws on the diplomatic analysis of the concept found in Duranti's *Archivaria* articles and the UBC project findings.

[78] The significance of custody to the authenticity of older records is reflected In the U.S. Federal Rules of Evidence, where the ancient documents rule has been extended to electronic records. As the importance of appearance diminishes (an unsuspicious appearance will certainly be deceptive in the case of electronic records), the importance of custody increases correspondingly. See *Wigmore on Evidence*, (Chadbourn rev., 1978), vol. 7, para. 2129, n. 1, example 7.

[79] For the structure and functioning of medieval chanceries see Giry, *Manuel de Diplomatique*, 661-820. For the structure and functioning of modern bureaucracy according to the classical organisational theory of Weber, see Max Weber, *The Theory of Social and Economic Organization*, trans. A.M. Henderson and Talcott Parsons (New York: The Free Press, 1947), 329-41. See also Kathleen Carney, "Managing Integrated Record Systems: A Conceptual Foundation," (Master of Archival Studies thesis, University of British Columbia, 1995), 11-31.

[80] Eugene Kamenka, *Bureaucracy* (Oxford: Blackwell, 1989), 1, 3.

[81] Jane Parkinson, "Accountability in Archival Theory," (Master of Archival Studies thesis, University of British Columbia, 1993), 25-26.

[82] In the discussion that follows, recordkeepers are understood to include persons responsible for making, modifying, and annotating records within a bureaucracy.

[83] Raffel, *Matters of Fact*, 91.

[84] *Ibid.*, 100. The use of hospital records specifically for auditing and supervisory purposes is discussed in Kai Erikson and Daniel Gilbertson, "Case Records in the Mental Hospital," in *On Record*, ed. Stanton Wheeler (New York: Russell Sage Foundation, 1970), 390 and in Phyllisis M. Ngin, "Recordkeeping Practices of Nurses in Hospitals," *American Archivist* 57 (Fall 1994): 616-30, *passim*

[85] Kamenka, *Bureaucracy*, 168.

[86] Raffel, *Matters of Fact*, 102

[87] Jack Goody, *The Logic of Writing and the Organization of Society* (Cambridge: Cambridge University Press, 1986), 152.

[88] Raffel, *Matters of Fact*, 110.

[89] *Ibid.*, 94.

[90] *Ibid., 95.*

[91] *Ibid.*, 112.

[92] H.H. Gerth and C. Wright Mills, eds. and trans., *From Max Weber: Essays in Sociology* (New York: Oxford University Press, 1946), 215-16, 228.

[93] Kamenka, *Bureaucracy*, 160. See also Robert K. Merton, "Bureaucratic Structure and Personality," in *Reader in Bureaucracy*, ed. Merton et al. (Glencoe, Ill.: The Free Press, 1952), 361-71.

[94] Max Weber, *Max Weber on the Methodology of the Social Sciences*, trans. and ed. Edward A. Shils and Henry A. Finch (Glencoe, Ill.: Free Press, 1949), 90.

[95] David Beetham, *Bureaucracy*, 2nd ed. (Buckingham: Open University Press, 1996), 19.

[96] Geert Hofstede, *Culture's Consequences: International Differences in Work-Related Values* (London: Sage Publications, 1980). See also Hofstede, "The Cultural Relativity of Organizational Practices and Theories," *Journal of International Business Studies* 14 (Fall 1983): 75-90; Hofstede, "Motivation, Leadership, and Organization: Do American Theories Apply Abroad?" *Organizational Dynamics* 9 (Summer 1980): 42-63.

[97] Hofstede, "Motivation, Leadership," 45.

[98] Richard Mead, *Cross-Cultural Management Communication* (New York: John Wiley and Sons, 1990), 25-28.

[99] Bearman, "Diplomatics, Weberian Bureaucracy, and the Management of Electronic Records," *American Archivist*, 178.
[100] Mary Douglas, *How Institutions Think* (Syracuse, N.Y.: Syracuse University Press, 1986), 92.

Conclusion

[1] *Wigmore on Evidence*, vol. 1A (Tillers revision, 1983), para. 37.7 at 1078.
[2] Quoted in Richard H. Gaskins, *Burdens of Proof in Modern Discourse* (New Haven: Yale University Press, 1992), 26.
[3] Leon J. Goldstein, *Historical Knowing* (Austin: University of Texas Press, 1976), 141.
[4] Luciana Duranti, "Diplomatics (Part IV)," 10.
[5] For a detailed philosophical examination of the coherence theory of truth and its relation to the correspondence theory of truth, see Ralph C.S. Walker, *The Coherence Theory of Truth: Realism, Anti-Realism, Idealism* (London: Routledge, 1989). For an examination of the theories in the context of historical methodology, see W.H. Walsh, "Truth and Fact in History," in *An Introduction to Philosophy of History*, 3rd ed., rev. (Atlantic Highlands, N.J.: Humanities Press, 1967), 72-92.
[6] The phrase is Paul Ricoeur's. As he puts it: "History ... wants to resuscitate and it can only reconstruct. It wants to make things contemporary, but at the same time, it has to restore the distance and depth of historical time that separates it from its object. ... These difficulties do not arise from defects of method, they are well-founded ambiguities." Quoted in Le Goff, *History and Memory*, 105.
[7] Dorothy A. Haecker, "The Historical Way of Knowing," (Ph.D. thesis, University of Kansas, 1981), abstract.
[8] *Wigmore on Evidence*, vol. 1A (Tillers revision, 1983), para. 37.7 at 1085.
[9] Jonathan Cohen goes so far as to argue, in relation to the law's pursuit of justice, that "only by producing generally acceptable verdicts on facts at issue can a legal system ensure that in the long term it will continue to retain the respect of the informed public. ... What is crucial here is not so much actual accuracy of trial outcomes, but rather the extent to which people believe in this accuracy, especially in criminal cases. Moreover *only by using broadly the same fact-finding procedures as those that the informed public respects can a legal system ensure that it will produce generally acceptable verdicts* [emphasis mine]." Jonathan Cohen, "Freedom of Proof," in *Facts in Law: Association for Legal and Social Philosophy Ninth Annual Conference at Hatfield College, University of Durham, 2nd - 4th April 1982*, ed. William Twining (Wiesbaden, Germany: Franz Steiner Verlag, 1983), 4-5.
[10] A recent example of a new way of looking at the world is the Supreme Court of Canada's overturning of the trial court's decision in *Delgamuukw v British Columbia*, and its specific rejection of the trial judge's decision to exclude or to accord no weight to oral histories of aboriginal peoples on the grounds that they constituted hearsay and were thus inherently unreliable. In its decision, the Supreme Court recognised the need for the legal system to "adapt the laws of evidence so that the aboriginal perspective on their practices, customs and traditions and on their relationship with the land, are given due weight by the courts. In practical terms, this requires the courts to come to terms with the oral histories of aboriginal societies, which, for many aboriginal nations, are the only record of their past." *Delgamuukw v British Columbia*, [1997] 3 S.C.R. 1010 at 64.
[11] Observational principles may also be read into the methods associated with assessing record authenticity, specifically in the preference for documentary originals over copies. If we consider the creation of the record itself to be the event, the original record is the one closest to the event.
[12] Raffel, *Matters of Fact*, 64.
[13] Cousins, "Practice of Historical Investigation," *Poststructuralism and the Question of History*, 132.
[14] R.J. Morris, "Electronic Documents and the History of the Late 20th Century: Black Holes or Warehouses – What do Historians Really Want?" in *Electronic Information Resources and Historians*, 311-12.
[15] Margaret Hedstrom, "Understanding Electronic Incunabula: A Framework for Research on Electronic Records," *American Archivist* 54 (Summer 1991): 340-41.
[16] *Ibid.*, 341.

Bibliography

Abdy, J.T. *A Historical Sketch of Civil Procedure Among the Romans*. Cambridge: Macmillan and Co., 1857.

Ambrosini, Maria Luisa, and Mary Willis. *The Secret Archives of the Vatican*. Boston: Little, Brown, 1969.

Barnes, Harry Elmer. *A History of Historical Writing*. Norman, Oklahoma: University of Oklahoma Press, 1938.

Barzun, Jacques, and Henry F. Graff. *The Modern Researcher*, 5th ed. San Diego: Harcourt, Brace Jovanovich, 1992.

Baum, Michael S. and Henry H. Perritt, Jr. *Electronic Contracting, Publishing, and EDI Law*. New York: Wiley, 1991.

Beard, Charles A. "Written History as an Act of Faith." In *The Philosophy of History in Our Time*, ed. Hans Meyerhoff. New York: Doubleday, 1959.

Bearman, David. "Archival Principles and the Electronic Office." In *Information Handling in Offices and Archives*, ed. Angelika Menne-Haritz. München: K.G. Saur, 1993.

————. "Record-Keeping Systems." *Archivaria* 36 (Autumn 1993): 16-36.

————. "Diplomatics, Weberian Bureaucracy, and the Management of Electronic Records in Europe and America." *American Archivist* 55 (Winter 1992): 168-81.

Becker, Carl. "What are Historical Facts?" In *Detachment and the Writing of History: Essays and Letters of Carl Becker*, ed. Phil L. Snyder. Ithaca, N.Y.: Cornell University Press, 1958.

Bedos-Rezak, Brigitte, ed. *Form and Order in Medieval France: Studies in Social and Quantitative Sigillography*. Aldershot: Variorium Reprints, 1993.

Beetham, David. *Bureaucracy*, 2nd ed. Buckingham: Open University Press, 1996.

Bentham, Jeremy. *An Introductory View of the Rationale of Judicial Evidence; Rationale of Judicial Evidence*. In *The Works of Jeremy Bentham*, ed. John Bowering, vols. 6 and 7. New York: Russell and Russell, 1962.

Bloch, Marc. *The Historian's Craft*, trans. Peter Putnam. New York: Alfred A. Knopf, 1963.

Blouin, Francis, and Bruno Delmas, eds. "Special Section on Diplomatics and Modern Records." *American Archivist* 59 (Fall 1996): 412-94.

Boüard, Alain de. *Manuel de diplomatique française et pontificale*, vol. 1. Paris: A. Picard, 1929.

Boyle, Leonard E. "Diplomatics." In *Medieval Studies: An Introduction*, ed. James M. Powell. Syracuse, N.Y.: Syracuse University Press, 1992.

Brierley, John E.C., and Roderick A. MacDonald, eds. *Quebec Civil Law: An Introduction to Quebec Private Law*. Toronto: Emond Montgomery Publications, 1993.

Burke, Peter. *The Renaissance Sense of the Past*. New York: St. Martin's Press, 1970.

Burns, Robert I. *Society and Documentation in Crusader Valencia. Vol. 1, Diplomatarium of the Crusader Kingdom of Valencia: The Registered Charters of Its Conqueror, Jaume I, 1257-1276*. Princeton, N.J.: Princeton University Press, 1985.

[Canada]. *Dishonoured Legacy: The Lessons of the Somalia Affair. Report of the Commission of Inquiry into the Deployment of Canadian Forces to Somalia*, vol. 5. Ottawa: Minister of Public Works and Government Services Canada, 1997.

Carr, E.H. "The Historian and His Facts." In *What is History*. Hammondsworth: Penguin, 1984.

Chartier, Roger. *On the Edge of the Cliff: History, Language and Practices*. Baltimore: Johns Hopkins University Press, 1997.

Chasse, Ken. "Appendix J: Computer-Produced Records in Court Proceedings." *Proceedings of the Seventy-Sixth Annual Meeting [of the] Uniform Law Conference of Canada*. [Edmonton: University of Alberta. Faculty of Law, 1995].

Cheney, C.R. "The Study of the Medieval Papal Chancery." In *The Papacy and England 12th - 14th Centuries*. London: Variorum Reprints, 1982.

Clanchy, M.T. *From Memory to Written Record: England, 1066-1307*. 2nd ed. Cambridge, Mass.: Basil Blackwell, 1993.

Cohen, Jonathan. "Freedom of Proof." In *Facts in Law: Association for Legal and Social Philosophy Ninth Annual Conference at Hatfield College, University of Durham, 2nd - 4th April 1982*, ed. William Twining. Wiesbaden, Germany: Franz Steiner Verlag 1983.

Collingwood, R.G. "Historical Evidence." In *The Idea of History: Revised Edition with Lectures 1926-1928,* ed. Jan van der Dussen. Oxford and New York: Oxford University Press, 1994.

Cousins, Mark. "The Practice of Historical Investigation." In *Poststructuralism and the Question of History,* ed. Derek Attridge, Geoff Bennington and Robert Young. Cambridge: Cambridge University Press, 1993.

Damaška, Mirjan. *Evidence Law Adrift.* New Haven: Yale University Press, 1997.

————. "Presentation of Evidence and Factfinding Precision." *University of Pennsylvania Law Review* 23 (May 1975): 1083-1106.

Davies, Wendy, and Paul Fouracre, eds. *The Settlement of Disputes in Early Medieval Europe.* Cambridge: Cambridge University Press, 1986.

Davis, Natalie Zemon. *Fiction in the Archives: Pardon Tales and their Tellers in Sixteenth Century France.* Stanford, Calif.: Stanford University Press, 1987.

Delaney-Beausoleil, Kathleen. "La valeur de preuve des documents d'archives: aspects théoriques." In *Les valeurs archivistiques: théorie et pratique. Actes du colloque organisé conjointement par la Division des archives et les Programmes d'archivistique de l'Université Laval, 11 novembre 1993.* Québec: Université Laval, 1994.

Dollar, Charles M. *Authentic Electronic Records: Strategies for Long-Term Access.* Chicago, Ill.: Cohasset Associates, 1999.

————. "Archival Science and Information Technologies." In *Information Handling in Offices and Archives,* ed. Angelika Menne-Haritz. München: K.G. Saur, 1993.

————. *Archival Theory and Information Technologies: The Impact of Information Technologies on Archival Principles and Methods,* ed. Oddo Bucci. Macerata: University of Macerata, 1992.

Dibble, Vernon K. "Four Types of Inference From Documents to Events." *History and Theory* 3 (1964): 203-19.

Ducharme, Léo. "The Rules of Evidence in Civil and Commercial Matters in Québec Law." In *Essays on the Civil Codes of Québec and St. Lucia,* ed. Raymond A. Landry and Ernest Caparros. Ottawa: University of Ottawa Press, 1984.

Duff, Wendy. "Ensuring the Preservation of Reliable Evidence: A Research Project Funded by the NHPRC." *Archivaria* 42 (Fall 1996): 28-45.

Duranti, Luciana. "Archival Science." In *Encyclopedia of Library and Information Science*, ed. Allen Kent. Vol. 59. Supp. 22. New York: Marcel Dekker, 1997.

———. "The Archival Bond." *Archives and Museum Informatics* 11 (1997): 213-18.

———. "Archives as a Place." *Archives and Manuscripts* 24 (November 1996): 242-56.

———. "Diplomatics: New Uses for an Old Science [Part I]." *Archivaria* 28 (Summer 1989): 7-27.

———. "Diplomatics: New Uses ...(Part II)." *Archivaria* 29 (Winter 1989-90): 4-17.

———. "Diplomatics: New Uses ...(Part III)." *Archivaria* 30 (Summer 1990): 4-20.

———. "Diplomatics: New Uses ...(Part IV)." *Archivaria* 31 (Winter 1990-91): 10-25.

———. "Diplomatics: New Uses ...(Part V)." *Archivaria* 32 (Summer 1991): 6-24.

———. "Diplomatics: New Uses ...(Part VI)." *Archivaria* 33 (Winter 1991-92): 6-24.

———. "Reliability and Authenticity: The Concepts and Their Implications." *Archivaria* 39 (Spring 1995): 5-10.

Duranti, Luciana, and Heather MacNeil. "The Protection of the Integrity of Electronic Records: An Overview of the UBC-MAS Research Project." *Archivaria* 42 (Fall 1996): 46-67.

———. "Protecting Electronic Evidence: A Third Progress Report on a Research Study and its Methodology." *Archivi & Computer* 6 (1996): 343-404.

Duranti, Luciana, Heather MacNeil, and William E. Underwood, "Protecting Electronic Evidence: A Second Progress Report on a Research Study and its Methodology." *Archivi & Computer* 6 (1996): 37-70.

Duranti, Luciana, and Terry Eastwood. "Protecting Electronic Evidence: A Progress Report." *Archivi & Computer* 5 (1995): 213-50.

Eastwood, Terry. "Should Creating Agencies Keep Electronic Records Indefinitely?" *Archives and Manuscripts* 24 (November 1996): 256-67.

Elton, G.R. *Return to Essentials: Some Reflections on the Present State of Historical Study*. Cambridge: Cambridge University Press, 1991.

———. *The Practice of History*. Gt. Britain: Fontana, 1969.

Erlandsson, Alf. *Electronic Records Management: A Literature Review.* Paris: International Council on Archives, 1997.

European Commission Directorate-General XIII. "Towards a European Framework for Digital Signatures and Encryption: Communication from the Commission to the European Parliament, the Council, the Economic and Social Committee and the Committee of the Regions Ensuring Security and Trust in Electronic Communication." COM (97) 503 [1997].

Evans, Richard J. *In Defense of History.* New York: Norton, 1997.

Ewart, J. Douglas, et al. *Documentary Evidence in Canada.* Agincourt, Ont.: Carswell, 1984.

Fogel, Robert William, and G.R. Elton. *Which Road to the Past?* New Haven: Yale University Press, 1983.

Franklin, Julian H. *Jean Bodin and the Sixteenth-Century Revolution in the Methodology of Law and History.* New York: Columbia University Press, 1963.

Fussner, Frank. *Historical Revolution: English Historical Writing and Thought, 1580-1640.* New York: Columbia University Press, 1962.

Gall, Gerald L. *The Canadian Legal System.* 4th ed. Ottawa: Carswell, 1995.

Gaskins, Richard H. *Burdens of Proof in Modern Discourse.* New Haven: Yale University Press, 1992.

Gerth, H.H., and C. Wright Mills, eds. and trans. *From Max Weber: Essays in Sociology.* New York: Oxford University Press, 1946.

Gilbert, Geoffrey, Sir. *The Law of Evidence,* 6th ed. London: W. Clarke, 1801.

Ginzburg, Carlo. "Checking the Evidence: The Judge and the Historian." In *Questions of Evidence: Proof, Practice, and Persuasion across the Disciplines*, ed. James Chandler, Arnold I. Davidson, and Harry Harootunian. Chicago: University of Chicago Press, 1994.

Giry, Arthur. *Manuel de diplomatique: Diplomes et chartes Chronologie technique: Éléments critiques et parties constitutives de la teneur des chartes Les chancelleries; Les actes privés.* New York: Burt Franklin, 1893, [1964].

Goldstein, Leon J. "Historical Facts." In *Historical Knowing.* Austin: University of Texas Press, 1976.

Goody, Jack. "The Letter of the Law." In *The Logic of Writing and the Organization of Society.* Cambridge: Cambridge University Press, 1986.

Gottschalk, Louis. "The Historian and the Historical Document." In *The Use of Personal Documents in History, Anthropology, and Sociology*, prepared for the Committee on Appraisal of Research, ed. Louis Gottschalk, Clyde Kluckhohn, et al. New York: Social Science Research Council, [1945].

Grafton, Anthony. "The Footnote from de Thou to Ranke." *History and Theory* 33 (1994): 53-76.

Gregson, Harold Anthony. "Records Management Attributes in International Open Document Exchange Standards." Master of Archival Studies thesis, University of British Columbia, 1995.

Guyotjeannin, Olivier, Jacques Pycke, et Benoît-Michel Tock. *Diplomatique médiévale*. Paris: Brepols, 1993.

Hacking, Ian. *The Emergence of Probability: A Philosophical Study of Early Ideas About Probability, Induction and Statistical Inference*. Cambridge: Cambridge University Press, 1975.

Hedstrom, Margaret. "Research Issues in Migration and Long-Term Preservation." *Archives and Museum Informatics* 11 (1997): 287-91.

————. "Descriptive Practices for Electronic Records: Deciding What is Essential and Imagining What is Possible." *Archivaria* 36 (Autumn 1993): 53-63.

————. "Understanding Electronic Incunabula: A Framework for Research on Electronic Records." *American Archivist* 54 (Summer 1991): 334-54.

Heywood, Heather. "Appraising Legal Value: Concepts and Issues." Master of Archival Studies thesis, University of British Columbia, 1990.

Himmelfarb, Gertrude. "Postmodernist History." In *On Looking into the Abyss: Untimely Thoughts on Culture and Society*. New York: Alfred A. Knopf, 1994.

Hofstede, Geert. "The Cultural Relativity of Organizational Praces and Theories." *Journal of International Business Studies* 14 (Fall 1983): 75-90.

————. "Motivation, Leadership, and Organization: Do American Theories Apply Abroad?" *Organizational Dynamics* 9 (Summer 1980): 42-63.

————. *Culture's Consequences: International Differences in Work-Related Values*. London: Sage Publications, 1980.

Holdsworth, W.S. "Documentary Evidence. " In *A History of English Law*, vol. 9. London: Methuen & Co., 1926.

Humphreys, R. Stephen. "The Historian, His Documents, and the Elementary Modes of Historical Thought." *History and Theory* 19 (1980): 1-20.

Huppert, George. *The Idea of Perfect History: Historical Erudition and Historical Philosophy in Renaissance France*. Urbana: University of Illinois Press, 1970.

Hutcheon, Linda. *A Poetics of Postmodernism: History, Theory Fiction*. London: Routledge, 1988.

Jenkins, Keith. *On "What is History": From Carr and Elton to Rorty and White*. London: Routledge, 1995.

———. *Re-Thinking History*. London: Routledge, 1991.

Johnson, Allen. *The Historian and Historical Evidence*. New York: Scribner, 1926.

Johnson, Mark A. "Computer Printouts as Evidence: Stricter Foundation or Presumption of Reliability?" *Marquette Law Review* 75 (Winter 1992): 439-466.

Joynt, Carl B., and Nicholas Rescher. "Evidence in History and the Law." *Journal of Philosophy* 56 (1959): 561-77.

Kamenka, Eugene. *Bureaucracy*. Oxford: Basil Blackwell, 1989.

Katsh, M. Ethan. *Law in a Digital World*. New York: Oxford University Press, 1995.

Kelley, Donald. *Foundations of Modern Historical Scholarship: Language, Law and History in the French Renaissance*. New York: Columbia University Press, 1970.

Langbein, John H. "Substantial Compliance with the Wills Act." *Harvard Law Review* 88 (January 1975): 489-531.

Langlois, Ch. V., and Ch. Seignobos. *Introduction to the Study of History*, trans. G.G. Berry. London: Duckworth & Co., 1898.

Landsman, Stephan. "The Rise of the Contentious Spirit: Adversary Procedure in Eighteenth Century England." 75 (March 1990): 497-609.

Le Goff, Jacques. *History and Memory*, trans. Steven Rendall and Elizabeth Claman. New York: Columbia University Press, 1992.

———. "Documento/Monumento." In *Enciclopedia Einaudi*, vol. 5. Turin, Italy: Einaudi, 1978.

Lester, Geoffrey S. "The Problem of Ancient Documents [Parts I and 2]." *The Advocates Quarterly* 20: 1/2 (January and March 1998): 101-131; 133-175.

Levy, Jean-Phillipe. "The Evolution of Written Proof." *American University Law Review* 13 (1964): 133-53.

Lowenthal, David. *The Past is a Foreign Country.* Cambridge: Cambridge University Press, 1985.

MacCrimmon, Marilyn T. "Developments in the Law of Evidence: The 1989-90 Term. Evidence in Context." *The Supreme Court Law Review*, 2nd series, vol. 2 (Toronto and Vancouver: Butterworths, 1991): 385-450.

———. "Developments in the Law of Evidence: The 1988-89 Term. The Process of Proof: Schematic Constraints." *The Supreme Court Law Review*, 2nd series, vol. 1 (Toronto and Vancouver: Butterworths, 1990): 345-403.

———. "Developments in the Law of Evidence: The 1987-88 Term. Fact Finding and the Supreme Court," *The Supreme Court Law Review* 11 (1989): 275-352

MacNeil, Heather. "Protecting Electronic Evidence: A Final Progress Report on a Research Study and Its Methodology." *Archivi & Computer* 7 (1997): 22-35.

———. "The Implications of the UBC Research Results for Archival Description in General and the Canadian *Rules for Archival Description* in Particular." *Archivi & Computer* 6 (1996): 239-46.

Martin, Raymond, Joan W. Scott, and Cushing Strout. "Forum on *Telling the Truth About History.*" *History and Theory* 34 (1995): 320-29.

McCrank, Lawrence J. "History, Archives, and Information Science." *Annual Review of Information Science and Technology (ARIST)* 30 (1995): 281-382.

Mead, Richard. *Cross-Cultural Management Communication.* New York: John Wiley and Sons, 1990.

Merryman, John Henry. *The Civil Law Tradition: An Introduction to the Legal Systems of Western Europe and Latin America*, 2nd ed. Stanford, Calif.: Stanford University Press, 1985.

Nance, Dale A. "The Best Evidence Principle." *Iowa Law Review* 73 (January 1988): 227-98.

Odgers, Stephen. *Uniform Evidence Law.* [Sydney, Australia]: The Federation Press, 1995.

Parkinson, Jane. "Accountability in Archival Theory." Master of Archival Studies thesis, University of British Columbia, 1993.

Petrucci, Armando. "The Illusion of Authentic History: Documentary Evidence." *Writers and Readers in Medieval Italy*, ed. and trans. Charles M. Radding. New Haven: Yale University Press, 1995.

Poole, Reginald L. *Lectures on the History of the Papal Chancery down to the Time of Innocent III.* Cambridge: Cambridge University Press, 1915.

Raffel, Stanley. *Matters of Fact: A Sociological Inquiry.* London, Boston and Henley: Routledge & Kegan Paul, 1979.

Reams, Bernard D. Jr., L.J. Kutten, and Allen E. Strehler. *Electronic Contracting Law: EDI and Business Transactions, 1996-97 Edition.* New York: Clark, Boardman, Callaghan, 1997.

Renier, G.J. *History: Its Purpose and Method.* New York: Harper & Row, 1950.

Ross, Seamus, and Edward Higgs, eds. *Electronic Information Resources and Historians: European Perspectives.* Göttingen and London: Max-Planck-Institut für Geschichte and the British Library Board, 1993.

Scheppele, Kim Lane. "The Ground-Zero Theory of Evidence." *Hastings Law Review* 49 (1997-98): 321-334.

Seigel, Michael L. "A Pragmatic Critique of Modern Evidence Scholarship." *Northwestern University Law Review* 88 (1994): 995-1045.

Shafer, Robert Jones, ed. *A Guide to Historical Method.* 3rd ed. Belmont, Calif.: Wadsworth Publishing Co., 1980.

Shapiro, Barbara J. *Beyond Reasonable Doubt and Probable Cause: Historical Perspectives on the Anglo-American Law of Evidence.* Berkeley and Los Angeles: University of California Press, 1991.

———. *Probability and Certainty in Seventeenth-Century England: A Study of the Relationships Between Natural Science, Religion, History, Law and Literature.* Princeton, N.J.: Princeton University Press, 1983.

Sharman, Robert C. "Causation in Historical Study." In *Debates and Discourses: Selected Archival Writings on Archival Theory 1951-1990* (Canberra: Australian Society of Archivists, 1995).

Sheppard, Anthony. *Evidence.* Rev. ed. Toronto: Carswell, 1996.

Skemer, Don C. "Diplomatics and Archives." *American Archivist* 52 (Summer 1989): 376-83.

Sopinka, John, et al. *The Law of Evidence in Canada.* Toronto and Vancouver: Butterworths, 1992.

Stanford, Michael. *The Nature of Historical Knowledge.* Oxford: Basil Blackwell, 1986.

———. *A Companion to the Study of History.* Oxford: Basil Blackwell, 1994.

Stevens, David O. "Electronic Record-keeping Provisions in International Laws." *Records Management Quarterly* (April 1997): 72-79.

Strong, John William, ed. *McCormick on Evidence.* St. Paul, Minn.: West Publishing Co., 1992.

Style, Christopher, and Charles Hollander. *Documentary Evidence*, 4th ed. London: Longman, 1993.

Tessier, Georges. "Diplomatique." In *L'Histoire et ses méthodes*, ed. Charles Samaran. Paris: Gallimard, 1961.

Thayer, James Bradley. *A Preliminary Treatise on Evidence at the Common Law.* Boston: Little, Brown, 1898.

Thompson, James Wesfall, and Bernard J. Holm. *A History of Historical Writing*, vol. 2. New York: Macmillan, 1942.

Treviño, A. Javier. *The Sociology of Law: Classical and Contemporary Perspectives.* New York: St. Martin's Press, 1996.

Tribe, Laurence H. "Triangulating Hearsay." *Harvard Law Review* 87 (1974): 957-74.

Twining, William. *Rethinking Evidence: Exploratory Essays.* Oxford: Basil Blackwell, 1990.

Uniform Law Conference of Canada. "Uniform Electronic Evidence Act and Comments," [n.d.], <http://www.ualberta.ca/alri/ulc> [September 1998].

———. "Uniform Electronic Evidence Act: Consultation Paper, March 1997, <http://www.ualberta.ca/alri/ulc> [March 1998].

United Nations Commission on International Trade Law. *UNICTRAL Model Law on Electronic Commerce with Guide to Enactment.* New York: United Nations, 1997.

[U.S.] Department of Health and Human Services. Food and Drug Adminstration. "21 CFR Part 11: Electronic Records; Electronic Signatures; Final Rule;

Electronic Submissions; Establishment of Public Docket; Notice." March 20, 1997.

Valla, Lorenzo. *The Profession of the Religious and Selections from the Falsely Believed and Forged Donation of Constantine*, trans. and ed. Olga Zorzi, 2nd ed. Toronto: Centre for Reformation and Renaissance Studies, 1994.

Van Caenegem, R.C. An Historical Introduction to Private Law. Cambridge: Cambridge University Press, 1992.

————. *Judges, Legislators and Professors: Chapters in European Legal History*. Cambridge: Cambridge University Press, 1987.

Vergari, James V., and Virginia V. Shue. "Computer-Based Information as Evidence." In *Fundamentals of Computer-High Technology Law*. Philadelphia, Pa.: American Law Institute--American Bar Association Committee on Continuing Professional Education, 1991.

Weber, *Max. Max Weber on the Methodology of the Social Sciences*, trans. and ed. Edward A. Shils and Henry A. Finch. Glencoe, Ill.: Free Press, 1949.

Weber, Max. *The Theory of Social and Economic Organization*, trans. A.M. Henderson and Talcott Parsons. New York: The Free Press, 1947.

Wigmore, John Henry. *Evidence in Trials at Common Law*. 11 vols. Boston: Little, Brown, 1972-83.

Wilkinson, James. "A Choice of Fictions: Historians, Memory, and Evidence." *PMLA* 111 (January 1996): 80-92.

Windschuttle, Keith. *The Killing of History: How Literary Critics and Social Theorists are Murdering Our Past*. New York: The Free Press, 1996.

Zuckerman, Adrian A.S. "Law, Fact or Justice?" *Boston University Law Review* 66 (May/July 1986): 487-508.

Subject Index